Laws for Dalit Rights and Dignity

Laws for Dalit Rights and Dignity

Experiences and Responses from Tamil Nadu

A. RAMAIAH

RAWAT PUBLICATIONS

Jaipur • New Delhi • Bangalore • Mumbai • Hyderabad • Guwahati

ISBN 81-316-0057-2

Published by
Prem Rawat for **Rawat Publications**
Satyam Apts., Sector 3, Jawahar Nagar, Jaipur 302 004 (India)
Phone: 0141 265 1748 / 7006 Fax: 0141 265 1748
E-mail: info@rawatbooks.com
Website: www.rawatbooks.com

New Delhi Office
4858/24, Ansari Road, Daryaganj, New Delhi 110 002
Phone: 011-23263290

Also at Bangalore, Mumbai, Hyderabad and Guwahati

Typeset by Rawat Computers, Jaipur
Printed at Chaman Enterprises, New Delhi

Contents

Foreword

Notwithstanding the oft-repeated, yet unsubstantiated, contradiction between the Fundamental Rights of individual and the Directive Principles of State Policy enshrined in the Constitution of free India, safeguarding the rights and dignity of the Scheduled Castes or the Dalits has been an issue persistently pursued by the Indian State through its well-specified organs or machinery. Yet, it is altogether a different matter that due to the continued hangover of the traditional nature of society, the vastness of its population and the vitality of the various issues involved in, particularly the issues pertaining to the rights and dignity of the Dalits, besides the State, by and large, being not devoid of the objective assessment of the phenomenon under reference, the rights and dignity of the Dalits have frequently been abused by the dominant vested interests. Situation has further aggravated on account of the continued animosity of the dominant vested interests, growing assertions of the aggrieved, and the perennial callousness coupled with the age-long prejudice and the partisan attitudes of the state machinery functioning at various levels towards the Dalit victims.

Nevertheless, exclusive laws have been enacted, in the forms of Acts and legislations, right from the days of the *Pax Britainnica* (1857-1947 A.D.) and even after India's independence. During the post-independent period, the Untouchability (Offences) Act (UOA) was passed in 1955, which was, in a way, the expansion of Article 17 of the Indian Constitution legally abolishing the practice of untouchability in any form against the earlier untouchables, constitutionally known as the Scheduled Castes (SCs), and socially and culturally as the Dalits. But, the Act could not prove to be effective due to the onus of proving the offence falling on the victims, and most of the UOA cases being tried under the Indian Penal Code (IPC) that is meant for countless number and types of other cases, including those pending for decades together. Over and above, due to constitutional propriety about the term 'untouchability', the UOA was amended as the Protection of Civil Rights (PCR) Act in 1976. Under this Act, the term 'untouchability' was replaced by a positive term 'civil rights' necessitating the need to specially protect the civil rights of the SCs/Dalits by the state. It may be mentioned here that by bringing in the term 'civil rights', not the economic and political rights, in the case of the SCs, not only the need of their civil rights, which was denied to them for centuries together, was realized but, at the same time, their such rights were also equated with the civil rights of others, and thereby making the state responsible for protecting the civil rights of both the SCs and others with equal importance, though civil rights of the latter are to be protected only under the IPC.

Since the PCR Act also could not prove to be much effective, another Act, namely, the Scheduled Castes and Scheduled Tribes (Prevention of Atrocities) Act was adopted in 1989, which is much more stringent in its punishment and wider in the nature of offences it covered. As per this Act, it is the accused who has to prove his/her innocence. However, dealing with the cases of atrocities – registering, challenging, and pleading in the Court of law – has remained so far with the various agencies of the government. Consequently, large numbers of cases go unregistered, and of the cases registered, challenged and pleaded in a Court of law, only a negligible percentage of cases end in conviction. This, in effect, belies the protection of rights and dignity of the SCs or Dalits and the Scheduled Tribes (STs, Adivasis) in the country.

The responsibility of recording or collecting data related to the nature and the number of cases of atrocities on SCs and STs is often left entirely with the government agency, and social scientists, particularly the sociologists and social anthropologists, have been using only these data in their studies on violence or atrocities against the Dalits and the Adivasis. Moving away from the existing practice of depending on the data collected by the government agencies, the present book on *Laws for Dalit Rights and Dignity* by Dr. A. Ramaiah relies primarily on the empirical data collected from multiple stakeholders to understand the efficacy of the Protection of Civil Rights Act and the Scheduled Castes and Scheduled Tribes (Prevention of Atrocities) Act. This study, located in three districts of the southern Tamil Nadu, focuses on the operation and effectiveness/ineffectiveness of the said Acts in protecting the rights and dignity of the Dalits. Based on the views of not only the victims and witnesses of atrocities but also the accused, the police officials and the NGOs/civil society organizations concerned, the book examines the various factors responsible for high rate of acquittal in cases registered under the two special laws. The book, being first of its kind, is not only a significant contribution to the theme of study but also a valuable addition to the knowledge base and for evolving appropriate policy measures.

Nandu Ram
Dr. Ambedkar Chair
Professor of Sociology
Jawaharlal Nehru University
New Delhi

Preface

Protecting Dalits (Scheduled Castes of SCs), who constitute a significant proportion of Indian population, from those who treat them as untouchables, subject them to inhuman brutalities and extreme forms of exploitation, has been a major challenge to both the state and the civil society organizations since India's independence. Despite special protective laws such as the Protection of Civil Rights Act, 1955 and the Scheduled Caste and Scheduled Tribe (Prevention of Atrocities) Act, 1989 and even after their implementation for several decades, atrocities on SCs continue to remain a day-to-day reality in most parts of India. While some argue that most of the cases registered under these laws are not given due attention by the police and others concerned, and therefore end in acquittal, others argue that most of the cases filed under these laws are false and that these laws are often misused. The latter have been agitating against these laws, particularly in Maharashtra, and also demanding their immediate withdrawal. Such a scenario, on the one hand, raises doubts on the will and commitment of the State, particularly its law and order machinery implementing these laws, and, on the other, emphasizes the urgent need of looking into the various factors responsible for the acquittal of most of these cases.

However, there has hardly been any study so far responding to these crucial questions.

The present volume entitled *Laws for Dalit Rights and Dignity: Experiences and Responses from Tamil Nadu,* is indeed a pioneering work responding to number of hitherto unanswered crucial questions regarding the uses and abuses of such special protective laws. On the basis of experiences of the victims, accused, the police, NGOs, judiciary and people in general, who were involved directly or indirectly in the 15 acquitted cases chosen for the study under reference, this book brings to light the various factors responsible for high rate of acquittal in the untouchability and atrocity cases. The views of two senior IPS officers – one from Tamil Nadu and the other from Maharashtra – who were in charge of implementing these special laws at the State level, have also been taken into consideration. The book offers practical suggestions also for implementing these laws effectively and to protect the interests of the SCs on a securely permanent basis. However, owing to budget constrains and paucity of time, the study had to be confined within southern Tamil Nadu.

Unlike most other evaluative studies, which rely heavily on empirical data, the present study is based mostly on qualitative data and has depth in its rigour. The unique feature of this book is also that it presents to the readers the views of the stakeholders and others concerned as they have expressed to the author. These views have however been grouped under different sub-headings with a view to avoiding repetition of ideas and views. Such an approach, on the one hand, gives an opportunity to the readers for making their own judgement on the ground reality and, on the other, restrains the author from interpreting the reality either by over-playing or under-playing the data, which are always there for the readers to check and recheck.

However, completing this book had not been an easy affair and I take this opportunity to thank everyone who has contributed to the fulfilment of my task. This book is based on the data of one of my recent studies funded by the Ministry of Social Justice and Empowerment, Government of India. I therefore thank the Ministry first. My thanks are due to Tata Institute of Social Sciences, Mumbai, where I have been working since 1991, for extending necessary support to complete this work, and to the Adi-Dravida and Tribal Welfare Department, Government of Tamil Nadu, and the Office of Inspector General of Police (PCR/HR/CID), Chennai, for their help in collecting necessary data from the police officials of southern Tamil Nadu. I heartily acknowledge the sincerity and frankness with which Mr. C. Balasubramaniyan, IGP (PCR/HR/CID), Chennai, and Mr. T. K. Choudhary, IGP (PCR), Maharashtra, shared their views on the issue. I am also thankful to Ms. Sivagamy, IAS and Mr. Shyam Sunder, IGP (PCR/HR/CID), who have helped me in collecting relevant data, and shared their views informally on the subject. I most specially thank Mr. P. Ramanathan, Mr. V. Prakash and Mr. E. Durai Raj, who carried out the most difficult task of collecting data, going to remote villages and putting even their lives at stake. My special thanks are due to Prof. Jayaram, my senior colleague in the Institute, who had offered valuable suggestions before finalization of this volume.

Finally, this book would not have been completed without the support and encouragement of Thamilarasi, my wife, and Lakshana and Monica, my daughters. I owe them more than what I can express in words.

A. Ramaiah

Glossary

ADGP	Additional Director General of Police
APP	Assistant Public Prosecutor
Dalit	Scheduled Caste
DGP	Director General of Police
DIGP	Deputy Inspector General of Police
DYSP	Deputy Superintendent of Police
HR	Human Rights
IGP	Inspector General of Police
MF	Mistake of Facts
PCR	Protection of Civil Rights
POA	Prevention of Atrocities
SC	Scheduled Caste
SI	Sub-Inspector of Police
SJ	Social Justice
SP	Superintendent of Police
SPP	Special Public Prosecutor
ST	Scheduled Tribe

List of Tables

1

Introduction

The Problem in Focus

India – one of the oldest civilisations and second largest populous country housing over 16 per cent of the world population – has achieved multifaceted progress since independence. It has become self-sufficient in agriculture production. Literacy rate has increased from 18.33 in 1951 to 52.21 in 1991. Among the industrialised countries it stands tenth. It is the sixth nation to have gone to outer space, and emerging as one of the most powerful nations in the world particularly in the field of information and technology. More importantly, in all international forums, India has stood against all kinds of discrimination including racial discrimination like apartheid. Yet, a section of its citizens, the *Dalits*[1] (Scheduled Castes or SCs), who constitute over 16 per cent of its population (*Census of India* 2001) are subjected to inhuman and invidious indignities, exploitations and brutalities, and treated as untouchables even today. Such a scenario defeats the very meaning of freedom from the British rule and also the ideals of Indian Constitution: justice, equality and fraternity.

The concern for protecting Dalits from untouchability, caste-based brutalities and extreme forms of exploitation has been a major agenda for governments till date. Such concern manifested itself, broadly, in two forms: (a) social reform and political intervention, and (b) legal measures. While some reformers appealed to the caste Hindus not to discriminate the Dalits, and, at the same time, persuaded the Dalits to keep doing their defiling and demeaning traditional occupations like scavenging and other tasks as their God-ordained means of livelihood; others have mobilised the Dalits to fight for their rights, self respect and dignity, and, at the same time, persuaded them to take up modern and more dignified occupations. The latter also advocated appropriate legislative measures both to change the mind-set of the exploiters or oppressors and to protect the interests of the oppressed. While the former approach is of Gandhiji, the latter is of Dr. Ambedkar. Intervention and initiatives of political leaders, both during pre- and post-independence periods, by and large, fall into these two categories (Ramaiah, 1998a).

The social relation between the Dalits/SCs and the caste Hindus has often been uncordial. It has been a contesting and conflicting one where the Dalits have always been the marginalised, oppressed and exploited category. They have been the victims of worst forms of violence for centuries, though the historical records had remained silent for long over this matter (Mendelsohn and Vicziancy, 2000: 45). As far the question, as to why atrocities against Dalits continue unabated, it has been well argued that it is the systemic defects in the social and village structure, in other words, the caste system and the caste based village system, that have been responsible for the prejudiced mindset of most Hindus resulting in frequent violence against Dalits. Ambedkar maintains:

> "Caste has killed public spirit. Caste has made public opinion impossible. A Hindu's public is his caste. His responsibility is only to his caste. His loyalty is restricted only to his caste. Virtue has become caste-ridden and morality has become caste-bound" (1979: 56).

He further says:

> "So long as the present (village) arrangement continues, it is impossible for the untouchables either to free themselves from the yoke of the Hindus or to get rid of their

> untouchability. It is the close-knit association of the untouchables with the Hindus living in the same village which marks them out as untouchables and which enables the Hindus to identify them as being Untouchables" (Ibid.).

He even proposed separate settlement for the Dalits as a means to permanently protect their interests (Ibid.: 425). Neither has such suggestion been given due importance by the social scientists and policy makers, nor has the violence against Dalits been mitigated through other means. The perpetrators of violence justify their action as if it were part of their tradition. Therefore, their violence is often known as "traditional violence"[2]. The Dalits suffer other forms of violence too. Such violence seems to flow mainly from the modern forms of resistance on the part of untouchables, which, in other words, may be understood as upper castes' violent response to changing situation of untouchables/Dalits.[3] More often than not, the increasing incident of violence against Dalits is attributed to the increasing level of consciousness among Dalits of their deprivation (Oommen, 1985). "Atrocities are...inflicted more on those Scheduled Castes who are socially mobile and who assert ...their rights and respectable status in the society than on those who compromise with the *status quo*" (Nandu Ram, 1995: 295). "The frequency and intensity of violence is an offshoot of desperate attempts by the upper caste groups to protect their entrenched status against the process of disengagement and upward mobility among lower castes resulting from affirmative action of State Policy" (Government of India, 2004: 1).

However, the concern here pertains to the legal intervention and its impact on mitigating violence against Dalits. Besides the efforts of many social reformers, a number of special laws had come into effect even prior to India's independence (see Annexure 1). Of the various protective measures undertaken after independence, mention may be made of the two special laws, viz., The Protection of Civil Rights Act, 1955 (PCR Act)[4] and its rules (see Government of India, 2000) and the Scheduled Castes and Scheduled Tribes (Prevention of Atrocities) Act, 1989 (POA Act)[5] (see Annexures 2 and 2A). These laws are exclusively meant for protecting the Dalits (SCs) from injustice and exploitations of the caste Hindus and others. Despite enforcement of these laws for several decades, violence against Dalits continues unabated in most parts of India. Therefore the crucial questions here are: Why do atrocities continue despite there being special laws? Does it mean that these laws themselves have some limitations and therefore ineffective? Is it due to a lack of will on the part of the police of the region or is it because of the lack of will on the part of the judiciary, which interprets the laws to ensure justice? Or are there other reasons?

Regarding the legal system that is meant to ensure justice to the victims, Emile Durkheim (1964) maintains that "in a complex society like ours, the legal system functions with the restitutive sanctions rather than the repressive ones" (quoted in Nandu Ram, 1995: 309). "It operates with the sprit of correcting the offender and not eliminating him or her from the social scene" (Nandu Ram, 1995: 309). It is for these reasons, Ambedkar argued that in a caste-ridden society like India it is ultimately the laws of caste-based panchayat that operates more vigorously than the laws agreed upon under the Constitution of India (Ambedkar, 1989: 120-121). On a similar line of thinking, it has been argued that:

> "At the theoretical level, the fundamental fallacy in understanding the role of law as an instrument of social change lies in viewing it as an independent agency of social control and social direction." As "it appears autonomous within society," it has become possible "to talk about law acting upon society rather than law as an aspect of society." As Cotterrel (1984: 48-49) rightly points out, "as long as law is seen as an aspect of society – a certain side of social life as whole – there can be no possibility of it 'standing apart' in some way and 'acting upon' society." It is the failure to recognize the fallacy underlying the law-society dichotomy which explains not only the critical faith reposed in the efficacy of the former as an agency to bring about change in the latter, but also the limitations of law as an instrument of social emancipation, as long as the basic social relations remain unaltered" (Jayaram, 1986: 34; 1981).

Regarding the special laws that are meant to protect the interests of Dalits, Marc Galanter opined that "the impact of anti-disabilities legislation is not to be measured merely by the few cases that are brought. The aim of such laws is not to prosecute offenders, but to promote new patterns of behaviour" (1972: 283). To the claim that the special laws such as the PCR Act are ineffective because most of the SCs and STs are not even aware of these laws[6], Galanter observed:

> "It is not unawareness of its existence that inhibits its use, but awareness of its hazards and weaknesses. Untouchables are, quite sensibly, more deterred by the formidable difficulties of the Untouchability (Offences) Act than caste Hindus are deterred by the remote and mild penalties that it threatens them with.... The conclusion seems to be inevitable that ...the working of the anti-disabilities legislation shows that it is of limited effect in eliminating disabilities...this is not because the legislation has reached the utmost limits of effective legal action, but because it stops far short of these limits. One would be foolish indeed to believe that legal measures alone could secure the elimination of untouchability from society" (quoted in Jayaram, 1981:11).

Pointing to what actually happens in the field with regard to implementing these special laws, it has been observed that:

> "....the implementation of the Act has largely remained tardy and SCs and STs have not been able to derive full benefits available under the Act. There appears to be a clear lack of will on the part of law enforcement officers to take action. The Supreme Court of India in 1992 in *State of Karnataka vs Appa Balu Ingale* said that more than 75 per cent of the cases under this Act are ending in acquittal at all levels. In Andhra Pradesh, in almost all the 226 incidents of atrocities reported, the accused could easily evade the arms of law because of technicalities and tacit connivance of law enforcement authorities.[7]

In a detailed article, Galanter noted that "those lower castes who wanted to carry their struggle into the legal arena probably diverted their efforts to bringing charges of ordinary crimes (assault, trespass, etc.) against their opponents. Success in such litigation would depend only on the competitive struggle to produce convincing evidence, not on securing from the judiciary favorable interpretations of existing law" (Galanter, 1972: 233).

The following conclusion of Cohn, which Galanter had quoted, is also worth noting:

> "The lower castes have generally been unsuccessful when, through the use of police or of the urban courts, they have sought to redress what they believe to be the corporate wrongs done to them by upper castes. The upper castes maintain their economic position; their knowledge of the courts and the intricacies of the law and better access to officials have thwarted attempts to change the position of the lower castes in the village society and economy."

However, the high caste people have been demanding immediate withdrawal of these special Acts on the ground that SCs and STs are misusing the Acts against the upper caste people. In such a scenario, on the one hand, doubts are raised on the will and commitment of the state to implement these laws and, on the other, emphasizes the urgent need of identifying the factors responsible for the acquittal of most of these cases.

However, there has hardly been any scientific study so far focusing on these vital issues. There is not even a single book for its comprehensive understanding. The one by S.K. Ghosh (1980) for which Justice V.R. Krishna Iyer has written the *foreword* is perhaps the only book that pertains to the issues under reference to some extent. However, this work is nothing but a compilation of various constitutional safeguards and protective legislations like the Protection of Civil Rights Act, 1955. It does not focus on factors leading to acquittal of the untouchability cases. Moreover, the book was published before the introduction of the SCs and STs (Prevention of Atrocities) Act, 1989. Similarly Vivek Pandit (1995) came out with a handbook reproducing all laws concerned with the protection of Dalits (SCs) including the POA Act, 1989, and the Scheduled Castes and Scheduled Tribes (Prevention of Atrocities) Rules, 1995, besides offering useful tips for the effective use of such laws. It also comprises the summary observations of a study on "Atrocities on Scheduled Castes and Tribes: Causes and Remedies" undertaken by the National Commission for the SCs and STs (Government of India, 1990). This study covered five states, viz., Bihar, Rajasthan, Madhya Pradesh, Andhra Pradesh and Tamil Nadu with a large sample of 1,000 cases – of which 100 cases were studied in depth. Though the study came out with a number of useful observations, the following one is more relevant for the present study and thus worth noting:

> "Delayed investigation, faulty and delayed charge-sheets, lukewarm prosecution and protracted proceedings have all contributed to a high percentage of acquittals in atrocity cases. The same fate will be for cases under the Prevention of Atrocities Act, unless special steps are taken" (Ibid: 45; also see Government of India, 1984; Das, 1995).

The above observation is however based on cases registered under the PCR Act during 1983 to 1987. The study had no scope of examining even a single POA Act case, since the POA Act came into effect only from September 11, 1989. Therefore, these observations cannot be considered suitable for or relevant to the understanding of the POA Act. Even the recent book of Naval focuses merely on causes of atrocities and the special features of the POA Act (Naval, 2001).

However, the interim observations and recommendations of the Jury of the National Public Hearing on Dalit Human Rights[8] set up by the National Campaign on Dalit Human Rights (NCDHR) are of immense importance. After hearing of over 50 cases of violation of Dalit human rights, the Jury made number of observations and recommendations. The following are some of those, that are directly relevant to the present study:

> "Despite the fact that in 1993 the Indian Government enacted the Protection of Human Rights Act and special machinery was created to enforce this Act as well as the Special Courts constituted under the SC/ST (Prevention of Atrocities) Act, 1989 for safeguarding the human rights of Dalits, it is made very evident from all the cases heard by the Jury that:
>
> (1) The state is continuing to perpetuate violence against Dalits;
>
> (2) The state is colluding with the dominant castes in several areas across the states. We heard depositions about the oppression of Dalits and the denial of their human rights by all state agencies, especially the police;

(3) The state, by its inaction, fails to implement all its laws and rules and to take stringent measures and action when dominant castes perpetrate atrocities on Dalits;

(4) The Judiciary has not responded to the violations of the rights of the Dalits with adequate sensitivity and urgency."

The other relevant observation is that:

"....we are constrained to observe that instead of aiding empowerment of Dalits, the law enforcing machinery has become the great abuser of the human rights of Dalits. ...we found that in case after case the police have actively colluded with caste Hindus to perpetrate and perpetuate violence against Dalits and have failed to provide them with adequate security against caste atrocities" (see Jayshree, et. al., 2000: 310-311).

What may be inferred from the above observation of the eminent Jury is that the police colluding with the accused had been one of the major factors responsible for most of the untouchability and atrocity cases ending in acquittal. However, these are the observations only of the Jury. In this entire exercise of public hearing for Dalits, the views of the police who play a major role in ensuring legal protection to Dalits had not been given due importance. Moreover, there may be other reasons for the high rate of acquittal in the untouchability and atrocity cases, which are yet to be identified. Thus arises the need of present study.

Objectives

In the above context, the present study aims at exploring the various factors responsible for high rate of acquittals in the untouchability and atrocity cases registered under the PCR Act, 1955 and the SCs and STs (Prevention of Atrocities) Act, 1989. The following are the specific objectives of this study:

1. To review the various legal measures introduced in favour of Dalits during pre and post independence periods and their impact;
2. To analyze the context in which the Dalit victims seek police protection;

3. To understand the attitude of the police towards Dalit victims approaching them for help;
4. To identify factors responsible for acquittal in untouchability and atrocity cases from the experiences of the Dalit victims, their witnesses and others who had sought justice through the two special laws;
5. To identify factors responsible for acquittal in untouchability and atrocity cases also from the experiences of police, Special Public Prosecutor, NGOs and others concerned; and
6. To make recommendations for effective enforcement of these laws.

Methodology

With a view to pursuing the above objectives, the following methodology was adopted. This includes areas of study, selection of samples, sources of data, tools of data collection, data analysis and chapterisation.

Areas of Study

The area chosen for the present study is southern Tamil Nadu, more specifically, the three southern districts, viz., Ramanathapuram, Virudhunagar and Sivagangai. While the choice on Tamil Nadu is based on the fact that this was the State which led a powerful anti-Brahmin movement in the early 1920s as a means to end caste based discriminations, and this was also the state which passed legislation as early as 1938 banning caste disabilities, but is yet witnessing violent crimes against the SCs. The choice of the three districts of southern Tamil Nadu is based on the fact that these districts not only witnessed inter-caste conflicts frequently, but also constituted a number of acquittal cases registered under the said Acts.

Selection of Samples

The thrust of the present study being the identification of factors responsible for high rate of acquittal in the PCR and POA Acts cases, the samples had to be selected in a manner that it would help us identify, if not all, maximum number of factors responsible for high rate of acquittal. As the context and the nature of offence or offences committed in one particular case may differ from that of the others, it was assumed that the factors responsible for the acquittal of such cases would also differ from one another. This assumption therefore made it necessary to choose only those samples of acquitted cases in which the context and nature of offences committed differed from one another, so as to identify maximum number of factors responsible for the acquittal of such cases.

Accordingly, the *theoretical sampling method* (Strauss, 1997), which aptly accommodates the above requirement, was adopted for the present study. Under this sampling method, each of the new sample selected is supposed to add new information/dimension to the existing knowledge on the issue under study. Irrespective of the number of samples being selected already, the process of selecting samples with such conditions is expected to continue until such time the new sample being selected reaches the saturation point as far as adding new information/dimension to the issue being studied is concerned. In other words, the process of adding new sample is to be stopped the moment the new samples start giving only such information/dimension, which have already been obtained through the samples selected earlier.

In the same way, samples of acquitted cases were chosen for the present study from amongst the acquitted PCR Act, 1955 and the SCs and STs (Prevention of Atrocities) Act, 1989 cases registered in the three southern districts of Tamil Nadu during 1991-1999. The three districts include: 1. Ramanathapuram district, 2. Sivagangai district and 3. Virudhunagar district. The unit of analysis for the study therefore refers to each of the chosen acquitted case.

In view of the fact that Ramanathapuram was the district which witnessed in 1957 the worst ever caste conflicts in the state killing over 42 people and damaging properties worth lakhs of rupees as a fallout of the murder of a Scheduled Caste leader Immanuvel, maximum number of samples were chosen from this district. The other reasons for the same were: (a) the researcher's familiarity with the district and (b) the willingness of the police officer, in-charge of the district's PCR unit, to share documents pertaining to more number of PCR and POA Act acquitted cases.

In the first phase of selection of samples, the Police Inspector, in-charge of the PCR Police Station/Unit, Ramanathapuram district was approached with formal order from the Inspector General of Police (PCR), Chennai for necessary support. When asked for the details of PCR and POA Acts acquitted cases for the purpose of research, the Inspector promised all possible support and showed the Case Register containing basic information particularly the nature of offences committed and the status of each registered case. Looking into the status of registered cases, over 45 acquitted PCR/POA Act cases were first identified, and were later on, grouped into different categories on the basis of the nature and place (district) of offences.

Considering the gravity and uniqueness of the nature of crimes committed, a few cases were chosen also from the adjoining districts of Virudhunagar and Sivagangai. In all, the total number of such cases that the researcher could lay hands on were 75, out of which 45 from Ramanathapuram, 15 from Virudhunagar and 15 others from Sivagangai. Out of these 75 acquitted cases, which constituted the universe, samples were chosen as per the theoretical sampling method. Every case that was unique in terms of the nature and place of offences committed was considered as a sample for the present study. Every case that was similar to cases already chosen was ignored and subsequently other unique cases were identified, with a view to understanding more number of factors responsible for the high rate of acquittal in PCR and POA Act cases.

In this way, 15 independent categories of unique cases were identified. Since there was no more unique case in the 75 cases that were looked into, the process of identifying unique cases was considered to have reached its saturation point. Though 15 independent categories of unique cases were identified, only 15 cases (one case from each category), for which the researcher was confident of getting not only necessary documents but also the views of those individuals associated with the cases, were chosen as samples. All other cases were ignored as they were very much similar in every respect to the chosen 15 cases and therefore could contribute nothing new. It may be noted here that out of the 15 cases, a maximum number of nine were from Ramanathapurm district, and three each from Virudhnagar and Sivagangai districts.

Each of these 15 cases of samples was unique and different from the other, as stated before, in terms of nature of offences committed. The unique cases of samples chosen from Ramanathapuram district include: (1) case of murder, (2) case of rape with murder, (3) denial of minimum wage, (4) stealing of firewood, (5) denial of equal rights in religious festivals, (6) false allegation of having dashed against the accused, (7) discriminatory and derogatory remarks against a SC government employee, and (8) discriminatory and derogatory remarks in response to an attempt on life case filed earlier. The cases chosen from the Sivagangai district include: (1) illegal occupation of land, (2) denial of access to common path leading to burial ground, (3) denial of access to common path in the village premise, and (4) threat to life and attempt of physical assault for apprehending the caste Hindus indulged in illegal fishing. And, the samples of acquitted cases chosen from the Virudhunagar district include: (1) a case of rape with murder, (2) physical assault on SC school boy for talking to a few caste Hindu school girls, and (3) harassment and discrimination meted out to SC school employee by the school authority (for more details, refer Table 1.1).

Sources of Data

The data relevant for the present study were collected from both primary and secondary sources. The primary data was collected from multiple stakeholders such as the victims, witnesses and the accused. Besides the Special Public Prosecutor, the primary data was collected also from the Inspector General of Police and the Additional Director General of Police – the state level police officers in-charge of the implementation of the PCR and POA

Table 1.1
Cases at a Glance

Case No.	*Crime No.*	*Names of Victim vs. Accused*	*Place of Incidence*	*Nature of Offence*	*Offence under*
1	26/98	Karuppaiah vs. P. Radhakrishnan	K. Meenakshipuram, Virudhunagar District	Rape with murder	POA Act 3(2)(v) IPC 302, 201
2	48/96	K. Karuppaiah vs. Parthiban, J.	Lakshmipuram, Ramanathapuram District	Rape with murder	POA Act 3(2)(v) IPC 376, 379, 302
3	176/97	K. Karuppan vs. C. Kumaravel,	Mosukudi, Ramnathapuram District	Murder	POA Act 3(2) 5(v) IPC 302
4	106/99	V. Nagaraj vs. S. Shekh Mohamad,	Rajakambiram, Sivagangai District	Illegal occupation of land	POA Act 3(1)(x) IPC 341, 447, 502(2)
5	34/98	K. Shanmugam vs. S. Mutthaiah	Allur, Sivagangai District	Denial of access to common path to burial ground	POA Act 3(1)(x)
6	9/98	V. Mani vs. S. Karuppaiah	Vadavanpatti, Sivagangai District	Denial of access to common path in the village premise and discriminatory and derogatory remarks.	POA Act 3(1)(x)
7	5/92	Mr. Pandi vs. Kannuchamy Servai	Yemaneswaram, Ramanathapuram District	Denial of due wage and discriminatory and derogatory remarks	PCR Act 7(1)(d)
8	9/91	M. Muniyandi vs. Vijayasamy Thevar	Paramakudi, Ramanathapuram District	Stealing of SCs' fire-wood and attempting to assault him with brooms and foot-wears.	PCR Act 7(1)(d)

Contd...

Contd...

9	8/91	K. Satthaiah vs. U. Ganapathi Thevar	Paranur, Mayilurani, Ramanathapuram District	Denial of equal rights in religious festivals, abuses and beating when demanded. .	PCR Act 7(1)(d)
10	27/99	M. Mutthu vs. P. Parthiban	Melaiyur, Virudhunagar District	Physical assault and discriminatory remarks on SC school boy for talking to caste Hindu school girls.	POA Act 3(1)(x) IPC 147, 342, 323
11	27/98	A. Alagan vs. M. Gurupatham	Sakanthi, Sivagangai District	Threat to life and discriminatory remarks for apprehending the caste Hindus indulged in illegal fishing.	POA Act 3(1)(x)
12	3/91	N. Veerachamy vs. C. Vinayagam	Thiruvadanai, Ramanathapuram District	False allegation of having dashed against a caste Hindu and in response, attempt to assault with footwears.	PCR Act 7(1)(d)
13	6/91	Balakrishnan vs. Sivasubramaniam	Rameswaram, Ramanathapuram District	Discriminatory and derogatory remarks on the SC government employee.	PCR Act 7(1)(d)
14	72/99	K.Pandyan vs. Veluchamy (HM)	Aruppukottai, Virudhunagar District	Discrimination and harassment to SC government servant at workplace.	POA Act 3(1)(x)
15	11/92	M. Kalimuthan vs. R. Mutthuchamy Chettiyar	Vettikulam, Mayilurani, Ramanathapuram District.	Discriminatory remarks and attempt of physical assault in response to a case of attempt on life filed earlier.	PCR Act (1)(d)

Acts, and the Deputy Superintendent of Police, the officer-in-charge of investigating POA Act cases. Informal discussions were held with a few Inspectors, Sub-Inspectors and Police Constables working at the local police stations. Views of common people representing the accused and victims and NGOs were also sought. The relevant data were collected also from the First Information Reports (FIRs) and copies of judgments of cases under study. It may be noted that out of the 15 chosen cases, copies of FIRs and judgments could not be obtained in respect of a few cases, since neither the concerned police stations liked to share the FIR copies, nor did the victims have these with them. Similarly, even the Special Court concerned did not share the judgment copies despite formal written request for more than once.

Secondary sources such as reports and other documents particularly of the National Commission for SCs and STs and the Ministry of Social Justice and Empowerment were extensively used. Other secondary sources such as relevant books, journals and other reports have also been referred to and used appropriately. Though the data collection process began as early as July 10, 2000, due to many unanticipated difficulties, it was not consistent and it had to be continued till mid-August 2002.

Tools of Data Collection

The tools used for collecting necessary data were in-depth interview, case-history method, observation, non-participant observation and questionnaire. While in-depth interviews were held with most of the stakeholders to understand the process that each case under study had gone through, the case-history method was used to take stock of how each incident of atrocity had actually taken place. While the "non-participant observation" method was used to record the views of those other than the victims and witness, particularly of the accused and their associates, as to how they managed to get acquitted of the PCR/POA Act, cases filed against them, the "observation" method was followed to understand the social relationship between the SCs and the non-SCs in general and between the victims and accused in particular. Most of the in-depth interviews held were in Tamil. These were recorded and later on translated into English and are presented in Chapters 3 and 4, as narrated/shared by the stakeholders concerned. A questionnaire consisting 17 questions focusing mostly on the four objectives of the study was prepared and used to collect authentic information/views of the top-level police officials in-charge of implementing the PCR and POA Acts throughout Tamil Nadu.

Analysis of Data

The study is basically qualitative in nature. Adopting a case study method, the chosen acquitted cases were examined in depth to understand the factors responsible for high rate of acquittal. The data collected from the multiple stakeholders and through secondary sources have been analysed under four broad areas reflecting the four objectives of this study. These include: (1) the context in which the victims seek justice through these special laws, (2) the attitude of the police towards the victims seeking their help, (3) factors responsible for high rate of acquittal in the PCR and POA Act cases, and (4) recommendations for better implementation of these laws. The views of stakeholders are sought on all these four areas. Since each stakeholder was encouraged to share whatever they liked with regard to the high rate of acquittal in the PCR and POA Act cases, the transcribed and translated version of their views presented in Chapters 3 and 4 are often not in the same order in which the objectives of this study being listed. Yet, care was taken in the process of in-depth interviews to record their views on all the four broad areas. For those cases for which the views of the victims or their witnesses on how the offence under reference took place could not be obtained in any way, for reasons of either their non-availability or unwillingness, hence relevant information were obtained from the copies of concerned First Information Reports. Though the views of each stakeholder have been presented in Chapters 3 and 4 in the same way and order in which they narrated, the important points emerged in each of these narrations have been grouped under the four broad areas and presented under the title "Case Highlights" at the end of every narration of the stakeholders. It may be noted that though all the stakeholders were requested to respond to all the four major questions, some of them responded only to some partly due to their lack of involvement in the case under study and being ignorant of the issue being discussed, and partly due to fear of possible dire consequences. Later, the views of the victims and their witnesses were compared and found at variance with the views of the police. This method was followed for almost every chosen case. For a few cases, the views of the NGOs, which followed up or associated with the case in one way or the other were also sought. The conclusions drawn by way of comparing and contrasting the views of the victims and their witnesses with that of the accused and their associates, were then juxtaposed in general not only with the views of the senior police officials in-charge of implementing and investigating cases registered under the PCR and POA Acts but also with the views of common people and NGOs in order to respond objectively to the objectives of this study.

Scope and Limitations

As a first ever study of its kind, incorporating the views not only of the victims, witnesses and the accused, but also of the officials in-charge, concerned NGOs and individuals, and in which scientific approach has been followed at every step, the findings of this study are bound to be very valuable and useful particularly for those who are grappling with the whole issue of ensuring protection to the SCs through the special laws. These would in addition, be helpful for formulating new policies, and for making necessary changes in the existing policies concerning the protection and development of the SCs. However, the fact that the views of the accused and others could not be obtained for some cases owing to certain field-level difficulties, and the fact that the cases studied pertains only to three districts of southern Tamil Nadu, one may however argue that the study has a limited scope.

This volume is based on the author's study entitled *"Factors Responsible for High Rate of Acquittal in Untouchability and Atrocity Cases Registered Under the PCR Act 1955 and the SCs and STs (Prevention of Atrocities) Act, 1989: The Case of Southern Tamil Nadu"*, which was funded by the Ministry of Social Justice and Empowerment, Government of India. With a view to converting the study report to its present shape relevant changes have been made in the titles and arrangement of chapters, besides the editorial revisions. This book consists of seven chapters. While the present chapter focuses on the relevance, objectives and the methodology of the study, the second chapter portrays the various legislative measures introduced in favour of Dalits/SCs during pre- and post-independence periods and their impact. The third chapter focuses on the initiatives taken by the Government of Tamil Nadu to combating crimes committed against Dalits and the impact of such initiatives, while the fourth chapter brings to light the various factors responsible for high rate of acquittal in untouchability and atrocity cases from the points of views of Dalit victims and their witnesses. The fifth chapter takes stock of the views and experiences of the police, Special Public Prosecutor, NGOs and others concerned with regard to issues pertaining to effective implementation of the two laws and the various factors responsible for high rate of acquittal in the untouchability and atrocity cases. While the sixth chapter compares the contesting views of respondents to arrive at logical conclusions, the last chapter highlights the major findings and recommendations emerge from the study.

Notes

1. Unless specified, the term "Dalit" is to be understood throughout the text as a synonym to "Scheduled Caste". The term "Scheduled Castes" (SCs) is the constitutionally recognised identity for those being subject to untouchability and social discrimination on account of their so-called low caste Hindu background. They are those whom the Hindu scriptures have identified as *Chandalas, Untouchables, Ati-Shudras* and *Panchamas.*

While Ambedkar identified them as *Protestant Hindus* and *Broken Men*, M. K. Gandhi as *Harijans*, and the British as *Depressed Classes* and *Untouchables*. Though such people are there almost in every religious denomination of India, all of them have not been recognised by the Constitution as Scheduled Castes. All SCs are Dalits, but all Dalits are not SCs. The Constitution of India recognises as Scheduled Castes only those who formally identify themselves as either Hindus, or Sikhs or Buddhists. While the Hindu Dalits were recognised as SCs as early as 1950 and the Sikh Dalits in 1956, the Buddhists Dalits got recognition as SCs only in 1990. The term Dalit or Dalits is otherwise a wider concept inclusive of not only the SCs, but also the Scheduled Tribes, Backward Castes, Working Class and some time even women as a whole.

2. The traditional violence is one in which the caste Hindus who feel that the untouchables are not only the embodiment of evil sprits but also have the power over such sprits that are responsible for most of the diseases. On this pretext, even the 'traditional' act of violence like rape of untouchable women seems to be justified (Mendelsohn and Vicziancy, 2000: 45).
3. The Dalits' resistance to discrimination arising from the practice of untouchability, together with more general claims to social respect, and their claims for agricultural land, housing sites, payment of statutory minimum wages, and demands for adequate representation in government jobs, and access to educational and economic development opportunities may be included as examples for the latter type of violence (Ibid. 46).
4. The PCR Act was earlier known as the "Untouchability (Offences) Act, 1955. This Act was passed in the Parliament on June 1, 1955.
5. Under these two special laws only those Dalits professing either Hinduism or Sikhism or Buddhism are eligible to seek protection since only they alone have been recognised as the Scheduled Castes under the Indian Constitution. In other words, those Dalits professing religions other than Hinduism, Sikhism and Buddhism are not eligible to seek protection under these laws, though they may suffer from untouchability and atrocity on account of their social or caste origin.
6. "Regretfully, despite more than 12-13 years of the enactment of the Act, many SCs and STs are not fully aware of the provisions contained therein. A recent study in Delhi has revealed that 33 per cent of SC employees suffer 'atrocities' in the hands of

non-Scheduled Castes, but only 13 per cent of them lodge complaint with the police. Most of them silently bear the humiliation and prefer not to complaint to the police, courts or senior officers fearing backlash. This sadly proves the point that SC and ST employees are either not aware of the provisions of the Act or they are afraid of harassment if they take protection under this Act" (visit http://www.dalitawaz.com/protection.asp#a1)

7. visit http://www.dalitawaz.com/protection.asp#a1
8. This national public hearing of NCDHR was held at Chennai during 18-19, April 2000.

2

Legal Protection to Dalits

An Overview

Eradication of the practice of untouchability and protecting Dalits from atrocities and humiliation have been the much-admired concern of most of the nationalists and political bigwigs even before India's Independence. Though there was hardly any law ensuring their basic human rights, safety and dignity, there were laws declaring them as untouchables. There were laws enforcing inhuman punishments against those Dalits declining to be untouchables. There were also laws prohibiting them from taking up occupations of their choice, and condemning them as slaves of others. This chapter focuses on the various laws that came into effect in different period of time, the context in which they came into effect and their impact particularly in the lives of Dalits.

Ancient Laws Favouring Untouchability and Atrocities

Before the advent of the modern age, it was largely the religion-based laws enshrined in the sacred books of Hindus such as the *Vedas, Smritis, Brahmanas,* and the *Puranas* that governed the people of India. Among these, the Hindu Code of Conducts, popularly known as the *Manusmriti,* written by the

Hindu law giver, Manu, is worth noting, particularly, in view of its deep influence among Hindus and the devotion with which the Hindus adhere to its teaching till date. That is why, Ambedkar too considered, the *Manusmriti* as the book of (Hindu) religion (Ambedkar, 1987: 336). What are Manu's teachings that particularly explain the unequal social status and power relations between Brahmins and other upper caste Hindus on the one hand, and the Shudras and Ati-Shudras on the other? What are those specific teachings of Manu that condemn some people by birth as untouchables and subject them to abject poverty and inhuman indignities and brutalities, and extol some others as gods on earth assuring undue status and power? Though Manu has propounded a number of provisions in *Munusmriti* justifying the unequal relation and status between Brahmins, on the one side, and the Shudras and Ati-Shudras on the other, only a few that explains such inequality more overtly, have been listed below.[1] According to Manu:

> The Brahmins are Gods on earth. ...A Brahmin is entitled to whatever exists in the world. In fact the whole world is his property, and others live in his charity" (see Ghurye, 1969: 47, 90).[2]
>
> (VIII. 380) Never shall the King slay a Brahman, though convicted of all possible crimes; let him banish the offender from his realm, but with all his property secure, and his body unhurt (see Ambedkar, 1987: 30).
>
> (VIII. 131) No greater crime is known on earth than slaying a Brahman; and the King, therefore, must not even form in his mind an idea of killing a priest (Ibid. 31).

But in the case of the Shudras and Ati-Shudras, Manu propounded altogether different policies. These are mostly unjust and discriminatory in nature. He denied Shudras and Ati-Shudras access to education, access to economic independence, and prevented them from marrying outside their caste. He also prescribed stringent punishments against those not adhering to these provisions. Besides, he made it obligatory on the part of the rulers/kings to implement these polices strictly. It is therefore necessary to look into some of these provisions:

For instance, Manu considered the Shudras as slaves (see Ambedkar, 1987: 26). (I. 91) Serving meekly all other classes/ castes is the only occupation prescribed for the Shudras (Ibid. 40). The Shudras' works (rites) are declared by implication to be unproductive of rewards either in this world or in the next" (see Ghurye, 1969: 60). The other such provisions include:

> (VIII.281) A man of the lowest class (Shudra), who shall insolently place himself on the same seat with one of the highest, shall either be banished with a mark on his hinder parts, or the king shall cause a gash to be made on his buttock (see Ambedkar, 1987: 29).
>
> (VIII.271) If he (Shudra) mentions their (Brahmins') names and classes with contumely, ... an iron style, ten fingers long, shall be thrust red into his mouth (Ibid. 28).
>
> A Shudra is not entitled to the rite of initiation, the study of Vedas, and the kindling of the sacred fire (Ibid. 60). (XII. 4) If the Shudra intentionally listens and committing to memorise the Veda, then his ears should be filled with (molten) lead and lac; if he utters the Veda, then his tongue should be cut off; if he has mastered the Veda his body should be cut to pieces (Ibid. 43).
>
> (X.129) No collection of wealth must be made by a Shudra even though he be able to do it; for a Shudra who has acquired wealth gives pain to Brahmins (Ibid. 41).

With regard to man-woman relationship between the Brahmins and Shudras Manu observed:

> (VIII 359) A man of the servile class (Shudra), who commits actual adultery with the wife of a priest, ought to suffer death (Ibid. 29) or shall be burnt alive tied up in straw (Ghurye, 1969: 62).

While this was the 'social dignity' Manu assured to the Shudras, the dignity he assured to the Ati-Shudras or Chandalas was even more deplorable. Who comprise the Ati-Shudras? The washer-men, leather-workers, cane-workers, fishermen, and the Bhils as *Antyajas* or outcastes come under this category (Ibid. 98). More stringent punishments have been propounded against them. Manu placed the Ati-Shudras below the level of Shudras in the social status/caste hierarchy by interpreting that the Ati-Shudras are the children born out of unholy and illegitimate alliance between Brahmin females and Shudra males, and thus labeled them as untouchables (Chandalas), and thus endorsed the practice of untouchability. The deteriorating condition of these caste groups that enjoyed relatively a better status before Manu is evident from the following observation:

> "the class of people called Chandalas, Svapachas and Mritapas had slowly but surely deteriorated in their social position between the time of Panini and that of Manu. In the former age they lived within the limits of the village in which other orders and castes lived. In the age of Manu (X, 51-2) they were not only excluded from the village but were assigned duties and perquisites which clearly show that they were looked upon as vile specimens of humanity." Ghurye (Ibid. 312): A householder is exhorted to throw some food for them (Chandala) and the outcastes along with that for crows and dogs outside the house, after all the members of the household have taken their meals.
>
> (X.51) The dwellings of the Chandalas shall be outside the village; they must be made Apapatras and their wealth (shall be) dogs and donkeys (see Ambedkar, 1987).
>
> On touching a Chandala or one who has touched a Chandala one must immediately bathe with one's clothes on. If a Brahmin unintentionally eats the food or accepts the presents given by a Chandala he is out-cast. But if he does so knowingly he becomes equal to a Chandala (see Ghurye, 1969: 79).
>
> According to Ushanas, the Chandala was to enter a village for sweeping, etc., in the first half of the day, carrying a broom under his armpit and a small pot hanging at his neck. ...A Brahmin, drinking water from the vessel of a Chandala, has to undergo the penance of living on cow's urine for a number of days (Ibid.: 98).
>
> (X.125) The remnants of their (Brahmins') food must be given to him, as well as their old clothes, the refuse of their grain, and their old household furniture (see Ambedkar, 1987: 41).

These codes of conducts of Manu did not remain as mere laws, but were strictly enforced for centuries by every ruler, and thus the notion of caste and untouchability got engrained in the very psyche and personality of the caste Hindus. And these notions and caste prejudices among caste Hindus often get reflected not only in their behaviour pattern, but also in their decisions that often decide the social, educational and economic status of the oppressed caste groups/Dalits. The Dalits also believed in Manu's commandments, and thus never questioned their pitiable existence. All these affected the interests of the oppressed groups to a large extent.

On the whole, the Dalits, the victims of such laws, had no option but to adhere meekly to these oppressive and discriminative laws of Manu. That these laws reduced them to be 'untouchables' for caste Hindus is not an exaggeration. To the question how these caste groups have been reduced to such a level, Ambedkar observed:

> "Untouchables were treated as slaves because: (1) they were so socialized as never to complain of their low state; (2) they never dreamed of trying to improve their lot, by forcing the other classes to treat them with the common respect; (3) the idea that they had been born to their lot was so ingrained in their mind that it never occurred to them to think that their fate was anything so irrevocable; (4) Nothing would ever persuade them that men are all made of the same clay, or that they have the right to insist on better treatment than that meted out to them." (see Iyer, K. 1989: 38-39).

However, protests against such laws and discriminatory practices became a reality over a period of time with the clarion call given by revolutionary social reformer like Ambedkar. Out of agony he once spoke to his fellowmen in the following words:

> "My heart breaks to see the pitiable sight of your faces and to hear your sad voices. You have been groaning from time immemorial and yet you are not ashamed to hug your helplessness as inevitability. Why did you not perish in the prenatal stage instead? Why do you worsen and sadden the picture of the sorrows, poverty, slavery and burdens of the world with your deplorable, despicable, detestable, and miserable life? You had better died and relieved this world

if you could not rejuvenate yourself. As a matter of fact, it is your birthright to get food, shelter and clothing in equal proportion with every individual, high or low. If you believe in living a respectable life you should believe in self-help which is the best help" (see Ibid. 41).

Pre-Independence Legal Initiatives Against Untouchability

Though a number of reformers from different parts of India attempted to eradicate untouchability and even devoted their entire life to this cause, the desired change could not be achieved owing to the fact that the notion of untouchability had got deeply ingrained in the Dalits' socio-cultural milieu, and there was no formal effort to abolish untouchability legally. However, the efforts of Ambedkar and a few others did result in enactment of a number of laws to protect the interests of the Dalits in the British India. For instance, in British India, Lord Ellenborough, prohibited the legal recognition of slavery in India. Following this Act, "The Caste Disabilities Removal Act XXI of 1850" was also passed aiming at removing disabilities arising out of Dalits' lower caste background.

However, it was only at the turn of nineteenth century the "depressed classes" became an important focus of concern with the reformers. It was only after 1909 that fears of threatened Hindu majorities and proposals for special legislative representation for "untouchables" shifted "untouchability" from the realm of philanthropy into the political arena. In 1917, the Indian National Congress reversed its long-standing policy of excluding "social reform" from its programme in passing a hesitant anti-disabilities resolution. And in 1923, the Bombay Legislative Council resolved that the untouchables be allowed to use all public watering places, wells, schools, dispensaries, etc. The National Congress' annual meeting at Karachi in 1931 concluded that

(a) No disability to attach to any citizen by reason of his or her ....caste ...in regard to public employment, office of power or honours, and in the exercise of any trade or calling.

(b) Equal rights of all citizens in regard to public roads, wells, schools and other place of public resort.

On September 25, 1932 a conference of caste Hindus which was held to ratify the Poona Pact adopted the following:

> "The Congress resolves that henceforth, amongst Hindus, no one shall be regarded as an untouchable by reason of his birth, and that those who have been so regarded hitherto will have the same right as other Hindus in regard to the use of public wells, public schools, public roads and all other public institutions. This right shall have statutory recognition at the first opportunity and shall be one of the earliest Acts of the Swaraj Parliament, if it shall not have received such recognition before that time.
>
> It is further agreed that it shall be the duty of all Hindu leaders to secure, by every legitimate and peaceful means, an early removal of all social disabilities now imposed by custom upon the so-called untouchable classes, including the bar in respect of admission to temples".

Besides, a number of temple-entry and anti-disabilities bills were introduced in the Central Legislative Assembly and in the Madras and Bombay Legislatures during 1932 and 1936. But these bills enjoyed only limited support within the Congress and met with stiff resistance from the orthodox, and a decidedly cool reception from the government. It may also be noted that none of these bills contained any penal provisions (see Galanter, 1972: 237-39).

In 1938, "The Madras Removal of Civil Disabilities Act 1938 (Madras Act XXI of 1938)" came into operation. It was in 1938, when Bombay and Madras had passed the temple-entry Acts, that for the first time in British India, did the governments intervene to secure the opening of temples for the untouchables. Between 1943 and 1950, 17 such laws were enacted by different provinces of India (see Annexure 1). But these laws brought no significant change about. Caste and untouchability continued as major social evils in India. Though the British established Legislative Bodies as early as 1861, it did not give due importance to eradicate these social evils.[3] It is therefore necessary to understand the extent to which the Dalits were protected from untouchability and atrocities through these laws?

It has been observed that these laws were applied not only not earnestly but also in contravention to their sprit. Regarding the use and abuse of such laws, Galanter observes:

> "During the period of British rule in India, the practices which came to be called "untouchability" received limited and for the most part indirect support from the law. ...The abolition of slavery in the middle of the nineteenth century extended elementary rights to many Untouchables. These lowest orders, then, enjoyed equality in the eyes of law and had access to it, at least formally. [But] In practice legal institutions often adapted themselves to prevailing patterns of disability.
>
> ...Courts granted injunctions to restrain members of particular castes from entering temples – even ones that were publicly supported and dedicated to the entire Hindu community. Damages were awarded for purificatory ceremonies necessitated by the pollution caused by the presence of lower castes; such pollution was actionable as a tress-passer to the person of lower castes" (Galanter, 1972: 228-29).

These observations aptly depict how the laws against caste disabilities were insincerely implemented. Before turning towards efforts initiated in Independent India, it may be noted that most of the laws passed in the British India were mainly region-specific, operating at the regional or provincial levels. And there was no law, which could cover the entire nation. Enactment of such laws became a possible reality only after India's Independence.

Constitutional Remedies

The post-independent India had a vision of egalitarian nation. Its "Constitution has emphasised the unity and integrity of the nation as a paramount value and insisted upon equality and dignity as a constitutional fundamental. In a powerful endeavour to produce a casteless society, the Constitution has promised equal protection of laws to the lowliest and the lost, forbidden *untouchability* and made free access to all places of public resort a fundamental right" (Iyer, 1989: 14). More specifically, Article 46 of the Indian Constitution unequivocally expresses:

> "The State shall promote with special care the educational and economic interests of the weaker sections of the people, and in particular, of the Scheduled Castes and the Scheduled Tribes, and shall protect them from social injustice and all forms of exploitation."

Many privileges, which were considered as serious offences in the case of the 'untouchables' under Manu's law, became the fundamental rights of these caste groups under the Constitution of India. For example, Manu denied them education, inter-dinning and inter-caste marriage, but the Constitution has guaranteed them access to all these privileges. Under the various provisions of Constitution, a number of programme have been planned and implemented encouraging inter-caste marriages and inter-dinning, and to protect them from the stigma of untouchability and caste-based discriminations. For instance, Article 17 of the Constitution declares:

> "Untouchability is abolished and its practice in any form is forbidden. The enforcement of any disability arising out of untouchability shall be an offence punishable in accordance with Law."

According to Article 15(2), No citizen shall, on grounds only of religion, race, caste, sex, place of birth or any of them, be subject to any disability, liability, restrictions or condition with regard to:

(a) access to shops, public restaurants, hotels and place of public entertainment; or

(b) the use of wells, tanks, bathing ghats, roads and places of public resort maintained wholly or partly out of state funds or dedicated to the use of the general public.

Article 29 (2) forbids persons in charge of "any educational institutions receiving aid out of state funds" to deny admission to an applicant "on grounds only of religion, race, caste, language or any of them". Similarly, Article 23 prohibits *begar* and forced labour.

Under these special constitutional provisions, number of social practices which were considered proper under Manu's laws became illegal under the modern laws. With a view to making those wrongs as right and those rights wrong, a number of enactments were passed.

PCR Act, 1955

To give effect to Article 17 and other such provisions of the Indian Constitution, the Parliament came out with a special law known as, "The Untouchability (Offences) Act, 1955". This Act was subsequently amended in 1976 and renamed as the "Protection of Civil Rights Act, 1955" to make the provisions of the Act more stringent. With a view to carrying out the provisions of this Act, the Government of India, as provided under the Act, notified the rules of the Act, viz., "The PCR Rules, 1977" (see Annexure 2; also see Government of India, 2000). The salient features of this law include the following:

1. Offences under the PCR Act are cognizable as well as non compoundable.
2. Under section 12 of the Act, if a member of non-SC commits any offence forbidden in the Act, the Court shall presume, unless the contrary is proved, that such act was committed on the ground of untouchability. In other words, under this Act, it is the accused who has to prove his innocence.
3. The Act provides for awarding minimum punishment of imprisonment for one month and a fine of Rs. 100 to the maximum imprisonment for six months and a fine of Rs. 500. For the second offence, the punishment may range from imprisonment for six months and a fine of Rs. 200 to imprisonment for one year and a fine of Rs. 500. For the third and subsequent offences the punishment ranges from one year imprisonment and a fine of Rs. 500 to imprisonment of two years and a fine of Rs. 1000. The offence, except when punishable with imprisonment for a minimum term exceeding three months, may be tried summarily by a Judicial Magistrate.
4. The Act has charged the Central Government with the responsibility of coordinating the measures taken by the

State Governments and placing a report on the table of each House of Parliament every year on the working of the PCR Act 1955. The Central Government has so far (up to 1997-98) laid 14 reports (Government of India, 1998: 200).

POA Act, 1989

Since cases of atrocities on SCs and STs were not covered under the provisions of the PCR Act 1955, and atrocities against SCs and STs continued unabated, the Parliament passed yet another important Act in 1989 known as the "Scheduled Castes and Scheduled Tribes (Prevention of Atrocities) Act, 1989" (POA Act), which came into effect from 30 October 1990 (see Annexure 3). For carrying out the provisions of this Act, the Government of India notified the Scheduled Castes and Scheduled Tribes (Prevention of Atrocities) Rules, 1995 on 31 March 1995 (see Annexure 4). Certain chapters and sections of the Indian Penal Code (IPC) and the Criminal Procedure Code (Code) have also been applied as required.

The offences covered under the SCs and STs (Prevention of Atrocities) Act, 1989 (POA Act) are cognizable and non-bailable (Government of India, 1998: 201). These include: (1) forcing to eat obnoxious substances, (2) dumping waste matter on land, (3) denudation, (4) wrongful occupation of land, (5) dispossession, (6) boded labour, (7) intimidation during voting, (8) mischievous litigation, (9) false information, (10) public humiliation, (11) outrage of modesty, (12) sexual exploitation, (13) fouling of water resource, (14) obstruction of entry to a place of public resort, (15) eviction from habitation, (16) mischief with explosives, (17) destruction of buildings, and (18) suppression of evidences.

Compared to the provisions of the IPC, the offences under the POA Act carry heavier penalties. For instance, the offences of custodial rape, highway robbery and house breaking by night which carry a minimum punishment of 10 years under the IPC are punishable with imprisonment for life and with fine under the POA Act. The Act also provides for forfeiture of property, externment, and collective punitive fine, and empowers Special

Courts and Special Prosecutors for expeditious disposal of cases (Government of India, 1998b: 232-33).

Under section 8 of this Act, if the accused is proved to have rendered any financial assistance to a person accused of, the Special Court shall presume, unless the contrary is proved, that such person had abetted the offence.

Under clause 4 of section 21 of the POA Act, the Central Government is required to coordinate the measures taken by the State governments and to place on the table of each House of Parliament every year, a report on the measures taken by itself and by the State Governments. Till 1999, the Government of India, Ministry of Social Justice and Empowerment has submitted six annual reports on the implementation of the POA Act (Government of India, 2001).

As per these laws, offences against the SCs and STs committed by members other than SCs and STs will be registered under the various provisions of either the PCR Act 1955 or the POA Act 1989 or under both these laws depending on the nature of offences committed. While the untouchability related offences are to be registered under the PCR Act, the atrocity related offences are to be covered under the POA Act.

Besides these two Acts, the Constitution of India also has a provision under Article 338 to appoint Special Officer to investigate all matters relating to the safeguards provided in various statues for the SCs and STs and to report to the President of India upon the working of these safeguards. Accordingly, on November 18, 1950, a Special Officer designated as Commissioner for the SCs and STs was appointed. But in view of the ever-increasing magnitude of issues to be handled, in 1978 a broad based multi-member body was thought of in place of the single Special Officer. Accordingly, the National Commission for the SCs and STs came into operation. In 1990 Article 338, which had already been amended twice (Forty-sixth Amendment Bill 1978 and Fifty-first Amendment Bill 1979), was once again amended, viz., Constitution (Sixty-fifth Amendment) Act, 1990 and received the assent of the President of India on 7 June 1990. And this Act, which came into effect from March 12, 1992, enabled the Government for the setting up of the National Commission for the SCs and STs. As per section (9) of Article 338 of the Constitution, it is mandatory for the Union and every State Government to consult the Commission on all major policy matters affecting the SCs and STs. According to clause 5(c) of Article 338, the Commission is required to participate and advise on the planning process of socio-economic development of SCs and STs, and evaluate the progress of their development under the Union or any state.

Incidents of Untouchability and Atrocities on SCs and STs

Despite such powerful legal provisions and government bodies to implement them, the SCs and STs continue to suffer from the stigma of untouchability and bear the brunt of worst forms of atrocities all over India. While recognizing the fact that most of the offences against the SCs and STs particularly those occurring in rural areas go unreported, recent data on cases of untouchability and atrocity as registered under the IPC and special laws, viz., the PCR Act and the POA Act reveal vividly that these are still very much a day-to-day reality. A survey undertaken in 1996 at 69 villages of Gujarat revealed that in as many as 46 villages, Dalits did not have access to common water source. Being treated as untouchables, they had to depend on separate/different source for water. The survey conducted during 1992-93 in 52 villages of Karnataka revealed that as high as 80 per cent Dalits were prevented from entering into village temples. In about 400 villages of Warangal district, Andhra Pradesh, still the two-tumbler system[4] is observed (see Sharma, M. 2004: 154). A recent sample study in Maharashtra – a state known for anti-untouchability campaign and Dalit mobilization – indicates that in about 50 per cent villages of the state, untouchability was strictly observed especially with regard to Dalits' entry into temples. In about 75 per cent villages of Marathwada region, Dalits were prohibited from entering into temples. In about 50 per cent villages of western Maharashtra, there was separate source of water for Dalits and the non-Dalits. In about 40 per cent villages of Maharashtra, Dalits had to use separate cremation grounds. It was also observed that the caste Hindu women avoided interacting with Dalit women (Action Aid, 2002: 9-11).

There is a gradual decline in the number of cases of atrocities against the SCs and STs. As can be seen from Table 2.1, even though the number of atrocities against the SCs rose from 24973 in 1993 to 33908 in 1994, it declined since then.

Table 2.1
Number of Crimes Against SCs and STs
(Cases registered under IPC and PCR & POA Acts)

Year	*SCs*	*STs*	*Total*
1993	24973	3652	28625
1994	33908	5019	38927
1995	32996	5498	38494
1996	31440	4973	36413
1997	27944	4644	32588
1998	25638	4276	29914
1999	25093	4450	29543

Source: Crimes in India, 1994:247; 1996:102; 1999:227.

It was 32996 in 1995, 27944 in 1997, and only 25093 in 1999. Almost a similar trend is evident even in the case of the STs. The total number of reported crimes against the STs rose, at the initial stage, from 3652 in 1993 to 5019 in 1994 and further up to 5498 in 1995. But from then onwards it declined to 4973 in 1996, 4644 in 1997, and 4276 in 1998. A marginal increase of 4450 in 1999 is however on record. Even when we look at specific crimes such as murder and rape, a similar trend is noticeable (Table 2.2). The number of reported cases of murder of persons belonging to the SCs by the non-SCs, though rose at the initial stage from 510 in 1993 to 571 in 1995, it declined later on to 543 in 1996, 516 in 1998 and 506 in 1999. A similar declining trend is evident even in the case of the STs.

However, with regard to incidences of rape of SC women, a disturbing trend is seen. The number of incidence of rape has gone up over the years both in the case of SCs and STs. For instance, the number of rape cases with regard to the SCs increased from 849 in 1992 to 992 in 1994, 1037 in 1997 and 1000 in 1999. Incidence of the crimes considered as offences only under the provisions of the PCR Act and the POA Act, also show a similar declining in occurrence trend. The number of such offences against the SCs as registered under the PCR Act declined from 2900 in 1992 to 1731 in 1994, 1417 in 1996 and 1216 in 1997. And it was only 678 in 1999. Offences registered under

Table 2.2

Incidence of Reported Crimes against Scheduled Castes and Scheduled Tribes during 1992-1999

Sr No	Crime-Head	Scheduled Castes								Scheduled Tribes							
		1992	1993	1994	1995	1996	1997	1998	1999	1992	1993	1994	1995	1996	1997	1998	1999
1.	Murder	616	510	546	571	543	513	516	506	103	105	105	75	94	95	66	80
2.	Rape	849	798	992	873	949	1037	923	1000	334	328	385	369	314	315	331	384
3.	Kidnapping & Abduction	213	246	251	276	281	243	253	228	62	44	64	74	50	41	56	59
4.	Dacoity	81	102	78	70	90	58	49	36	8	9	8	18	32	3	5	3
5.	Robbery	265	197	259	218	213	162	150	109	19	21	8	27	21	8	15	8
6.	Arson	406	369	553	500	464	389	346	337	47	26	36	40	51	29	38	43
7.	Hurt	NA	NA	4542	4544	4585	3860	3809	3241	NA	NA	699	688	694	706	638	646
8.	PCR Act	2900	2531	1731	1528	1417	1216	724	678	248	150	63	71	72	88	50	45
9.	SC/ST (POA)	NA	NA	14938	13925	9620	8070	7443	7301	NA	NA	1316	1480	754	643	709	574
10.	Others	19592	20220	10038	10492	13278	12396	11425	11657	3485	2969	2335	2656	2891	2716	2368	2608
11.	Total	24922	24973	33908	32996	31440	27944	25638	25093	4306	3652	5019	5498	4973	4644	4276	4450

Source: Crimes in India, 1994, 1996, 1999.

the POA Act, also declined from 14938 in 1994 to 9620 in 1996, 7443 in 1998 and 7301 in 1999. Although an increasing trend was evident all along with regard to number of crimes against the SCs and STs, from 1994 onwards a declining trend is seen in almost all crime heads (Table 2.2).

When all other conditions with regard to the existing social relations between the SCs and others, and the government approaches to deal with issues pertaining to these communities remain the same all along, why is there a declining trend in the incidence of crimes against the SCs and STs specifically from 1994 onwards? In answering this moot question, one can not ignore the deterrent role that the special laws, such as the Protection of Civil Rights Act, 1955 and the Scheduled Castes and Scheduled Tribes (Prevention of Atrocities) Act, 1989 would have played, in particular, the stringent penal provisions of the POA Act which came into operation from 1990, but more effectively from 1992 onwards.

Though a declining trend has been the common feature from 1995 onwards in most the states and Union Territories including states such as Uttar Pradesh, Rajasthan, Madhya Pradesh and Gujarat, it has not been so in the case of a few other states such as Bihar, Orissa and Tamil Nadu where an increasing trend is noticed (see Table 2.3). As regards the former category, Uttar Pradesh, which experienced at the initial stage, an increasing trend in the incidence of crimes against the SCs and STs, it started declining gradually from 16263 in 1994 to 11299 in 1996, 7095 in 1998 and 6917 in 1999. Rajasthan, which experienced an increasing trend during 1993-96, started declining from 8016 in 1996 to 7069 in 1997, 6858 in 1998 and 6838 in 1999. But in the case of Bihar, which falls in the category of "increasing trend", the number of reported crimes against the SCs and STs rose from 827 in 1993 to 892 in 1994, 1000 in 1996 and 1407 in 1998, though the number declined marginally during 1996-97 (868) and during 1998-99 (1258). Similarly, the state of Orissa also experienced an increasing trend.

It is, however, shocking to find almost a similar trend even in a state like Tamil Nadu, which is known for its anti-Brahmin movement in the early 1920s, and aimed at eliminating the supremacy of Brahmins in all socio-economic and

Table 2.3

Incidence of Crime Against Scheduled Castes and Scheduled Tribes (under IPC as well as Special Laws)

Sr. No.	States/Union Territories	No. of Reported Crimes						
		1993	1994	1995	1996	1997	1998	1999
1	Uttar Pradesh	10390	16263	14310	11299	8586	7095	6917
2	Rajasthan	5251	6193	6981	8016	7069	6858	6838
3	Madhya Pradesh	5191	5519	5669	5541	5669	4138	3990
4	Gujarat	2001	2366	2210	2133	2215	2138	1846
5	Maharashtra	1604	1921	2127	1689	1020	1069	927
6	Andhra Pradesh	795	1395	1929	1881	2116	540	721
7	Tamil Nadu	539	1593	1333	1897	1630	897	1011
8	Karnataka	936	1024	1267	1269	1305	1279	1239
9	Bihar	827	892	979	1000	868	1407	1258
10	Kerala	567	805	881	762	894	716	NA
11	Orissa	268	680	472	665	916	1332	1449
12	Himachal Pradesh	71	83	87	69	62	15	13
13	Haryana	57	67	82	64	98	32	28
14	Sikkim	25	43	73	60	49	0	0
15	Jammu and Kashmir	20	14	33	23	19	*	*
16	Pondicherry	15	16	24	13	23	1	2
17	Punjab	14	10	12	13	11	17	19
18	Dadra & Nagar Haveli	15	12	3	1	1	1	1
19	Delhi	4	8	6	11	19	7	14
20	West Bengal	14	1	Nil	Nil	Nil	15	9
21	Chandigarh	Nil	14	Nil	Nil	1	0	0
22	Goa	6	2	4	1	2	2	1
23	Meghalaya	6	1	4	1	13	0	0
24	Manipur	3	2	3	Nil	Nil	2	NA
25	Daman and Diu	2	Nil	3	Nil	Nil	0	1
26	Arunachal Pradesh	1	2	2	5	0	0	0
27	Mizoram	3	Nil	Nil	Nil	Nil	0	0

Contd...

Contd...

28	Nagaland	Nil	1	Nil	Nil	Nil	0	0
29	Assam	Nil	Nil	Nil	Nil	Nil	0	0
30	Tripura	Nil	Nil	Nil	Nil	Nil	0	0
31	Andaman and Nicobar Islands	Nil	Nil	Nil	Nil	2	0	1
32	Lakshdweep	Nil	Nil	Nil	Nil	Nil	0	0
	Total	28625	38927	38494	36413	32588	27561	26285

* The POA Act does not extend to Jammu and Kashmir State; NA= information awaited.

Source: Annual Report on Scheduled Castes and Scheduled Tribes (Prevention of Atrocities) Act, 1989; (Reports of 1995:2, 1997:4-5; 1997:4-5; 1998:4-5; 1999: 5-6), Government of India, New Delhi.

political spheres as a panacea for all issues concerning not only the non-Brahmin Backward Castes but also the SCs who suffered from untouchability and atrocities and experienced innumerable indignities and exploitations. It is shocking also for the reason that it was Tamil Nadu state which took the formal effort as early as 1938 of passing a legislation, "The Madras Removal of Civil Disabilities Act, 1938 (Madras Act XXI of 1938)", to ban the practice of untouchability and to protect the interests of the SCs. While it will definitely be of interest looking into the uniqueness of states like Tamil Nadu for experiencing increasing incidence of crimes against the SCs and STs, one would also wonder at and question as to why atrocities on SCs and STs at all, despite legislations against such crimes. It has been observed well ahead of time, that such crimes are, reflective of nothing but the unhealthy social relations operating in rural areas. In fact, according to Ambedkar:

> "A perpetual war is going on everyday in every village between the Hindus and the Untouchables. It is a contest between the Hindus who are economically and socially strong and the Untouchables who are economically poor and numerically small" (Ambedkar, 1979: 426). "Most often they [untouchables] are composed of a few families and their number is very small, too small to give them any power to repel an attack of the caste Hindus". Besides, "they are a disunited body infested with the caste system in which they believe as much as do the caste Hindus. This has

given rise to mutual rivalry and jealousy and made common action impossible" (1989: 265-266).

Though this observation aptly depicts the root cause for the frequent caste conflicts between caste groups in villages, the National Commission for the SCs and STs, has indicated "land" as the most important single cause for atrocities against the SCs and STs. In other words, atrocities against the SCs are reaction of the upper caste Hindus towards the SCs' assertion over ownership of land (Government of India, 1990:7). None can of course rule out these factors as major sources of caste conflicts particularly in villages, our concern in the context is to know the impact of the two special laws at the national level in curbing down the crimes committed against the SCs and STs. This cannot be understood better unless we know the extent to which these laws have been used successfully in punishing the accused. It is therefore necessary to look into the nature of disposal of cases registered under these laws.

It is often argued that most of the cases registered under these special laws are false and therefore ending in acquittal. How far is this argument valid?

Before evaluating the validity of this argument directly, it is necessary to clarify a few points as far as the disposal of PCR and POA Act cases is concerned. It is to be noted that every case registered either under the PCR or POA Act or under both have to pass through two constitutionally recognized bodies, viz., the "police" and the "judiciary", before reaching its logical end, which could be either "conviction" or "acquittal". In this process of taking each case to its logical end, one needs to bear in mind that all reported cases are not necessarily registered, and when registered, not necessarily under these special laws; and all cases so registered are not necessarily charge-sheeted by the police and sent to courts for trial, and all cases tried in the courts, not necessarily end in conviction. Some of the reported cases get closed at the police station itself through negotiation between the victims and accused, facilitated by the police, while some others are closed after due police investigation. Even after investigation, the police cannot close the case unless they subsequently seek the consent of the courts for the same by filing the "referred charge sheet" in the courts concerned. And the Court cannot give consent for the closure of such cases without the consent of the victims/complainants. Cases so closed are technically known as "referred cases". It may also be noted here that in a situation where the complainant is not satisfied with the investigation, he/she can request the concerned Court for another order for investigation, and accordingly, the Court can order the police concerned.

We may now focus on the validity of the argument cited above. In 1993, as seen in Table 2.4, out of 24236 reported cases including cases brought forward from the previous year, as many as 21656 (89.35%) cases were disposed of by the police, and only about 11 per cent pending with the police at the year end. But for the year 1996, though the number of cases to be disposed of rose to 32131, the cases actually disposed of were only 25555 (79.53%), that is about 9 per cent less than that of 1993. Except for the year 1998 in which the number of cases disposed of declined to as low as about 74 per cent and raising the pending cases to about 26 per cent, a more or less similar picture of gradual decline in the percentage of cases disposed of is seen from 1995 onwards.

More crucial in the present context is the data pertaining to the nature of disposal of cases by the police. It is evident from Table 2.4a that in 1993 out of the 21656 POA Act cases disposed of, only about 22 per cent cases were referred, i.e., closed after investigation, and for about as high as 78 per cent cases charges were framed against the accused (charge-sheeted cases) and subsequently sent to courts for trial. Most important point to be noted here is that *"in the eyes of the police all the charge-sheeted cases are true cases"*. The police generally do not frame charges against any accused unless they are satisfied with the validity of the case registered and confident about securing necessary evidences to prove the case in the Court of law. The percentage of charge-sheeted cases remained by and large the same for the rest of the period as well. The average percentage of cases charge-sheeted every year works out to be about 76 during 1993-99. This means even from the point of view of the police, as high as about 76 per cent of the POA Act cases disposed of by them every year are true cases. This conclusion negates in the most unequivocal terms the cliché that most of the cases

Table 2.4

Disposal of POA Act Cases by Police in India during 1993-99

Sr. No.	*Item*	*1993*	*1994*	*1995*	*1996*	*1997*	*1998*	*1999*	*1993-99 Average*
1	Total number of cases (including brought forward)	24236 (100)	27343 (100)	29867 (100)	32131 (100)	35017 (100)	34988 (100)	34799 (100)	31197.28 (100)
2	No. of cases actually disposed (cases closed + cases charge sheeted)	21656 (89.35)	23623 (86.39)	23677 (79.27)	25555 (79.53)	28076 (80.17)	25857 (73.90)	28572 (82.10)	25288 (81.06)
3	No. of cases pending with the police at the year end.	2580 (10.64)	3720 (13.61)	6190 (20.73)	6576 (20.47)	6941 (19.82)	9131 (26.10)	6227 (17.89)	5909.28 (18.94)

Figures in parentheses represent column percentage.

Source: Annual Report on Scheduled Castes and Scheduled Tribes (Prevention of Atrocities) Act, 1989 (Reports of 1995:5; 1997:9; 1998:8; 1999:8), Government of India, New Delhi.

Table 2.4a

POA Act Cases Disposed by the Police in India during 1993-99

Sr. No.	*Item*	*1993*	*1994*	*1995*	*1996*	*1997*	*1998*	*1999*	*1993-99 Average*
1	No. of cases actually disposed (including those brought forward and excluding those pending with police at year end)	21656 (100)	23623 (100)	23677 (100)	25555 (100)	28076 (100)	25857 (100)	28572 (100)	25288 (100)
2	No. of cases closed after investigation	4660 (21.51)	4716 (19.96)	4967 (20.97)	4585 (17.94)	7236 (25.77)	7522 (29.09)	8985 (31.44)	6095.86 (24.10)
3	No. of cases charge sheeted in courts	16996 (78.48)	18907 (80.03)	18710 (79.02)	20970 (82.05)	20840 (74.22)	18335 (70.91)	19587 (68.55)	19192.14 (75.89)

Figures in parentheses represent column percentage.

Source: Worked out of Table 2.4.

registered under the POA Act are false cases. Even the remaining 24 per cent cases which represent the cases closed after investigation, and which are usually alleged as false, are not necessarily false ones. Unless each case is looked into in detail, the validity of the closure of the cases cannot be taken for granted.

The second major stage that each registered case has to pass through is the stage of trial in the Court of law. Do all charge-sheeted cases, which in the eyes of the police are true, stand in the Court of law as true ones and accordingly, end in conviction? To answer this moot question, we shall have to look into the data on disposal of POA Act cases by the courts. Table 2.5 gives an alarming percentage of cases pending trial in the courts at the end of every year. According to Table 2.5, the percentage of cases pending trial during 1993-99 ranged from 78.95 to 90.83 and exhibits an increasing trend over the years except for the year 1998. The average annual percentage of cases pending trial at various courts in India works out to be as high as 87.8 per cent during the said period. This undue delay in the courts in disposing of the charge-sheeted cases adds to the agony and anguish of the victims, and causes them enormous hardships, economic loss, uncertainties and anxiety. The delay in a way exposes the limitations of the Session Courts (designated Special Courts) in disposing of POA Act cases and brings to light the urgent need to establish more of exclusive Special Courts to expedite the trial of pending POA and PCR Act cases.

Though during 1993-99 the police considered, as stated earlier, on an average, about 76 per cent of the cases they disposed of every year as true ones, and accordingly, charge-sheeted them for trial. On an average, only about 10 per cent of the cases disposed of by the courts every year ended in conviction, and the rest, about 90 per cent cases, ended in acquittal. It may be reiterated here that *acquitted cases* do not mean in any way *false cases* as often alleged and taken to be. It only means that these cases could not be proved in the Court of law beyond doubt. It is sometimes surprising that even a number of the POA Act cases of "rape with murder" get acquitted on the ground of the victim's inability to prove his or her case beyond doubt in the Court of law. As a result, the victims feel further intimidated and exploited. The question now is, why are the SCs

Table 2.5

Disposal of POA Act Cases by Courts in India during 1993-99

Sr. No.	*Item*	*1993*	*1994*	*1995*	*1996*	*1997*	*1998*	*1999*	*1993-99 Average*
1.	Total number of cases to be disposed (including brought forward)	41359 (100)	56002 (100)	67209 (100)	132463 (100)	139447 (100)	147340 (100)	133577 (100)	102485.28 (100)
2.	No. of cases disposed by courts	4678 (11.31)	7581 (13.54)	7191 (10.70)	13226 (9.98)	12781 (9.17)	31011 (21.05)	12864 (9.63)	12761.71 (12.45)
3.	No. of cases pending with the courts at the year end.	36681 (88.69)	48421 (86.46)	60018 (89.30)	119237 (90.02)	126666 (90.83)	116329 (78.95)	120713 (90.37)	89723.51 (87.54)

Figures in parentheses represent column percentage.

Source: Annual Report on Scheduled Castes and Scheduled Tribes (Prevention of Atrocities) Act, 1989, (Reports of 1995:5-6; 1997:10:1998:9; 1999:9), Government of India, New Delhi.

Table 2.5a

Extent of Conviction and Aquittal in POA Cases Disposed by Courts in India during 1993-99

Sr. No.	*Item*	*1993*	*1994*	*1995*	*1996*	*1997*	*1998*	*1999*	*1993-99 Average*
1	No. of cases disposed by courts	4678 (100)	7581 (100)	7191 (100)	13226 (100)	12781 (100)	31011 (100)	12864 (100)	12761.71 (100)
2	No. of cases ending in conviction	490 (10.47)	711 (9.38)	713 (9.91)	1827 (13.81)	2017 (15.78)	1677 (5.41)	1545 (12.01)	1282.85 (10.05)
3	No. of cases ending in acquittal	4188 (89.52)	6870 (90.62)	6478 (90.08)	11399 (86.18)	10764 (84.22)	29334 (94.59)	11319 (87.99)	11478.85 (89.95)

Figures in parentheses represent column percentage.

Source: Worked out of Table 2.5.

and STs, despite having powerful laws, unable to protect their interests?

Regarding the effectiveness of the special laws, it has been stated that these laws are "perfect on paper!" Nevertheless, Operation Agnivesh, the Puri Acharya and the lunacy and the untouchability syndrome are with us, whatever the Protection of Civil Rights Act, 1955 and the Constitution may proclaim" (Iyer, 1989: 14). It has also been observed that these laws have the limitation of procedural delay, to be followed by concrete evidences to punish the guilty (Nandu Ram, 1986: 112). For effective implementation of the two laws, the National Commission for the SCs and STs has made a number of valuable recommendations (see Annexure 5). The Commission has also expressed its dissatisfaction over the fact that the police, who are supposed to be the protectors of the SCs/STs, have themselves indulged in inhuman crimes against the SCs and STs. It has therefore appealed to the State to initiate strict measures against the concerned police officers. But till April 1998 only the State of Rajasthan and Orissa have sent information regarding involvement of police officials in crime and atrocities against the SCs and STs (*Government of India*, 1998: 243).

The Dalit Human Rights Monitor-2000 for Andhra Pradesh, published by Sakshi (August 2001: 138-41), has also made useful recommendations: 15 recommendations to the police, 19 to the Executive, 3 to the Judiciary, and 7 to the Central Government.

"The Bhopal Declaration" of the Bhopal Conference, which was held in 2002, proclaimed that unless its 21 points of action agenda are implemented earnestly, no amount of activism on the part of the Dalits/SCs and pro-active measures from the State can liberate these communities from the scourges of untouchability and exploitation. Out of its 21 demands, the following are directly related to the protection of the Dalits/SCs in general and effective implementation of the two laws in particular:

1. The state must assume sole responsibility in protecting the SCs and STs. The state must identify the atrocity-prone areas and deploy forces. In addition, provide arms and licenses to the SCs and STs as stipulated in the POA Act for self-defense purposes, make the setting up of Dalit self-defense groups from village onwards mandatory, and

specially train Dalit women to handle weapons in self-defense against the perpetrators of crimes and atrocities.

2. Implement effectively in letter and spirit the SCs and STs (Prevention of Atrocities) Act, 1989 and Rules 1995, especially with regard to atrocities against Dalit women, and accordingly prosecute the dominant caste leaders and their minions who stoke the fire of caste clashes and the police officials acting in connivance with them. In case of atrocities against SCs/STs, a system of collective punishment has to be evolved as oppressors enjoy community's support and protection and escape the law.
3. Enforce with stringent measures the Bonded Labour System (Abolition) Act, 1976 and abolish forthwith child labour to ensure freedom with dignity for all Dalits, and accordingly, make suitable amendments in the appropriate legislations.

Though the above, and many other recommendations noted earlier, will go a long way, if implemented earnestly, ensuring the basic human rights of the SCs and STs, yet the fact that cannot be easily ignored is that throughout India most of the cases registered under these special laws and tried in the Special Courts have ended in acquittal. Such a state of affair, on the one hand, indirectly encourages the accused to continue with their discriminatory attitudes towards and to commit more and more atrocities against the SCs and STs, and, on the other, demoralizes the victims hoping to seek justice through the Court of law. Such a high rate of acquittal also speaks covertly volumes of hardship and inconvenience that the victims and many others associated with their cases personally and officially would have been forced to face from the time the case gets registered to the time it receives its final pronouncement by the Court concerned. One may, therefore, hypothetically argue that during the crucial period of seeking justice through established formal institutions there may be many factors forcing the victims in many ways to say and do things that would ultimately go against their own interest. It is therefore important to study as to what factors, and at what stage, operate against the interests of the victims leading to the acquittal of large number of cases registered under the PCR and POA Acts.

Notes

1. For those quotations of provisions which have their respective sections along, refer to Ambedkar (1987) and for other provisions to Ghurye (1969).
2. The Brahmins had also been declared as "The Gods are invisible deities, the Brahmins are visible deities". "...Kautilya suggested that in order to avert such providential calamities as fire, flood, and pestilence, the people should worship gods and Brahmins". "... The Brahmins sustain the world. It is by the favour of the Brahmins that the Gods reside in the heavens; a speech uttered by Brahmins (whether a curse or a benediction) never fails to come true" Ghurye (1969: 90).
3. These bodies never even mentioned issues concerning the 'untouchables', except on two occasions: first, in 1916, a Parsi gentleman Sir Manakji Dadabhoy asked through a resolution in Central Legislation for more material and educational provisions for the "untouchables". Second, in 1928, Mr. Jayakar moved a resolution in the Central Legislation demanding reservation for the 'untouchables' in matters of education and public services, particularly in the police department. Interestingly enough, both these resolutions were opposed by the high caste Hindus. One was Pandit Madan Mohan in 1916 and the other G.S. Bajpai in 1928 (see Ambedkar, 1993: 133). It may be noted here that Mahatma Jyotiba Phule went a step ahead by proposing a policy of reservation, which Rajashri Sahu Maharaj had first implemented in his Kolhapur State as early as July 26, 1902.
4. In tea-stalls the Dalits are usually not offered tea/coffee or any such beverage things in common tumblers. For them there are tumblers kept separately in every tea-stall which the Dalit himself has to take, clean and show to the caste Hindu man preparing tea. The man pours tea without touching the tumbler held by the Dalit. After having tea, the Dalit himself has to clean the tumbler and keep it back in the same place where it was picked up from. Shops where such practices were not observed, no caste Hindu will visit (Ramaiah, 1998: 102).

3

Combating Crimes Against Dalits

The Tamil Nadu Experiences

The previous chapters focussed on the need for studying the factors responsible for high rate of acquittal in cases registered under the two special laws, and the methodology adopted for the same, and the various efforts taken to protect the interests of these communities particularly through the PCR Act and POA Act. The present chapter looks into the various measures undertaken by the Government of Tamil Nadu to protect the interests of the SCs, and projects the plight of the SCs in Tamil Nadu in general, and in the chosen southern districts, Ramanathapuram, Virudhunagar and Sivagangai, in particular.

The Scheduled Castes in Tamil Nadu

The social status of the SCs cannot be fully understood unless one looks at their relationship with other castes. Unlike in other parts of India where castes can be understood within the broader framework of *varna* system that divides the Hindus by birth into five categories viz., the Brahmins, Kshatriyas, Vaishyas and Shudras and the Ati-Shudras/SCs, castes found in Tamil Nadu in general and Ramanathapuram and its adjacent districts in particular, may broadly be categorised into three caste groups: Brahmins, non-Brahmins and Scheduled Castes. While the Brahmins are considered the highest in the caste hierarchy, the non-Brahmin castes are considered the middle level castes. The more visible middle level castes include the land owning castes such as Vellalar, the Ahamudayar (*Servai)*, Maravar (*Thevar*), Kallar; Konar (Yadavar), and the Telugu speaking Naidus; trading castes such as Chettiyar; artisan castes like Kusavar or Kuyavan (potter), Kotthan (mason), Thachchan (carpenter), Kollan (blacksmith), Thattans or Nahai Aasari (goldsmith); and the servicing castes such as Ambattans (barbers), and Vannan (washermen).

While most of the Brahmins strictly observe vegetarianism, most of the middle level castes, except the Vellalar and to some extent the Chettiyar, do not adhere to such restrictions. They however maintain, even today, except in urban areas, complete distance from the non-Brahmin castes, the Scheduled Castes in particular. Among the middle level castes, a few such as *Ahamudyar, Maravar* and *Kallar* together known as *Mukkulathor* (three castes) are more in number in Ramanathapuram district. They are not only large in number and more assertive but also notorious for their atrocities on the SCs.

Social Relation between the SCs and Caste Hindus

The social relation between the SCs and the caste Hindus has often been less than cordial. It has been a contesting and conflicting one where the SCs/Dalits has always been the oppressed and exploited category. They have been the victims of worst forms of violence. Most of this violence may be called as "traditional violence"[1]. The other forms of violence seem as a reaction to modern ways of resistance on the part of the untouchables, which, in other words, may be understood as upper castes' violent response to the changing situation of untouchables/Dalits[2]. Though the upper castes resort to both the types of violence, what has been observed to be more dominant till recent past is the second category of violence (Mendelsohn and Vicziancy, 2000: 45). However, what seems to be the driving common factor in both types of violence is the upper castes' desperation to maintain their caste supremacy over the SCs.

Though the upper castes in general resort to both the types of violence, what may be noted, particularly in States like Tamil Nadu, which is known for anti-Brahmin movement, is that those indulging in violent crimes like murder and raping of Dalit women, are generally the Backward Castes or the middle level caste Hindus (Ramaiah, 1992; 1999). When the Brahmins and a few upper level middle castes such as the Vellalars and Chettiyars treat the SCs as untouchables, the SCs do not consider them as their direct enemies. For them the real enemies are a few middle level "dominant castes"(Srinivas, 1987) or the Backward Castes (BCs) such as the Ahamudayar, Maravar and Kallar who commit worst forms of atrocities against them. "These middle castes have now become economically and politically dominant snatching away such dominance enjoyed by the upper castes in the past" (Nandu Ram, 1995: 286). The relationship between the Dalits and the BCs has always been hostile and uncordial. This is evident from the fact that throughout Tamil Nadu most of the violence against the SCs has been perpetrated by the people belonging to middle castes. These include the murder of a Scheduled Caste leader Inamanuvel at Paramakkudi and 42 Scheduled Caste persons at Mudukulathur in Ramanathapuram district in 1957, 44 at Keelavenmani in Tanjaur district in 1968, 5 at Unjanai in Pasumpon Muthuramalingam district in 1979 and 16 at Vilupuram in Chengalpat district in 1983. Besides, there were a number of murders of Scheduled Castes at Kudaloore and Vilupuram in Chengalpat district in 1987 and at Podi in Maduri district in 1988. In 1992, two more persons were killed at Paramakkudi in Ramanathapuram district (see Ramaiah, 1998: 90-92).

Besides the above incidents of atrocity on the SCs, there have been many incidents that have gone unreported or misreported. Except the PCR/Social Justice office at Chennai, in charge of implementing the PCR Act and the POA Act, there is no authorised body to maintain the data on such atrocities and the details of how such cases are handled.

However, according to the data provided by the said office (see Table 3.1), it is clear that about 3 to 5 per cent of atrocities committed against the SCs throughout India during 1988-1999 are from the state of Tamil Nadu. Yet, the state's percentage share to all India total was only 1.88 in 1993, though it reached the maximum of 5.21 per cent in 1996 (see Table 3.1). Tamil Nadu stood 6th in 1994, 5th in 1996, 9th in 1998 and 8th in 1999 as far as the maximum number of atrocities committed against the SCs in different states of India is concerned (refer Table 2.3).

Table 3.1

Percentage Share of Tamil Nadu to Total Incidence of Crimes Against SCs in India during 1988-99

Year	*All India Total*	*Tamil Nadu*	*Percentage Share*
1988	15207	709	4.61
1989	15799	482	3.05
1990	17737	544	3.07
1991	18336	562	3.06
1992	24922	550	2.21
1993	28625	539	1.88
1994	38927	1593	4.09
1995	38494	1333	3.46
1996	36413	1897	5.21
1997	32588	1630	5.00
1998	27561	897	3.25
1999	26285	1011	3.85

Source: Government of India (2000, 2001), Annual Report on Scheduled Castes and Scheduled Tribes (Prevention of Atrocities Act, 1989, Ministry of Social Justice and Empowerment, New Delhi, (Report for the year 1990:25; 1991-92:43; 1993-95:2; 1996-97:4; 1999:6).

The figures and the data in Table 3.1 indicate that though there seems a declining trend in the number of atrocities committed against the SCs in Tamil Nadu, one can never be sure that such trend would continue in future given the fact that during 1988-1999 the number of such crimes kept changing year after year. This unsteady trend found in the state of Tamil Nadu is, by and large, similar to that of the nation. In all, what remains, as a reality, is that, the SCs in Tamil Nadu are, as it is with many other States, still subjected to discrimination and atrocities. It is, therefore, important to take stock of the existing system and the various initiatives made by the Government of Tamil Nadu to protect the SCs from such crimes.

State Initiatives

Appointment of Officers

As with other states of India, Tamil Nadu too is legally bound to implement the PCR Act and the POA Act earnestly. For this purpose, the Government of Tamil Nadu has its central office at Chennai headed by two senior police officers – Additional Director General of Police (Social Justice) and the Inspector General of Police, Human Rights, Social Justice (CID), Chennai (see Government of India, 2001:45-49). Equipped with the necessary staff, this office is in charge of monitoring and enforcement of the PCR Act and the POA Act. It also supervises the functioning of the Mobile Squads. Under the ADGP and IGP (SJ/AR), there are three Supervisory Squads each headed by a Deputy Superintendent of Police with necessary supporting staff having the Head quarters at Chennai, Trichy and Madurai respectively.

Besides the Supervisory Squads, six prosecuting wings consisting of one Sub-Inspector, one Head Constable and a grade II Police Constable in each wing operate in the districts of Tanjavur, Trichy, Madurai City, Tirumelveli, South Arcot and Chithambaram (Rural). On the basis of "one in each district", as many as 34 Protection of Civil Rights Mobile Squads, each headed by an Inspector, one Sub-Inspector of Police, and two police constables function for the registration of cases under the two Acts and prosecution of the accused. For the collection of statistical information regarding cases registered under the two Acts and for conducting survey in atrocity prone villages, a Statistical unit consisting of one Sub-Inspector of Police and one Statistical Inspector are posted in each police district.

The Superintendent of Police in the districts have been instructed from time to time to adopt various measures for the Scheduled Caste victims such as immediate registration of cases, arresting of accused, expeditious and appropriate investigation and trial of the cases, posting of police pickets in vulnerable areas, immediate sanction and provision of relief and rehabilitation measures in co-ordination with the District Administration, formation of peace committees, and initiation of strong disciplinary action against the delinquent officials. The Sub-Divisional Officers and Deputy Superintendents of Police have been instructed to conduct case-by-case critical review of such cases under investigation (under trial). For investigation they are provided with a checklist. Extensive personal contact is maintained by the Inspector General of Police (PCR) with the Deputy Superintendent of Police and range Deputy Inspector General (DIG) of Police, apart from maintaining a regular correspondence with them for individual cases and for general matters to ensure effective and efficient enforcement of the PCR Act and the SCs and STs (POA) Act. The District Collectors also revise the cases of atrocities bi-monthly with the Superintendent of Police, Public Prosecutors along with the Chief Judicial Magistrates of the districts and issue suitable instructions to ensure safety and security of the members of SCs and STs.

Special Courts

For the trial of cases registered under the PCR Act and the POA Act, the Principal Session Court of Madras, N. Arcot, S. Arcot, Coimbatore, Periyar, Madurai, Ramanathapuram, Salem, Tiruchirapalli and Tirunelveli, and the Session Court of Changai, Nilgiri, Dharamapuri, Kanyakumari, Quaid-e-millit, Pudukottai, Thanjavur West, Thanjavur East have been designated as Special Courts.

Legal Aid

The SCs and STs receive free legal aid and other assistance from the Tamilnadu State Legal Services Authority, which, having taken over the policies and programmes of the erstwhile Tamilnadu Legal Aid and Advice Board, has been functioning from 1 November 1997. The said Authority has 151 constituent units spread over Tamil Nadu. It provides legal aid as per Article 39A of the Constitution. The Legal aid programmes include, apart from legal aid assistance to the victims to prosecute the accused or to defend cases before civil and criminal courts and tribunals, a variety of programmes such as relief through authorities, conciliation, mediation, centres for woman, assistance to prisoners, legal aid cum legal literacy promotion camps, and *lok adalats*. Out of 30177 applications received during 1997, the total number of applications received from SCs was 2427 and from STs 330. Out of 46502 applications received from various parts of India for legal aid during 1998, 4002 were from the SCs and 339 from STs. For the year 1999, the number of applications from SCs and STs were 3849 out of the total number of 47117 applications received. And, the expenditure on the provision of legal aid to persons belonging to SCs and STs was Rs. 1916048 during 1998, and Rs. 2247432 during 1999 (see Government of India 2000:35; 2001:43). However, these figures indicate only the number of SCs and STs who applied for legal assistance. The report does not indicate as to how many people actually received such assistance.

TA, Monetary Relief and Housing

To meet the travel and maintenance expenses of the victims and their witnesses as provided in the SCs and STs (Prevention of Atrocities) Rules, 1995, the expenditure of a sum of Rs. 228 lakh in 1998 and Rs. 106 lakh in 1999 was incurred. The Superintendent of Police at the district level, as given in the POA Act, initiates the necessary monetary relief to the victims through a formal proposal. The grievances of the SCs and STs regarding allotment of house site *pattas* and construction of free houses, extension and expansion of available basic amenities are redressed by the District Collectors.

Vigilance and Monitoring Committees

As per the Section 21(2)(v) of the SCs and STs (POA) Act 1989 and section 16 and 17 of the SCs and STs (POA) Rules 1995, the Government of Tamil Nadu has constituted a State Level Vigilance and Monitoring Committee consisting of 24 members under the chairmanship of the Chief Minister. The State Level Vigilance and Monitoring Committee is supposed to conduct it's meeting periodically. Such committees have been constituted also at the district level, and their meetings are held once in a quarter. The Secretary to Government, Adi Dravidar and Tribal Welfare Department review the reports of the District Level Committees received from the Collectors, and subsequently suitable instructions are issued to the Collectors concerned.

Review Meetings

The District Collectors review every month all the cases registered under the Protection of Civil Rights Act, 1955 and the Scheduled Castes and the Scheduled Tribes (Prevention of Atrocities) Act, 1989 and send their reports. The Secretary, Adi Dravidar and Tribal Welfare Department with the Inspector General of Police (PCR) discuss 'discuss in detail' the review reports received from the District Collectors and necessary instructions on the follow-up action are issued to the District Collectors.

Periodic Survey

The respective district PCR units in Tamil Nadu conduct periodic surveys in the atrocity prone villages with the following objectives:

(a) To find out whether or not caste discrimination exist in any form in any of those villages;
(b) To know whether basic amenities have been provided in those villages;
(c) To know whether there were cases reported but not registered;
(d) To ascertain whether ill-feeling exists between Scheduled Castes and other communities;
(e) To hear grievances like non-functioning of street lights etc.; and
(f) To find out the extent of awareness among the public about the provisions of the PCR and POA Acts.

The Statistical Inspectors of Protection of Civil Rights Mobile Squads conduct survey in the atrocity prone villages identified every year with the assistance of the Police Staff. Based on the suggestions and recommendations of the survey reports, the Collectors and Superintendent of Police in the districts are addressed with copies marked to the Secretary, Adi Dravidar and Tribal Welfare and to the Director, Adi Dravidar and Tribal Welfare for suitable follow-up action.

Identification of Atrocity-Prone Areas

A village is considered atrocity prone (a) if in a mother village or its hamlets three or more cases are reported within a period of three successive calendar years or (b) even a single grievous case like murder or rape or case which attract a punishment of seven years of imprisonment or more is reported then the village is declared as an atrocity-prone village.

Atrocity-prone villages thus identified are declared highly sensitive in nature, even if one case of heinous offences, such as murder, rape, arson or offences, like grievous hurt has been reported.

Atrocity-prone villages are kept in the active list for a period of two years from the last reported cases and then transferred to the dormant list for further period of three years. During the dormant period, if any case is reported it will be brought back to atrocity-prone villages list.

According to fifth (2001:47) and sixth reports (2001:49) on the SCs and STs (POA) Act, 1989, 214 villages in 1998 and 238 in 1999 were identified as atrocity-prone and 102 in 1998 and 128 villages in 1999 as dormant atrocity-prone villages. These villages are visited frequently by the Staff of PCR units in the districts and they bring to the notice of Superintendent of police and Collector the grievances or problems of public for taking precautionary and ameliorative measures to avoid any untoward incidents/clashes between the Scheduled Castes and others.

Trend in PCR and POA Acts Cases Reported and Disposed

Despite well-established systems not only for effective implementation but also for monitoring the functioning of the PCR and POA Acts, atrocities on the SCs have continued. What has then been the contribution of these laws? What has been the fate of cases registered under these laws?

Table 3.2

Number of Cases Reported Under PCR Act and POA Act in Tamil Nadu during 1990-1999

Year	*Reported PCR Act Cases*	*Reported POA Act Cases*	*Total*
1990	787	4	791
1991	867	14	881
1992	961	310	1271
1993	132	980	1112
1994	78	922	1000
1995	96	750	846
1996	45	721	766
1997	68	757	825
1998	48	897	945
1999	32	1011	1043
2000	38	996	1034

Source: As per the information sent by the office of the Inspector General of Police, Human Rights/Social Justice ICID, Chennai, 21 December 2001.

As evident from Table 3.2, the number of offences committed against the SCs and STs in Tamil Nadu as reported under the PCR Act increased from 787 in 1990 to 867 in 1991 and 961 in 1992, but declined drastically to just 132 in 1993 and further down to mere 78 in 1994. While the number of offences reported under the POA Act which were just four in 1990 (the year in which the POA Act came into effect), and 14 in 1992 recorded an unprecedented increase of 310 in 1992 and further increased to 980 in 1993, but declined gradually to 922 in 1994 and 721 in 1996. With 757 in 1997, 1011 in 1999 and 996 in 2000, the number of offences committed against the SCs and ST in the State as reported under the POA Act once again recorded a similar trend of *increase in the beginning* and *gradual decline later on*. Looking at the fact that the number of cases reported under the PCR Act started declining from 1992 onwards and at the same time the number of cases reported under the POA Act which came into effect from 1990 onwards recorded an unprecedented increase from 1992 onwards, it can be said that the SCs and STs who had all along registered crimes committed against them under the PCR Act, now prefer registering under the POA Act, perhaps for its stringent penal provisions and financial compensation to the victims.

Table 3.3

Disposal of Cases Reported under the PCR Act in Tamil Nadu during 1990-1999

Year	*Reported Cases*	*Referred Cases*		*Charged and P.T. Cases*		*U.I.*	*Cases Tried in Court*	*Acquitted Cases*		*Convicted Cases*	
		No.	*%*	*No.*	*%*			*No.*	*%*	*No.*	*%*
1990	787	267	33.92	5	0.63	—	515	479	93.01	36	6.99
1991	867	313	36.10	4	0.46	—	550	510	92.73	40	7.27
1992	961	509	52.96	7	0.72	—	445	415	93.26	30	6.74
1993	132	51	38.63	3	2.27	—	78	52	66.66	26	33.34
1994	78	24	30.77	4	5.13	—	53	35	66.04	18	33.96
1995	96	31	32.29	7	7.29	—	58	48	82.76	10	17.24
1996	45	20	44.44	5	11.11	—	20	18	90.00	2	20.00
1997	68	18	26.47	6	8.82	—	44	42	95.45	2	4.55
1998	48	4	8.33	11	22.91	—	33	32	96.97	1	3.03
1999	32	3	9.37	10	31.25	—	19	19	100.00	—	—
2000	38	9	27.27	22	66.66	—	7	7	100.00	—	—
Average	287	114	30.96	8	14.30	—	166	151	88.81	15	12.10

Source: As per the information sent by the office of the Inspector General of Police, Human Rights/Social Justice/CID, Chennai, 21 December 2001.

Table 3.3 and 3.4, which detail the nature of disposal of cases registered under the PCR Act and POA Act respectively during 1990-2000, reveal that though the number of cases reported, cases referred (cases closed after investigation), and the cases convicted shows on the whole a declining trend, particularly from 1992 onwards in the case of PCR Act cases, and from 1993 onwards in the case of POA Act cases, the decline has not been gradual. For instance, in the case of cases reported under the PCR Act, though the number rose from 787 in 1990 to 867 in 1991 and 961 in 1992, it declined drastically to just 132 in 1993 and to mere

Table 3.4

Disposal of Cases Reported under the SC/ST (PA) Act in Tamil Nadu during 1990-1999

Year	Reported Cases	Referred Cases		Charged and P.T. Cases		U.T.		Cases Tried in Court	Acquitted Cases		Convicted Cases	
		No.	%.	No.	%	No.	%		No.	%	No	%
1990	4	3	75.00	—		—	—	1	1	100	00	00
1991	14	9	64.28	—		—	—	5	4	80.00	1	20.00
1992	310	160	51.61	13	4.19	—	—	137	106	77.37	31	22.63
1993	980	615	62.75	36	3.67	—	—	329	309	93.92	20	6.08
1994	922	517	56.07	68	7.37	1	0.11	336	321	95.54	15	4.46
1995	750	378	50.39	85	11.33	—	—	286	264	92.31	22	7.69
1996	721	324	44.93	101	14.01	—	—	296	283	95.61	13	4.39
1997	757	319	42.14	166	21.92	5	0.66	267	248	92.88	19	7.12
1998	897	375	41.80	254	28.31	2	0.22	266	242	90.98	24	9.02
1999	1011	372	36.79	379	37.48	4	0.39	256	235	91.80	21	8.20
2000	996	296	29.72	491	49.29	7	0.70	202	196	97.03	6	2.97
Average	669	306	50.50	145	17.61	—	—	217	201	91.58	16	8.41

Source: As per the information sent by the office of the Inspector General of Police, Human Rights/Social Justice ICID, Chennai, 21 December 2001.

78 in 1994. Again it rose to 96 in 1995. Likewise, 1996 witnessed a decline, while 1997 witnessed an increase. Similarly, unlike the years 1998 and 1999, the number rose in the year 2000 in respect of cases reported under the PCR Act. More or less, a similar trend is seen even in the case of cases referred, and cases tried in the courts. The frequent change in the trend of disposed PCR cases is more overt in the cases of percentage of convicted cases. It was only 6.99 per cent in 1990, but rose to 7.27 per cent in 1991, again declined to 6.74 per cent in 1992. It rose to as high as 33.34 per cent in 1993 and further to 33.96 in 1994. It once again declined to 17.24 per cent in 1995 but increased to 20 per cent in 1996, and then onwards there was a drastic decline. And there was no case of conviction at all during 1999 and 2000 though 19 and 7 cases were tried in the courts during these years respectively. All these cases ended in acquittal.

But, in the case of cases pending trial in the courts and those ended in acquittal, an increasing trend is seen. With regard to the former, though the percentage declined in the beginning from 0.63 in 1990 to 0.46 in 1991, it rose to 2.27 in 1993, 7.29 in 1995, 11.11 in 1996 (but declined to 8.82 in 1997), 22.91 in 1998 and 66.66 in 2000.

Similarly, the average percentage of PCR cases ended in acquittal during 1990-2000 was about 89 per cent. Though the percentage of cases acquitted declined marginally in the beginning from 93.01 in 1990 to 92.73 in 1991, it rose to 93.26 in 1992 only to decline again to 66.66 in 1993 and further down to 66.14 in 1994. But the percentage went up significantly to 82.76 in 1995. Since then, an increasing trend is noticed. There were hundred per cent acquittals in the PCR cases tried in the courts during 1999 and 2000. On the whole, an increasing trend is evident in respect of cases acquitted (refer Table 3.3).

With regard to the disposal of cases registered under the POA Act (see Table 3.4), the situation is different. On the whole, an increasing trend is noticed in the number of POA Act cases reported, the percentage of cases pending trial in the courts and the percentage of cases ended in acquittal. But a declining trend is evident in the number of cases referred, cases tried in the courts and even in the cases ended in conviction However, the trend is again not consistent and gradual. For instance, the number of cases reported under the POA Act rose from 4 in 1990 to 980 in 1993, but declined to 721 in 1996. Since then the number of reported cases gradually increased and reached the maximum of 1011 in 1999. However, it declined subsequently to 996 in 2000. The average percentage of cases reported under the POA Act during 1990-2000 works out to be 669. Though it is encouraging to see the increasing trend in the percentage of cases charge-sheeted, it is disappointing that the percentage of cases acquitted has also gone up over the years. Except for first three years (1990-1992) during which the percentages of cases ended in acquittal declined from 100 (only one case was tried and ended in acquittal, and therefore 100% acquittal) in 1990 to 77.37 in 1992, it started increasing from 93.92 in 1993 to 95.61 in 1996. It declined again to 91.80 per cent in 1999, but has shown at the end an increasing trend with the percentage reaching as high as 97.03 in the year 2000. This increase in the percentage of acquitted cases has resulted in the decrease in the percentage of cases convicted.

Though the percentage of cases ending in conviction was 'zero' for the year 1990, it rose to 20 in 1991 and 22.63 in 1992 but declined to the low 6.08 in 1993. And during 1993-1997 the percentage of cases ended in conviction ranged from the minimum of 4.39 to the maximum of 7.69. However, it went up to 9.02 per cent in 1998 and declined gradually to mere 2.97 per cent in the 2000. The average percentage of cases, which ended in conviction during 1990-2000, was merely 8.41 per cent. That is, out of 669 reported cases (average number of cases reported during 1990-2000), only as many as 217 cases were tried in the courts, of which only 16 cases ended in conviction and the rest of as many as 201 cases ended in acquittal.[3]

The foregoing analysis brings into focus the fact that despite the Tamil Nadu government's well-established system to implement effectively the two special laws, atrocities on the SCs of Tamil Nadu continued to be a day-to-day reality. With regard to cases registered under the PCR Act, it may be concluded that though on the whole there appears a declining trend both in the matter of cases reported and cases referred, it is disappointing to see, on the whole, an increasing trend in cases ending in acquittal and those pending trial in the courts.

When it comes to cases registered under the POA Act, the situation is not the same. Here, an increasing trend is witnessed. Further, since the number of cases referred has shown a declining trend which means more cases are charge-sheeted and sent to courts for trial, it gives some hope of justice to victims. However, it is very discouraging that, on the one hand, the number of cases pending trial and those ending in acquittal have gone up, and on the other, the number of cases tried in the courts and cases ending in conviction have gone down over a period of time. The fact that the POA Act being more powerful and more preferred, the number of acquitted cases has gone up and the conviction rate has come down, calls for an in-depth understanding of the various factors responsible for the high rate of acquittal.

Notes

1. The traditional violence occurs when the caste Hindus who feel that the untouchables are not only the embodiment of evil sprits but also have the power over such sprits that are responsible for most of the diseases. On this pretext, even the 'traditional' act of violence like rape of untouchable women seems to be justified (Mendelsohn and Vicziancy, 2000: 45).
2. The Dalits' resistance to discrimination arising from the practice of untouchability, together with more general claims to social respect, and their claims for agricultural land, housing sites, payment of statutory minimum wages, and demands for adequate representation in government jobs and access to educational and economic development opportunities may be included as examples for the latter type of violence (Ibid. 46).
3. For details regarding the number of PCR and POA Act cases under investigation and those pending trial as on 30 November 2001, and for more specific details regarding the PCR and POA Act cases pending trial during 1984-2001, refer Table 2.5, Table 2.6 and 2.7 in Ramaiah (2001: 38-39.1)

4

Law and Justice

Experiences and Responses of Victims and Witnesses

In chapter three the focus was on the plight of the SCs in Tamil Nadu and the various efforts made by the Tamil Nadu Government to protect the SCs from atrocities and caste discrimination, particularly by way of implementing the PCR and POA Acts. The objective of present chapter is to bring to light the various factors responsible for high rate of acquittal in cases registered under the two special laws. This is attempted by way of identifying the factors that lead to the acquittal of the 15 cases chosen for study. For this purpose, as noted earlier, in-depth interviews were held with the victims and/or their witnesses, and documents relevant to each case such as the victims' First Information Report (FIR), and Courts' judgments were also examined. The responses of the victims and others to various questions posed by the researcher were tape-recorded, and were later translated from Tamil to English language. The same has been reproduced here in direct speech without making any change. Though the attempt was to record the views of everyone connected with the chosen cases viz., the victims, witnesses, accused, the police, and representatives of NGOs, it could not be done in respect of every case owing to one or more reasons such as: (a) the non-availability of the concerned individual, (b) their unwillingness to share views, (c) their limited knowledge on the information sought, and (d) their fear of possible dire consequences. Such an approach was considered necessary with a view to collecting maximum information for each case and identifying maximum number of factors responsible for the acquittal of untouchability and atrocity cases. Of the 15 acquitted cases chosen for the study, details pertaining to severe offences have been presented first, followed by relatively less severe ones. Accordingly, the cases of *rape with murder* have been presented first, followed by the case of *murder* and then the lesser crimes. For each case, details pertaining to: (a) the nature offence, (b) crime number and sections under which the case had been filed, (c) names of the victims and accused, and (d) the place where the incident took place have been presented in the beginning. Presented at the end of each case under the sub-title "Case Highlights" are the important points that emerged in the entire analysis of the case which revolved around: (a) the context in which the particular offence took place, (b) the attitude of the police towards the victims who approached them for help and (c) the main factors identified as the cause for the acquittal of the case. We may now examine each case in-depth.

Case No. 1

Offence: Rape with murder; *Crime No.* 26/98 (Karuppaiah Vs. P. Radhakrishnan); *Offence under sections*: POA Act: 3(2)(v), IPC: 302, 201; *Victim:* Karuppaiah, K. Meenakshipuram, Virudhunagar District.

Victim's View

Could you please narrate the entire incident?

The twenty years old Mrs. Muthulakshmi was married to Mr. Karuppaiah, resident of K. Meenakshipuram, a village located near Thiruchuli town in Virudhunagar district. She, like other members of the family, was involved in farming and other related activities to earn her living. On June 8, 98 around 5 o'clock in the evening, she, having worked the entire day in the field, went to one Mr. Poovalingam's pump-set (irrigation well) to have a bath. There, she was caught, dragged into Poovlingam's room and raped by Poovalingam's son. A few others were also party to it. Fearing that she might report to others, they killed her by hitting on her head with the help of an iron rod and by piercing the rod into her body. To give an impression that she died of lightning and thunder, they passed into her body electric current. They later slit open the trunk of a *neem* tree standing nearby and burnt it. Later, they placed the dead body in front of the burnt *neem* tree. This was to convince people that the tree got burnt due to the lightning and Muthulakshmi also died likewise.

Witnessing this incident of horror, one of the accused fainted on the spot. Since the car, which was called to the spot, came through the village to take the person to a hospital, others came to know the incident. The victim's mother, brother and husband came to know the incident only on the next day through someone. Immediately, the incident was brought to the notice of the *Thalayari* (one who collects land tax from the individual families). Subsequently, a formal complaint was lodged with the police. All the officials concerned were also informed, and accordingly they too came to the spot to verify the case. Then around 4.30 in the evening, the body was taken to the hospital, Aruppukkotai for post-mortem. Though it was a case of rape and murder, the police refused to register the case under the POA Act. It was done only when the NGOs staged protests. The police arrested the accused only when the latter was caught and handed over to former by the victims.

Though one of the victim's sisters happened to be there around the time of incident, she inadvertently failed to notice the incident carefully. Another witness Mr. Solayappan, the only main witness who happened to pass through that area at that time, also could not depose the case properly fearing dire consequences from the accused. Solayappan was threatened by the caste Hindu accused that he would not be allowed to stay anymore in the village and be killed if he would be a witness in the Court. He was threatened not only by the accused but also by the police who were bribed by the accused. The police had overtly told the victims in the police station itself, "We would not pursue the case unless you pass on to us our share (money/bribe)".

Case Highlights

Context

The victim's husband, mother and brother came to know about the killing through someone only on the next day. Subsequently, the matter was taken to the police, and a formal complaint under the POA Act was filed.

Police Attitude

1. Though it was a case of rape with murder, the police refused to book the case under the POA Act. It was done only when the victims' relatives and NGOs concerned resorted to public protest.
2. The police arrested the accused only when the latter were caught by the victims and handed over to the former.
3. There was an overt demand of money from the victims by the police to pursue the case.

Factors Responsible for the Acquittal

1. The witnesses were threatened by the accused of dire consequences including death, if they would give evidences in the Court of law in favour of the victims.
2. The witnesses were threatened not only by the accused but also by the police and therefore the former could not depose the case properly.

Case No. 2

Offence: Rape with Murder; *Crime No:* 48/96, K. Karuppaiah Vs. J. Parthiban; Sections: POA Act: 3(2)(v), IPC: 376, 379, 302; Witness: Mr. Thanskodi, Theveneri, Paramakudi Taluka, Ramanathapuram District.

Witness' Views

1. *Could you, as a witness, narrate the incident and the case filed later under the POA Act?*

The incident of murder of Mrs. Panchavarnam is four years old now. This woman belonged to our village Thevaneri. She was the daughter of Mr. Karuppan and Mrs. Kaliyammal. She belonged to the Scheduled Caste (SC). Along with her parents, she used to go everyday to Lakshimpuram village, located 5 km away from our village *Theveneri,* to earn her living through charcoal making. Once, Mrs. Panchavarnam alone went to the field carrying food for her parents. In Lakshmipuram village, most of the people belonged to Naidu caste. They have no respect for the SC people over there. We were aware that these wealthy Naidu's children indulged in atrocious activities. When Panchavarnam went alone, she was caught, raped and murdered by the Naidu caste man. Since it took two days to locate the body, we could not inform the police immediately. When we inquired with the Naidus, they said that they had no knowledge of her. Then our entire village people of about 200 went into the field/bushes searching for her. We finally found her body in a bush, fully naked and in a decomposed state. We took the matter to the police. But they did not bother, and took no action. They refused to register a case. We were left with no option but to form a group and organize a *dharna* (protest) at the nearby town Parthibanur and demanded that the case be registered. Only then the police registered the case under the POA Act. Since the accused generally had, besides money power, the support of politicians and high-level high caste officers, the police did not take any action against the accused. They convinced the victims saying, "We will give you money. Whatever happened has already happened; what can we do now? You take money". They discouraged the victims in all possible ways from pursuing the case further. At this stage, the victim having no other option gave up pursuing the case.

2. *Are the accused afraid of this law?*

They are not all afraid of the POA Act, since they are getting lots of money from abroad. They also have lots of lands and pump-sets for irrigation purposes. They settle all such cases by bribing the officials concerned.

3. *Do you think you need the POA Act?*

We cannot live in this place if we do not have this law. There is no other support for us to remain alive here except this law. This law has to be implemented vigorously, only then we, the oppressed people, can live here. This law is a must.

4. *Some say, this law is misused. What is your opinion?*

There is no reason for misusing this law. The caste Hindus do not let the law function on its own using their money and muscle powers. The upper caste people often purchase this law. This law is very useful for the SC people.

5. *How was the case conducted in the Court? Were the witnesses allowed to give evidence in the Court?*

They did not allow anybody to give proper evidence in the Court. The accused met the witnesses individually and bribed them. They not only gave them money but also threatened them not to give evidence in the Court. So, the witnesses did not come to Court at all. The victim's parents and myself alone stood as witness finally. I went to the Court as the fifth witness. They interrogated me well. But one person's evidence could not help win the case. Since most of the witnesses did not come to the Court to give evidence, we lost the case.

Whatever be the nature of complaint that the Scheduled Caste people lodge, the police do not take it seriously. Instead of conducting proper inquiry and reprimanding the accused, they accept bribe from the accused and threaten the SCs, and also file false or counter cases against them. Due to this law, it is not the SCs but the police who benefit more as they could extract a lot of money particularly from the caste Hindus. Not only that, if the accused give little more money, the police also file case against the victims themselves. In this way, we get beating not only from the caste Hindus but also from the police. Since there seems none to support us, we are forced to give up the case. We have to put up with all these things since we are small in number in our village and cannot oppose the caste Hindus openly.

The police have punished neither the accused, nor the parents of the accused in any manner under the POA Act. The police gave some compensation to the parents of the victim. That is all.

6. *Was there any such case in your village prior to the case of Panchavarnam?*

There was a case three years before. One old Scheduled Caste lady of this village went one day to the nearby place to collect firewood. Covering her mouth with cloth they killed her. She was buried there itself. Though the matter was taken to the police, no one was arrested. Moreover, there was none in her family to follow up the case. The case was covertly closed down.

After the case of Panchavarnam, there was an incident in Mosugudi village, which is nearer to Parthibanur town and also nearer to our village Thevaneri. One Mr. Arumugam belonging to Pallar caste (SC) was killed, during sunset, when he was busy putting fertilizer to his paddy crops, by Maravars (dominant Backward Caste) from the nearby villages: Vahainendal, Meenakshipuram and Chaiyamangalam. The Maravers caught hold of Arumugam and severed his head off. This case was also taken to the police. But nobody has been punished even in this case till date.

All these things have been happening because the police do not consider these laws as laws. They do not punish anyone. They do not even consider these as serious cases or offences. The police are not honest. If they were honest in their duties, it would be better.

After Panchavarnam incident, these Naidus in many ways harass us. We cannot do our agricultural work after 4 in the evening. They threaten us. When our girls stand alone anywhere, they abuse them with all possible filthy words. They destroy our crops. They let their cattle rampage our farms and damage all our crops. When we try to chase these cattle away, we, particularly our women and daughters, are abused. If we raise voice against such acts, they threaten us with dire consequences. They say, "we would cut you into pieces and nobody could stop us. What can you do to us with your law?" All these experiences make us question ourselves as to why at all we stay in this village, and why not move into other places.

7. *Do you think the PCR and POA Acts are needed for the SCs?*

Yes. The POA Act is good. Police should honestly implement it. The intervention of politicians and high caste people should be stopped. Unless the upper caste people are punished and made to be afraid of such punishment, we cannot live peacefully in this village. This law is a must.

8. *It is said that sometimes, the police do not even respect the Court judgement and they do not do what the Court has directed them to do. Do you know any such case?*

As far as I know, there is a case in Rajakambiram. There is only one SC family. About 5 to 6 acres of land belonging to that family was illegally occupied by the non-Dalits. Houses were also built over there. He (Mr. Nagarajan) went to the Court, and the Court gave judgement in his favour. Yet, those who illegally occupied his land, have not vacated. When he went to the police as directed by the Court, the police refused even to register the case under the POA Act. Though the Court gave judgement, the accused do not abide by it. The police is also extending support for such an act. The revenue department also supports such an act of contempt of Court. All these departments expect only money.

Officials including the police who disrespect the laws should be punished. Only then such laws can bring justice to the needy people. If this Act is removed, it is not possible for the Dalits to live here. They will be enslaved and subjected to all forms of atrocities. So this Act has to continue.

Case Highlights

Context

1. Since the victim, who went to the field around the nearby village carrying food for her parents, did not return home for two days, the victim's relatives reported it to the police. Then all her village people searched for her and found only her naked dead body inside a bush. It was understood that she had been raped and murdered. Then they decided to file a case under the POA Act.

2. NGOs came to her family to support to file a case under the POA Act.

Police Attitude

1. When the incident was first reported, the police did not even bother to take any action.
2. The police refused to register the case under the POA Act even when the relatives of victims themselves located the naked-dead body of the victim in the field and pleaded the police to register a case.
3. The victims and NGOs had to resort to public protest at the nearby town demanding legal action under the POA Act.

Factors Responsible for the Acquittal

1. The accused being economically more powerful and with this money power they could also influence the support of higher-level police officials, the victim could not pursue the case beyond a point.
2. The victim needed the support of the village members of the accused for earning their livelihood and therefore could not oppose the accused overtly.
3. The witnesses were not only bribed heavily with money but also threatened with dire consequences, and thereby prevented from coming to the Court to give evidence.
4. Since most of the witnesses did not come to the Court to give evidence, the case ended in acquittal.

Other Highlights

1. The accused were not at all bothered even after the registration of a case against them under the POA Act, since they were very much confident that with their money power and political connections they could easily stop the police from taking any action against them and could also defeat the case.
2. Whenever the victims insisted on filing a case, the police filed either a false or counter case against the victims.

3. More than the SCs, the police benefited a lot out of the POA Act since they could extract a large amount of money particularly from the accused.
4. The police did not attach any importance to the POA Act. They did not punish the guilty. If they were honest in their duties, the law could be better implemented.
5. Officials, including the police, who disrespect the POA Act should be punished.
6. When even the genuine cases were defeated by the caste Hindus with their money power, there was no point in SCs seeking protection under such laws. This law was often purchased by the upper caste people by bribing the police.
7. Since the accused were confident that with their money power, they could defeat all POA Act cases against them, they harassed the SCs more particularly after defeating the cases against them.

Case No. 3

Offence: Murder of a SC man; *Crime No.* 176/97:. K. Karuppan Vs. C. Kumaravel, *Offence under* POA Act: 3(2)(v), IPC: 302; *Victim:* Mr. K. Karuppan, Mosukudi, Paramakudi Taluka, Ramanathapuram District.

Victim's Views

1. *Could you narrate the incident of murder and the case that was filed subsequently - as narrated by the victim Arumugam's brother-in-law?*

Mr. Arumugam, my uncle, resident of Mosugudi village, was murdered by a group of 7 persons – 3 from Meenakshipuram village and 4 from Chaiyamangalam. These accused confessed in the police enquiry that they murdered Arumugam in retaliation of the Pallars' attack on the Thevars of the nearby town Parthibanur a few days back. Subsequently, all of them were arrested. Two of them – Kumaravelu and Poomi – were booked under TADA. On the way to the police station, the police let two of the accused free after accepting money from them on the pretext that they were government employees. Three others were bailed out. But the victims could not win the case just because there was no witness who had seen the incident of murder though they were very much present in that area at that time. "Though the accused themselves accepted that they were the guilty, the case could not be fought successfully since the accused bribed the concerned officials at various levels. Money made all the difference. Moreover, money was mobilised from various Marvar caste Sangams (Associations) to defeat the case and to support the accused financially. Though Kumaravelu was booked under TADA, he was not punished for being guilty of murdering the Scheduled Caste person. The accused escaped punishment successfully by bribing the advocates and others in the Court".

2. *How did the police help you in this case?*

The SP first came to the spot and completed the preliminary formalities. Later, when the investigation began, the police called us, and said, particularly, to the mother of the victim, "Your son has been murdered. We need to make zerox copies of all these documents. Give us money". We gave them money. Secondly, the circle Inspector called for us and told what we should be telling in the Court in order to win the case. We said in the Court what exactly he had asked us to say. The Inspector did not tutor us properly to win the case, but only to get defeated. We realised it only when the Court gave verdict in favour of the accused. Our witnesses were totally illiterates. They sincerely followed the advice of the police, but only to get defeated.

3. *What is the caste background of your witnesses?*

Two belonged to Maravar caste, the caste the accused belonged to, and two others belonged to the Pallar Caste, the caste the victims belonged to. The Maravar caste witnesses, resident of our village, refused to give evidence in the Court with a view to supporting their caste men, the accused, whereas the three Pallar caste witnesses gave evidence in the Court in favour of the victims. They said in the Court that they saw the accused taking bath after murdering the person. This case was lost mainly because the police had tutored the witnesses wrongly.

As narrated by the victim's mother:

Kumaravelu s/o. Chellaiah Thevar confessed that he murdered Arumugam. Later, Poomi s/o. Periyasamy Thevar also confessed that he too was involved in the murder. In the police interogration Kumaravelu said, "First Poomi only started beating and cutting Arumugam. When the victim started shouting, crying and running here and there for help, I caught him and severed his neck". When we were there at the police station, we heard him telling this.

As narrated by the victim's brother-in-law:

When I was in the nearby town Parthibanur, I was told around 7 in the morning that my *mama's* (uncle's) neck had been severed off in the village. I immediately consulted our caste leaders and an advocate. They advised me to give a complaint about the incident at the Parthibanur police station and also to inform the same to the SP over phone. We did as advised. The SP rushed to the spot all the way from the district headquarter, Ramanathapuram. But the local police did not bother to go to the spot. The SP came to the spot first. As a result, the local police took out their anger on us. They questioned us, "how dare, you informed the matter to the SP". They alleged, "That means, you have only done this murder". The police had arrested seven of us and kept us in the police station at that time. When the SP started beating one of the accused Kumarvelu, the later agreed that he had done the murder. Then only the police let us go out of the police station.

Had the SP not been there, the local police would have turned the entire case against us. But they kept us in lock-up for 11 days. Every day, the police used to beat us and forced us to say that it was we who had murdered. But we used to plead them saying, "how we can be the guilty, when we had not killed the person". All our legs were swollen due to continuous beating by the police. They tortured me questioning why I informed the SP. The victim's brother and wife, who were there with the victim till a few minutes before the murder, were also tortured and forced to be the guilty. The police abused us with all possible vulgar words. The person from our adjacent village (ottha-veedu) told the police the truth that he heard them talking about the murder.

He said, "it was done by Poomi, s/o. Periyasamy Thevar and Kumaravelu, s/o. Chellaiah Thevar. Others involved were from the nearby villages. When Kumaravelu was interrogated by the police, he agreed, but Poomi escaped from the police custody. After about 20 days, he surrendered at the Madurai Court with the help of his caste people.

We had no support from anyone or any group. We believed that the government would support us. But we were cheated. The police whom we trusted tutored us wrongly with regard to what is to be said in the Court, and cheated us nefariously. Those who murdered my uncle are very much staying in the near-by village, Meenakshipuram. They often come here too. Since we are just 30 households, we cannot do anything against them. If we do so, we cannot live here.

The family members of the accused and also the Village Administrative Officer (VAO) often told the police to beat us further, to keep us under custody for more number of days and to force us to be the guilty of the murder. Yet, we did not yield to their inhuman torture. Once the accused accepted their guilt, the VAO did not turn that side. The same VAO came to our home demanding his 'share' out of the money given by the LIC in the name of victim. We gave him Rs. 3,000/- out of that money. I confronted him at that time asking as to why he forced us to be the guilty. Since then he has not been talking to us.

As narrated by the victim's elder brother Mr. Karuppan:

1. *Could you tell me how the incident took place?*

On the day of the incident, my wife and myself were busy weeding our paddy field. At that time, my younger brother (the victim) was coming towards us carrying fertiliser to be put in his paddy field which is next to ours. Once he reached his field, we left the place and were walking towards our village. On the way, we saw a *Thevar* caste man Mr. Palanichamy, S/O. Mr. Ammasi, resident of Meenakshipuram village, coming towards us by the same way. We asked him whether he was going to his field which was also around that place only. But for some reasons, he did not respond to us. When we reached very closer to him, he tried to go aside ignoring us. But after crossing him, I once again asked the same question. He said, 'yes' this time. But near him we also saw a few people who had covered their heads with towels and were walking towards the eastern side. We then left for home. It was around 6 o'-clock in the evening. The street lights were on when we were in the field itself. I ate and slept.

Since, he (the victim) did not turn up at home for a long time, his wife and others went to the field and nearby places looking for him. But they found him no where. Then, they went to the nearby village – *Valimarichan.* There too, he was not found. After sometime, my younger brothers' wife woke me up and enquired about her husband. He would have probably gone to nearby village – Valimarchan – to confirm availability of labourers for the next day's work in his field, I replied. He is not there, she said. The whole night we searched but could not locate him. The next day early morning I went to my field. There, one Mr. Chellaiah who was going around his field which is nearer to the field of my brother found my brother dead and his head severed and thrown aside. Then everyone got to know. We all then rushed there crying.

I along with others decided to report to the police. A few of us went ahead of us and reported to the SP. When some of us were walking towards Parthibanur police station, we found the SP and his officials coming towards our village in their vehicles. Mr. Kannappan was the SP. We rushed back. They enquired us all on the spot. Then they took me and my wife to the Parthibanur police station. The police started beating us and asked, "Who killed your brother. You alone were present there at that time". But we kept telling the same that we were not there when my brother was killed. We only found there a few persons at that time. But they kept on beating and abusing my wife and me. They alleged us, "you only killed your brother. They (the caste Hindu members) did not do". The police tortured us. They forced us to admit that we only killed our own brother. We said, "how can I kill my own brother. You can check with our VAO and the Thalayari about our family. We don't indulge in such a thing". But they paid no heed to our plea. The Sub-Inspector and the police constable of Parthibanur police station did this to us. They thought they could threaten us by their coercive method of enquiring and make us accept the same. But we stuck to the fact, telling only what had actually happened on that day.

In the meantime, with the intervention of the SP, the people of entire Meenakshipuram village including those involved in the murder came to the Parthibanur police station to put their signature as required. They came to the police station with an impression that none would be taken into task. As soon as they all reached the station, the SP ordered the police to round them up. Then he asked both of us to see whether there was anyone in the crowd whom we had seen on the day of the incident. But that person whom we expected i.e., Palanichamy, S/O. Ammasi Thevar was not there, though about 40 persons from that village had come at that time. We said, "The person is not here". The police again started beating us as to why we could not identify the person. We did not know what to do. We asked Ramu, the eldest son of Ammasi, "where is your younger brother Palanichamy". They showed all other brothers, but not the one who had come to our field. Then the police asked Ramu, "where is your brother Palanichami?" They showed to the police another person as Palanichamy and said, "these people (witnesses) did not see the person properly. No member of our family went there on that day". Then the police started beating Ramu insisting that he should bring his younger brother or else he would be sent to jail. Ramu went running to the village called Kanniseri near Mudukulathur town where his younger brother had been sent to escape legal punishment. On the second day, he brought his younger brother Palanichamy to the police station at about 10 o'-clock at night. Palanichamy had made his head completely clean-shaven and also shaved off his mustache to confuse us from identifying him as the guilty. At the police station, we were about to sleep though feeling extremely hungry. They brought the person at that time. I was not able to recognise the person. But my wife immediately identified him and informed the police. Then, I could also recognise him. Then they let us sit outside the station. Then police started beating Palanichami. He refused to admit the charges against him. Again they started beating him. He pleaded the police not to beat him any further and confessed that he was not involved in the killing but he knew who did it. Kumaravelu, S/o. Chellaiah Thevar and Poomi, S/o. Periyasamy Thevar were the ones who murdered Arumugam, he said. The moment he uttered these two names, Poomi, who was very much present among those 40 persons, but we were unaware of his involvement in the murder, left the place telling that he would get back after having tea. He went to the shopping area of Parthibanur and escaped from the police custody. But Kumaravelu was caught and subjected to coercive inquiry. He finally admitted that he was involved in the killing of Arumugam. He said, "I did it along with Poomi and two others from Chaiyamangalam village." When asked as to why he did so, he said, "we did it to teach a lesson to the Pallar caste people in this area who challenged our caste supremacy". My wife, three others and myself were present at that time and heard the above confession of the accused.

We were then sent out. A case was filed. Trial was conducted. In case the guilty had not admitted the charge, we would have been punished and sent to jail. During the interrogation, the police kept on beating us and told, "Why can't you fellows admit that you had killed the person. We know, this killing was only the result of enmity between you and your younger brother over a land". Till the accused confessed the truth, we were tortured everyday in the most inhuman manner in the police station. Only when the guilty were identified, they set us free. But now the guilty are not in the jail since the case got acquitted.

2. *How did the case get acquitted when the murderers themselves had accepted the charge and that too in front of the concerned police officers?*

The judgment has been in their favour, because the witness did not depose the case properly. Witnesses were my relatives and myself only.

3. *When you were the witness, how come you did not give proper evidences to punish those who murdered your own brother?*

In all villages around our village, the Maravar caste (Thevar) people are more in number. These people do most of the cultivation in our Mosukudi village itself. I was scared of being the witness against their wish as they might even kill me or other members of my family. So, I did not, rather could not, give proper evidence in the Court as a witness.

Another reason for not giving proper evidence in the Court is that the Circle Inspector and police men at Parthibanur police station kept insisting me to tell in the Court only those things which were told by them. They, time and again, said, "you were not there on the spot when the murder took place, so you should not tell that Kumeravelu, S/o. Chellaiah Thevar killed your brother. You may tell that you saw a few people there taking bath". They further said, "you can win the case only when you tell what we have asked you to tell". We did the same thing. But the case got acquitted. It is all because of heavy bribing of officials at all levels by the accused. How can a government case be rejected without the involvement of bribe?

4. *Did the government give any money to the wife of the deceased and how far was this money useful to her?*

Yes, the government gave money. They gave this money because of his death. They gave it through Bank/Taluka office. This amount was useful to her. But she has gone back to her parents' place.

5. *Do you think that this POA Act is useful to you?*

Yes, because of this law, we could get some financial compensation, which help us manage our children and family.

Case Highlights

Context

The murder of Arumugam of Mosukudi village is an evidence of the caste Hindus' violent nature and their discriminatory attitude towards the Scheduled Castes.

Police Attitude

1. When the incident of murder was formally brought to the notice of the local police, the police paid no heed to the aggrieved, as if nothing had happened. They swung into the action only when the SP, who was also informed, came all the way from the district head quarter Ramanathapuram.
2. The local police kept in lock-up the elder brother of the deceased and a few others closely related to the victim for 11

days, subjected them to inhuman torture and forced them to be the guilty of the murder.

3. The police demanded bribe and the victims had to give them money.
4. Had the accused not admitted their guilt, the aggrieved would have been sent to jail.
5. The victim's relatives felt that the police cheated them.

Factors Responsible for the Acquittal

1. Despite being a case of murder, a blatant violation of the POA Act, and the accused themselves admitted their guilt and that too in front of the concerned police officials, the guilty could not be punished.
2. The victims made the police officials who handled the case responsible for the defeat of the case in view of their callous handling of the case and antagonistic attitudes towards the victim in particular.
3. Since both the police and the accused threatened the witnesses with dire consequences, the latter could not depose of the case properly and confidently. Even the victim's own brother was unable to give evidence in favour of the case as he had already been warned that he and his family members would be killed if he ignored the warning.

Recommendations

1. The POA Act is to be implemented more earnestly.
2. The police demand money from the victim to pursue the case, and from the accused to free them and to punish the victim who dared to seek justice through the POA Act. So, there should be some mechanism to check such an unlawful acts on the part of the police.

Case No. 4

Offence: Illegal occupation of land; *Crime No:* 106/99: Nagaraj Vs. S. Shekh Mohammad; Offence under POA Act: 3(1)(x), IPC: 341, 447, 502(d); *Victim:* Mr. V. Nagaraj, Rajakambiram (village), Sivagangai District.

Victim's View

1. *Could you narrate the incident for which you registered a case under the POA Act?*

I stay at Rajakambiram village, Manamadurai (taluka), Sivagangai (district). We are only a few families, belonging to Pallar caste (SCs). Most of the villagers belong to Muslim community. A few Muslim members encroached on our land, and we have all necessary documents for the land. They also built houses on our land. I then filed a case under the SC and ST POA Act in 1990 (A.N.N. 185/90). The matter went to the Special Court, Madurai. The Court declared that the land belonged to me and therefore to be given back to me. Against this judgment, the accused appealed (A.N.S.54/93) to the District Court, Sivagangai. Again the judgment on 23.11.94 was in our favour.

In contravention to the direction of the Court, on 11.11.98 at 11 AM when I was busy cutting the *Karuvel Maram* (juri flora trees) grown in our land and putting fences around our land, our opponents appeared there and started abusing me. "How dare, you entered our premises and erecting fences in our land. Why do you – Pallar caste fellows – need land and property? You dogs. How can you live as our equals?" Yet another person ordered me to remove the fence. Another one said, "We made a mistake of not chasing you away from this village in the beginning itself". They further threatened, "You dogs. You have to live under our subordination only. If you don't leave this place, we, all together, will humiliate you and your family members and chase you away from here. The Panchayat President of this area is our man (Muslim). Though the Court has given judgement in your favour, we are not going to leave this land. You may go to any Court". I then complained to the police on the same day.

Since there was no response from the police to my complaint on 11.11.1998, I once again submitted a petition at the PCR police station, Sivangangai seeking protection for myself and to have access to my land. Though this complaint was lodged on 3.1.99, the police made an FIR only on 5.1.99. The SI who made the FIR also went through other relevant documents including the judgement of the Special Court. Having been convinced, he said he would register the case on humanitarian ground. He then registered the case under section 3 (1) (x) of the POA Act. Once again, nothing happened. None visited the spot to verify the case. I again complained at the PCR police station on 9.8.99 reacting to this complaint, one woman from the accused family, whose house is also located in our land, just 200 feet away from our house, came to our house on the same day (9.8.99) and started abusing everyone in derogatory terms. She said, "you, *Pallapayale*, you need land? If we wish, we can completely destroy you all". On the same day i.e. 9.8.99, she, without our knowledge, filed a case against us at the local police station, as if we misbehaved with her. She did so to force us to withdraw the complaint.

At this juncture, the SI of the PCR police station did a mischievous act. He deleted the date i.e. 9.8.99 written on the top of my complaint sheet. He said, "Date should not be written like this". He then asked me to sign at the bottom of the petition. There he wrote the date 13.8.99 instead of 9.8.99. He did another mischievous thing. He said that he would file an FIR, and the copy of the same I could collect from the local (Manamadurai) police station. Instead of making an FIR, he had actually prepared a memo against me and sent the same to Manamadurai police station. I was not aware of the difference between an FIR and a memo. Later, I was asked to come to the Manamadurai police station. I went there with all necessary documents. I showed them all including a copy of the judgement. But the Inspector did not show any interest to look into any of my documents or to listen to what I was telling, since they had already planned to file a counter case against me. I said, "We have registered-documents (pattas) for 3 ¾ acres of land. We got it in 1974 itself. This is our grand father's land. But they have forcefully occupied our land and built about 8 houses on it. We did not go there to occupy any body's land". Though I tried to explain the matter in details, the Police Inspector was determined to file a case against me. He immediately contacted the then DSP, who, in turn, suggested him to make a counter petition and file an FIR against me. Accordingly, he changed the date of my PCR complaint from 9.8.99 to 13.8.99. Without even conducting an enquiry for the PCR case that I had filed, the Sub-Inspector (SI), on his own, forged documents stating that it was a case of *mistake of facts* (MF) and produced the same to the

Court without giving any importance to my appeal. Accordingly, the Court later on informed me. I therefore once again appealed to the Court seeking to know as to why the Court took such a decision when I already had all necessary documents and evidences. I requested an advocate to plead for me. He showed no interest. So, I myself appeared in the Special Court and deposed the facts. The Judges said that I should approach the concerned Session Court at the district level where there was a counter case filed against me. Till date, there has been no communication either from the police or from the Court with regard to the cases under Crime No.1/99 and crime No.446/99. For both these cases they have given MF though these incidents took place in broad daylight.

My earlier petition (on 11.11.98) on the same issue, i.e., denial of access to my land despite Court's positive verdict to this effect, was submitted to the SI Mr. Kumarasamy at the Manamadurai police station. He accepted my petition and gave only a receipt. Since there was no action from his side for more than 4 days, I went to the District Collector. The Collector accepted my request and forwarded the same to the SP for necessary action. But even the SP did not seem to be bothered. I sent the petition to the SP four times by registered post and pleaded for necessary action under the provisions of the POA Act. Six months passed. Nothing happened. Then I directly approached an advocate and with his advice we filed a case under the POA Act. We were then approached for police enquiry. The next day we all went to the Madurai Special Court to give evidences. We did that so well. But in the proceedings, the whole issue was misconceived and recorded differently. The Court concluded that there was a link between the incident of caste-based abuses and the issue of the land. Accordingly, the Special Court Madurai acquitted the case.

Though I have all necessary documents, including a judgment in my favour, the Court acquitted the case. It is all because, I belong to the Scheduled Caste and have none to support me. They, the accused, have muscle power and money power. The police support them. The police register false cases against the SCs, and the revenue department produces false records in favour of the accused.

When we go to the Court for justice, it favours the accused, and thereby uphold unjust practices as if the judiciary were meant for unjust practices. In this scenario, it is doubtful that we will ever get justice through the POA Act. If this has been the experience of a person like me who is educated to some extent, what would be the fate of common village men who are illiterate and ignorant? In all, I would say that the police do not implement this Act completely. For every registered case, the police propose a compromise. When this fails, the police do not hesitate to file a counter case against the victims and make all possible contacts to defeat the case.

Views of the Witness 1: (Mr. Ramanathan, S/o. Karuppaiah, Rajakambiram village):

POA Act is needed. But in our village, we are governed by the verdict of our *Zamat* Court. Being only two families, we, the Pallars, have no option but to depend on the Muslims for our day-to-day living and redressing our grievances. We cannot violate the pronouncement of our *Zamat* Court.

Untouchability is there in our village, Rajakambiram. Pallan should carry the light during religious festival. And the Parayars should play the drum. We cannot stop performing these defiling tasks since we depend on them for our survival.

Views of the Witness 2: (Mr. Chellaiah, S/o. Chellam, Rajakambiram village).

"Though we have all necessary documents for our land, due to their money and muscle power and our ignorance and illiteracy, we are cheated and defeated. They have encroached our land and also built houses over there. Our repeated appeals to the Collector and the Revenue department have not yielded any positive results. They use their money and muscle power to defeat all our efforts. They continue to harass us. They easily occupy our land assuming that we cannot do anything. The Revenue department, the police and the Collector – all work in their favour, and take immediate steps as desired by them. But they do not respond to any of our petitions and initiatives. The police do not register case against the caste Hindus encroaching on the SCs' land as they are being bribed heavily. Since we are only two families here, they try their best to chase us away from here. Though the Court has given the verdict that the land belonged to us, the police and the revenue departments have not taken necessary steps to free the encroached land and hand it over to us".

Case Highlights

Context, Police Attitude, Factors Responsible for the Acquittal

1. Unlike the usual cases, the accused in this case were not the caste Hindus, but members belonging to Muslim community. They exploited the SCs by forcefully occupying their land.
2. The accused did not value much the verdict of the Special Court. The accused regarded very high the verdict of the *Jamat* Court (traditionally constituted body of the Muslims whose verdict is regarded as final by its members).
3. Though the Special Court declared that the land belonged to the victim Nagaraj, neither the concerned police department nor the revenue department performed its lawful duties to this effect. By doing so, they in fact dishonoured the Court's verdict. It is thus not only a clear case of contempt of Court but also an offence under the POA Act. But who will initiate the litigation process?
4. The accused influenced the concerned officials of both the police and revenue departments using their money and muscle power to work in their favour.
5. The police instead of being the protectors of the victims, played with their ignorance and socio-economic vulnerability. They diluted and diverted the case through their mischievous acts, and manipulated the case covertly in favour of the accused. The revenue department officials also helped them in the process.
6. The police framed charges against the victim through their mischievous acts instead of helping him to get justice.
7. Even the Special Court did not seem to be free from caste prejudice. This was evident not only from its subsequent unjust judgement after the first one but also from the

prejudiced attitude of most of the Court officials in general and of the Judges as well.

Recommendation

These experiences of the victim with the police, revenue department and the judiciary, which denied the victim's legitimate right over his land, in spite of his possessing all necessary documents, and also a favourable judgement from the concerned Session Court, have clearly proved that no Scheduled Caste person can obtain the due protection from the these structures of power. It is so viewed due to the fact that the people of oppressive and dominant castes predominantly represent these departments and their loyalties and commitments are more towards the people of their own caste than towards their profession as custodians of law and justice. So, unless there is sufficient representation of SCs and STs in these powerful government bodies, protecting the SCs and STs from atrocities and exploitation will ever remain a distant dream.

Case No. 5

Offence: Denial of access to common path; *Crime No.* 34/98, Shanmugan Vs. Mutthaiah; Offence under POA Act: 3(1)(x); *Victim:* Mr. Mr. Shanmugam, S/o. Mr. Karuppan, Allur village, Sivagangai District.

Victim's Views

1. *Could you narrate the incident for which you filed a case under the POA Act?*

The Allur village is dominated by the caste Hindus such as Kallars, Maravars, Valayars, Konars and Vellalars. In all, there are about 200 families. The only family belonging to the Scheduled Caste is my own.

I filed a case against a *Valayar* caste person not merely because he denied me access to a common path but mainly because, he abused me in derogatory terms referring to my low caste background. In fact, the land through which the road (common path) passes is not a *purampoku* land (unused government land) and it is so mentioned in all relevant documents. The land remained unused for a long time, and the road was laid on it at a later stage. Since the accused had purchased this land including the road, he did not give us access to the road.

However, since I am poor, old and staying alone with none to support but three daughters to be looked after, and depend entirely on the caste Hindu villagers including the accused for food and physical security, I did not want to antagonise the accused. Moreover, the accused himself realised his mistakes and came to a compromise. Having no support to fall back upon, I compromised.

2. *Do you need the laws such as the POA and PCR?*

These laws are very essential because victims like me who is poor get financial compensation for the loss suffered, and others are also afraid of us now.

Case Highlights

Context

The victim despite living in a vulnerable condition, dared to file a case under the POA Act, mainly because he was very much conscious and particular about his self-respect, and he was deeply hurt by the derogatory and discriminatory remarks made by the accused.

Factors Responsible for the Acquittal

1. The victim could not pursue the case to its logical end, since he was poor, alone in the village and depended entirely on the caste Hindu villagers for his livelihood and protection.
2. The accused himself realised his mistakes and offered the victim for a compromise which a Scheduled Caste person could never even think of in such villages. So, the victim compromised his plea for punishing the accused.

Recommendations

The POA Act and PCR Act should continue as these help the victims in two ways:

(a) Financial compensation for the loss suffered.

(b) The caste Hindus who are once booked particularly under the POA Act and subjected to trial procedures, would not think of committing atrocity against the SCs again. And this will also be a lesson for other caste Hindus. But, what is more important, is that these laws should be enforced properly and earnestly.

Case No. 6

Offence: Denial of access to common path; *Crime No.* 9/98: V. Mani Vs. S. Karuppaiah; *Offence under* POA Act: 3(1)(x); Mr. Mani, S/o. Veeran, Vaduhanpatti Village, Sivagangai District.

Victim's Views

1. *Could you narrate the incident of caste discrimination?*

We have been struggling for the last 30 years to lead a dignified life free from caste oppression by the *Kallar* caste (CHs) people. Recently, two of our village caste Hindu men Karuppaiah, S/o. Solaimalai and Alahan, S/o. Ravi troubled us a lot. They belonged to Kallar caste. They have blocked a common path without which we cannot go anywhere. They claimed that it belonged to them and therefore closed it. We now walk miles together round the village whenever we need to go out of the village. Then we filed a case under the POA Act. But the case failed, because the police accepted money from the accused and overtly favoured the Kallar caste people. It is also because, two of the policemen in charge of this case themselves belonged to the Kallar caste. The police suppressed all the important documents to be sent to the Court and kept them to themselves. And in the absence of these vital documents, the case automatically got acquitted. The police do such thing in a well-planned manner with a view to helping the accused escape legal punishment.

2. *Do you think the POA Act is needed?*

In fact we did not even know that there was such a law. Only recently when our children started going to nearby towns and started interacting with the educated people, we got to know about it. It is because of such laws, we are at least able to walk like human beings. Otherwise, they would have oppressed us even more inhumanly. It is with the help of this law that we are able to infuse some amount of fear in them saying, "if you trouble us further, we shall file a complaint against you under the PCR Act". They now think twice before attacking us, as they may also have to face problems and spend Rs. 5000 to 10,000/- once a case is filed against them under this law. Whether we win the case or not, we need this law. It is with this law that we can counter their attack and also infuse a sense of fear in them.

Case Highlights

Context

Since the closed common path was the only way for the SCs to go anywhere in or outside the village, the SCs faced immense difficulties and had no option but to file a case under the POA Act to have access to the common path.

Police Attitude

1. The police covertly favoured the accused accepting money from them.
2. The police favoured the accused also because two of them belonged to the same caste that the accused belonged to.

Factors Responsible for the Acquittal

The police nefariously removed a few vital documents from those to be sent to the Court for trial, and therefore the case got acquitted.

Recommendations

These special laws should continue since they are the only hopes for the SCs to counter an attack by, and also to infuse a sense of fear among the caste Hindus intending to discriminate against and commit atrocities on the SCs.

Case No. 7

Offence: Denial of due wage and discriminatory remarks; *Crime No.* 5/92; Pandi Vs. Kannuchancy; *Offence under* PCR Act: 7(1)(d); *Victim:* M. Pandi, S/o Mr. Muniyandi, Naganathapuram, Perumpacheri, Paramakudi, Ramanathanpuram District.

The Incident (as per the FIR)

On 16.3.92 Pandi S/o Muniyandi, resident of Naganathapuram village was busy cutting the juri-flora trees (fire-wood trees) for wage along with 5 others who also belonged to the same Pallar caste on the request of one Mr. Ramasamy who belonged to Marvar caste (Backward Caste Hindu) and was a resident of Burma colony, Paramakudi. When they were cutting the trees, one Mr. Kannu, S/o Chellam Servai, resident of Malaiyan Kudiyiruppu village went there and asserted that the trees being cut and the land on which the trees had grown belonged to him, and said further that he had already filed a case against Ramasamy in the High Court to this effect. Kannu then loaded all the wood that had been cut in the bullock cart and took them away. Then Ramasamy left the place saying that he would lodge a complaint against Kannu at the police station, Paramakudi. Since then, Pandi went many times to Kannu asking for the due wage of Rs. 210/-. Since the latter did not give the wage as assured, on 30.3.92 Pandi went in the morning to Kannu's house and said that since he was not given the due wage, he would cut the latter's trees worth the due wage. When Pandi was standing at the Kannu's field, Kannu, came over there, shouted, "You, mother fuckers, degraded Pallan caste fellow (*yeena chadhi palla payale*); how dare, you come and stand on my land". He also attempted to beat him. Being scared, Pandi ran to the nearby house of one Mr. Satthaiah. But Kannu came over and caught his hand and said, "Pallan caste mother fuckers, who can stop me if I beat you". He again attempted to beat him. At that time Mrs. Lakshmi, W/o Ramasamy Thevar and Saathayi, who were there, intervened and took away Pandi from there. A formal case was then filed to take appropriate legal action against Kannu Servai who not only refused paying due wage to Pandi but also insulted him referring to his low caste background.

Accordingly, a case was filed on 02.4.92 at 11 a.m. under crime No. 5/92, section 7(1)(d) of PCR Act at the PCR Police station, Ramanathapuram. This case was registered by Mr. S. Murugesan, Inspector, PCR Police station, Ramanathapuram.

As required, the original of FIR along with the victim's petition was sent to the Judge, PCR Special Court, Madurai, and copies of the same were sent to the concerned officials.

Case Highlights

Context

The victim had no other demand except the wage due to him. He could claim the wage neither from the person who (Ramasamy) asked him to cut the trees for wage, nor from the person (Kannu Servai) who not only claimed that the trees being cut belonged to him and took away them all but also abused him in discriminatory and derogatory terms and also attempted to assault him. There was none to support him. It was in this context that the victim filed a case under the PCR Act.

Police Attitude

1. Though the victim reported the incident, which took place on 30.3.92, on 31.3.92 itself, the police registered the case only on 02.4.92.
2. Though the police registered the case on 02.4.92, they sent to the Special Court the relevant documents, which should have been sent on the same day itself, only on 08.4.92 (after 6 days), as evident from the judgement itself.

Factors Responsible for the Acquittal

1. Examining the various documents that the researcher could get and comparing them with circumstantial evidences, the researcher could arrive at the following conclusions regarding factors responsible for the acquittal of the case: The first reason for acquitting the case under reference is

that the case was reported late. The incident that took place on 30.3.92 was reported to the police only on 02.4.92, according to the Inspector who registered the case, and the reason for the delay that he acknowledged was that the complainant, not knowing the jurisdiction, went to the PCR Unit of Sivagangai instead of Ramanathapuram. However, the victim claimed that he had reported to the police on the very next day (31.3.92) of the incident.

However, who was at fault? Was it the fault of complainant or of the Inspector who registered the case? The Court has categorically said that though the Inspector admitted that he registered the case on 02.4.92, he did not send the relevant documents on the same day as required, but only on 08.4.92, i.e. after 6 days. The Court has further argued that the Inspector also did not give any valid reasons for the delay.

This callous attitude of the police as recognised by the Court is not only a violation of the provisions of POA Act and therefore punishable, but, in a way, negates the credibility of the police's claim that the incident was reported to him only on 02.4.92 and not on 31.3.92 as claimed by the complainant.

2. Another reason for acquitting the case was that the third witness Mrs. Lakshmi turned hostile instead of standing by the side of the victim. But the Honourable Judge would very well understand that in a society like ours where caste is a reality and caste sentiments, loyalties and affinity are much more strong than any other thing, it is no surprise that the third witness, who belonged to Thevar caste which is deadly against the Pallar caste which the victim belonged to, turned hostile and gave evidence in support of the accused.
3. Compared to the above reasons, other reasons such as the doubt with regard to the timing of the incident and the reason for the victim asking for his due wage from the accused instead of the person who had asked them to do that particular work are of relatively less important.

However, all these leaves a room for doubt with regard to the validity of the case. And, as usual, the benefit of doubt was given to the accused and accordingly, the case was acquitted. But the crucial issue is, Why should the benefit of doubt in respect of the cases tried in courts be always given to the accused, who is, more often than not, more powerful and influential, instead of being given to the victim who are mostly without any power, economic, political and bureaucratic, illiterate, and often ignorant of the strength and weakness of their cases and of the procedures to be followed at various stages of seeking justice through the Court of law. It is perhaps because of such an approach, the Honourable Judge often seem to be more concerned with the accused and accordingly look for some gaps or loopholes and turn the table of justice against the victims. This situation has to be altered and the benefit of doubt be given to the victim whose protection the police is concerned with and whose welfare the Constitution is committed to.

Recommendations

1. The police not only delayed the case by registering the case only on 02.4.92 instead of 31.3.92, but also failed to send the relevant documents to the Special Court on the same day as required by the law. These documents were sent only on 08.4.92 instead of 02.4.92. Instead of acquitting the case, the Court could have ordered necessary punitive action against the police for having failed to perform their lawful duties and as a result the case could not be proved in the Court of law beyond doubt.
2. When there are difficulties in proving beyond doubt the validity of any PCR and POA Act cases, which usually happen, given the vulnerable condition of the victims, the Honourable Judge, may give the benefit of doubt to the victims instead of the accused.

Case No. 8

Offence: Stealing of SCs' firewood and attempt to assault with brooms and foot-wears; *Crime No.* 9/91: M. Muniandi Vs. C.Chellathurai; *Offence under* PCR Act:7(1)(d); *Victim:* Mr. M.Muniandi, S/o Muttuhukarupppan, Aatrupaala Vadaharai, Paramakudi town, Ramanathapuram District.

Victim's Views: (as per the FIR)

Mr. Muniandi, the victim under reference, belonging to Pallar caste was an ex-army man (soldier). After retirement, he was involved in agriculture related activities and buying and selling of firewood trees (juri-flora) to earn his livelihood. Once he had purchased the juri-flora trees belonging to one Mrs. Gyanambal, resident of Valayanendal village. She belonged to Maravar caste (caste Hindu). Since Muniyandi could not cut the juri flora trees in time as agreed upon, Gyanambal, with the help of one of her caste members Mr. Vijayasamy Thevar, resident of a nearby town, Thelichaathanallur, cut the trees and took them away without the knowledge of Muniandi who had already purchased them. A formal case of theft was registered at the police station, Paramakudi on 29.9.91. Subsequently, the SI concerned asked the accused to give in writing that henceforth he would not indulge in such an act.

A few days later i.e., on 8.10.91 around 6 in the evening when Muniandi was bringing the fire-wood in bullock-cart purchased from Gyanambal, the same Vijayasamy Thevar S/o Chellathurai along with Mr. Krishnan, Kaliyappa Konar, Kaliammal and Padma of Valayanendal village i.e., the village of Gyanambal from whom the victim had purchased the fire-wood trees, came in the way and insulted him saying, "you, degraded Pallan caste fellow. You registered a case of theft against us. But what could you do to us registering a case?"

Both Vijayasamy Thevar and Krishnan shouted at him saying, "how dare you, Pallan caste fellow, gave a complaint against us", and attempted to beat him with their footwears. Subsequently, Kaliyammal and Padma humiliated him saying, "you, degraded Pallan caste fellow, you will come to sense only when you are beaten with brooms".

At that time one Mr. Ramu S/o Velu Konar, resident of Perumpacheri village and Mr. Arumugam, resident of Valayanendal village, intervened and asked both the parties to leave the place. This incident was well known to one policeman who was the son of one Mr. Raju Thevar.

Due to this incident, Muniandi felt extremely pained and humiliated. Therefore, he registered a case under the PCR Act on 9.10.91 at 10 in the morning. The copy of FIR was sent to the Court and higher-level officials concerned on 15.10.91 for necessary action.

Case Highlights

Context

The victim was an ex-army man and therefore not only had the knowledge of the PCR Act but was also confident of punishing the accused under this law without anybody's support.

Police Attitude

1. The Offence under reference is an outcome of the police's failure to take prompt and timely action with regard to an offence committed earlier by the same accused.
2. Though the earlier offence that was very much an offence under the POA Act, the police concerned did not register the case under the said law. Instead, they merely got in writing from the accused that he would not do such thing in future.
3. Such an attitude of the police failing to perform their lawful duties in earnest can be said to have, encouraged the accused to behave the way he behaved in the present case.

Factors Responsible for the Acquittal and Recommendations

According to the researcher, the Honourable Special Court acquitted the above case for the following reasons:

1. The Court concluded that the firewood that had been stolen were the ones that had already been cut and left in the field. Those were not the ones cut by the accused as claimed in the FIR.

   But the learned Judge would very well understand that the case under reference was not about 'who had cut the trees?" but about "who had stolen them". Whoever had cut the trees, there was no doubt that the trees belonged to the victim, and there was also no doubt that the firewood had been stolen by the present accused. This was evident from the fact that this incident of theft had already been reported to the police on 29.9.91 by the present complainant. This complaint against the present accused prior to the present case was a clear case of an offence under the POA Act. The concerned police officer should have registered the theft case under the POA Act. But he did not do so. He merely got in writing from the accused that he would not repeat such an illegal act in future. As per the law the Court could have questioned the police as to why they did not register that case under the POA Act. The Court could have also punished them for not performing their lawful duty. Instead, the Court simply acquitted the case.

2. The fact that during the trial the victim was unable to recall the name of the 4th accused whose name had been mentioned in the FIR, can not be a valid reason for acquitting the case.
3. Moreover, the victims and witness were not tutored properly by the police, which was very much a part of their lawful duty, as to how they should face the trial and what all they should be telling during the trial.
4. Though the incident took place on 8.10.91 at 6 o'-clock in the evening, the victim gave a complaint at the police station only on the next day (9.10.91) morning at 10 a.m. This delay is another reason for the learned Judge to doubt the very occurrence of the incident, as mentioned in his judgement. But the Judge would very well understand that no one would take the decision of initiating any formal action in a hurry, particularly when the opponent party is more powerful economically and politically. He would obviously consult others, collect all necessary facts and only then he would take up the matter formally. This would certainly take time. That is what would have happened in this case as well. Moreover, no one would prefer going to the police station to lodge a complaint during night-time, and that too against the dominant caste members. Therefore, the delay in reporting the incident cannot be a valid reason for acquitting the case.
5. The reasons for the acquittal of the case seems to have been based mostly on the incident that took place prior to the present one which the victim had mentioned in his FIR merely to indicate how the present case is related to the previous one.

6. On the whole, it gives an impression that the learned Judge seemed to have looked only for some gaps/reasons or the other, however relevant or valid they may be, to acquit the case and protect the interests of the accused.

Case No. 9

Offence: Denial of equal rights in religious festival; *Crime No.* 8/91: K. Satthaiah Vs. U. Ganapathi Thevar; *Offence under* PCR Act: 7(1)(d); *Victim*: Mr. Sathaiah, s/o. Mr. Marimuthu, Mayilurani village, Ramanathapuram District.

Victim's Views

1. *Could you please narrate how the incident took place?*

The Iyan Kovil (temple) festival is celebrated every year together by the people of Mayilurani and Paranur (Panchayat) villages of Ramanathapuram district. For this festival, like the *Thevar* caste (CHs) people, we (SCs) too, as usual, contributed Rs. 100/- per family and also participated in the Jallikattu event which means chasing the bulls and snatching away whatever tied around their necks as a mark of demonstrating one's courage and physical prowess. Though we make equal financial contribution every year, only the *Thevar* caste families get four to five (sometimes even more) pieces of half coconuts as Koil prasad. We, each SC family, get only a few broken pieces of coconuts, which is not even equivalent to one piece of half coconut.

Being unhappy over this discriminatory practice, one day I, along with my *aiah* (maternal grand father), met the *Thevar* caste man Mr. Ganapathi and asked as to why such a discrimination should prevail. He, in reply, said, "This has been the tradition. We will give only what has been given to you all along. You have to accept what we give. You, Pallan caste people, are meant only for this much". Ganapathi is a government servant. Ever since he became the Village Administrative Officer (VAO), the SC people here face number of problems. On that day, the CHs did not use vulgar words. But on the next morning when we, about 5 to 6 members, were returning from another place, they caught us though we tried to run away to protect ourselves. They abused us, telling, "how dare you, Pallans and Parayans, asking for equal share in the prasad". They beat us severely. They thought even to the extent of burning us alive and destroying us. They however spared us when we became submissive and meek and pleaded for mercy. We then lodged a formal complaint at the PCR Police station, Ramanathapuram. The police registered our case. The Inspector came to the spot, but the inquiry was conducted at the Ramanathapuram PCR office. However, we were not happy about the way the case was handled. We were asked to go here and there. Finally, the case was referred to the Madurai (Special) Court for trial. But we lost the case.

2. *What were the reasons for loosing the case in the Court?*

They (the accused) have the officers on their side. The accused enjoyed the support of one Mr. Sethupathi Thevar, whose father is known to the Magistrate handling our case. Through this connection, they bribed and convinced the Magistrate to deliver judgement in their favour. Our witnesses were prompt. My own brothers were the witnesses. I even opposed the Magistrate's stand on the case.

The Magistrate overtly favoured the accused saying whatever the accused did was correct. After the first trial, we don't even know what happened to the case. But they have spoiled our case. Later, there was a suspension order to the accused. They even showed the order. But we don't know whether the suspension order was an outcome of our case or on some other charges.

Afterwards also, we filed cases against him. But we could not do anything against him since in this entire area everything is happening under his headship. He is the one who often ignites caste clashes in this area.

3. *Do you think the POA Act is needed?*

We need it, because my caste people are not there as officers. The police work only for those who gives them more money. When the Thevar caste people give more money, the police do not even file a case; there is no case at all. They have more money and also belong to upper caste. How can we fight against them in the absence of such laws?

Views of the Accused (Mr. Ganapathi)

1. *What about the case filed against you? How did you manage the case?*

   What case? It was a false case against me. They (SCs) wanted to spoil my name. I am a big person in this area and have been working as a Village Administrative Officer (VAO). Here, whatever I say, my caste people will listen. The Pallar caste fellows simply filed a case against me. But, If we give money, the police will talk in our favour. We have closed the case with the help of a Magistrate. They suspended me. But then and there I paid money and settled the matter, and I immediately resumed my duty. I am now working as VAO.

2. *What do you think about the PCR and POA laws. They should be there or not?*

   Whether these laws are there or not, it is immaterial for us. In this area, whatever we like, that is the law to be abided by everyone.

Researcher's View on Judgment

According to the researcher, the Special Court acquitted the case under reference mainly for the following reasons:

1. First of all, the case under reference, which had been registered under the PCR Act, should have been registered under the SCs and STs (POA) Act, 1989 considering the nature of offence committed. This in itself is an offence under the POA Act on the part of the police who registered the case.
2. The first charge is that though the incident took place on 15.8.91 at 8.20 in the night, and the same was reported to the police on the next day i.e., 16.8.91 at 12.45 in the afternoon, a case, to this effect, was registered only on 21.8.91. And no reason has been given by anyone from the government side i.e., the police for this delay of about 6 days.

   But why should the Court victimize the victim by acquitting his case for the blunder of the police who refused to perform their lawful duty of registering the case as soon it was reported to. The delay was only due to the police. Instead of punishing the police under section 4 of the POA Act 1989, why should the Court acquit the case?

3. The second main charge of the Court is that though the Inspector claims that he had requested the victim to hand over a copy of the complaint to the concerned SI to investigate the case, there is no evidence to prove that the SI received the said complaint and investigated the case accordingly and also sent the necessary documents to the officials concerned.

If there was no evidence to prove the above, it was obviously the fault of the police who charge-sheeted the case. The Court could have given one more chance to the police to prove the case with necessary evidences. Why should the case be acquitted?

Case Highlights

Context

1. The victims filed a PCR case not only because they were denied equal share in the religious festival (koil prasad) and debarred from participating in the Jallikattu/bull-chasing event, but also because they were abused, beaten and threatened to be killed.
2. They filed a case mainly to protect themselves from possible dire consequences.

Police Attitude

1. The police registered the case, but did not pursue the matter earnestly.
2. In view of the nature of offences committed, this case should have been registered under the POA Act, instead of the PCR Act.

Factors Responsible for the Acquittal

1. Refer the "researcher's views on judgement" noted before.

2. Not only the victims but also the accused himself had disclosed that the Magistrate was influenced by the accused through bribe and political powers to give verdict in favour of the accused.
3. Despite concrete evidences and witnesses, the Magistrate rejected the case and gave judgment as desired by the accused.
4. The accused, despite being the government servant overtly avowed that he and his caste Hindus could influence and also take the support of not only the police but also of the Magistrate to win cases filed against them with their money power and caste affiliation.
5. Though the victim emphasized the need for such protective laws, the accused proclaimed that he and his caste people had no respect for such laws, and even asserted that whatever he and his caste people (caste Hindus) want to be the laws, would be the laws in their area. And all others would have to obey such (unjust) laws which are meant to perpetuate untouchability, caste discrimination and the inhuman living condition of the SCs.

Case No. 10

Offence: Physical assault and making discriminatory remarks on SC schoolboy for talking to caste Hindu school girls; *Crime No.* 27/99: M. Muttu Vs. P. Parthiban; *Offence under* POA Act: 3(1)(x), IPC:147,342,323; *Victim:* Mr. M. Mutthu, S/o Moorkan, Melaiyur, Virudhunagar District.

The Incident (as per the FIR)

On 12.3.99 Mr. Muniyasamy S/o. Mr. Mutthu belonging to the Pahadai caste (one of the SCs) and resident of Melaiyur village teased Nayakar caste (one of the Backward Castes) girls, Miss. Nagadevi, D/o Palchamy and Miss. Anita, D/o Mr. Ramamurthi, resident of the same village, while they were going to and coming from school.

On 13.3.99 at 12.00 p.m. Nagadevi's angered brother Parthiban, S/o Palchamy and their caste men Babu S/o. Balakrishnan caught and forcefully dragged Muniyasamy to the Melaiyur panchayat office and beat him severely.

Alleging that on 16.3.99 at 5.30 p.m. Muniyasamy beat Parthiban while the latter was standing at the Melaiyur bus stop, Parthiban along with Sathiya, Sakthi and Babu and a few others reached the residence of Muniyasamy at 6.30 p.m. on the same day. They humiliated his father, Mr. Mutthu, and abused saying, "dey chakiliyapayale" meaning "you, the low caste fellow". While Parthiban hit him and injured the right hand, Sathiya hit the forehead and stomach of Mutthu using wooden sticks.

Later, Mutthu was taken to Nayakar street and tied along with the street lamp post. This incident was informed to the nearby police station at Paralachi, a small town, by one Mr. Susai. Subsequently the police came to the spot and rescued him and took him to the police station. An FIR was formally lodged and the case was registered by Mr. T. Nelson (SI) on the same day (16.3.99) at 7.45 P.M. under section 147, 342, 323 of IPC and under 3(1) x of SC/ST Act 1989. As required, FIR original and victim's statement were sent to the PCR Court, Madurai and other necessary documents were also sent to the concerned officials.

Victim's Views

In the morning the police and Mr. Gyanaprabu came to Melaiyur village and took me to the police station and lodged a formal police compliant. But nobody else came to support. We later went to the Court (PCR Special Court, Madurai). There we met our "Aiya" (Saheb/Sir) (Son of Mr. Karuppaiah Thevar), who was a known advocate from our village.

We reported to him our problem. He promised to resolve it. He then asked us to sign a few documents, which he claimed, necessary for punishing the accused. We did so without knowing its content and consequences. Then he asked us to go for a compromise. We refused. Then he started abusing and threatened us with dire consequences. He rebuked saying,

"Chakiliya pundamayengala, oungalukellam evalavu mappuda, yidha vittu neenga poiruvengelada". (This means, "You, sons of those born from the vagina of Chakilians, the low caste people. How dare, you refuse me. Let me see, how you can go away from here?) We had then no option since we had already signed all the documents meant for compromise. We did not know anything as to what happened later. The Court declared that we agreed for a compromise. The police also did not tell us anything in advance in this regard. We were provided with *dosa* and also Rs. 50/- each and asked to go home. That was all happened. We felt terribly cheated.

Views of the Accused

The accused (Sakti) said, "It became a problem as one of the Chakiliyan boys teased our girl". We beat him. They went to the police. Prathiban, one of the main accused, was arrested. We (Caste Hindus) went to the police to bail him out. We gave two mild slaps to Parthiban at the police station itself to show that we are concerned about the problem, and said, we are now united and the problem stands resolved. We then brought Parthiban home.

They (Dalits) cannot do anything, because we, the caste Hindus live together. We resolve our problem with the help of the police. All money; everything is money. We have so much money because we are together. They have no money. Someone must have instigated them to go to the police. What case that we have not seen? The policemen are with us and so we have no problem.

Case Highlights

The case of Mutthu S/o Mookan (Victim) Vs Parthiban S/o Palchamy Nayakar and others (accused) of Melaiyur village of Virudhunagar district registered under sections 147, 342 and 323 of IPC and 3(1) (x) of POA Act 1989 at Paralachi Police Station got acquitted in an unjust and illegal manner. After a careful perusal of necessary documents and taking into consideration the views expressed by the victims, accused and others related to the case, the following are the major factors responsible for the acquittal:

1. *Errors in the FIR*:

   (a) As per the information given by Mr. Gyanaprabu, president of Dr. Ambedkar, Emmanuel Mandram (NGO), though the police was informed on the 16.3.99 at about 9.00 p.m., i.e. 21 hours, the police came to the rescue of the victim, who was beaten up and tied to a street lamp post at Nayakar street of the same village, only on the following day morning (17.3.99). But the FIR indicates that the victim was rescued by the police on the same day and taken to the police station and FIR was also filed at 19.45 hours on the same day. How could the FIR be filed in the police station (at 19.45 hours) even before the incident was reported to the police which happened only at 21 hours on 16.3.99?

   (b) The FIR does not indicate the fact that the victim remained tied the whole night and a bucket full of cow-dung mixed with water was poured on his head and tortured the whole night of 16.3.99 by the accused.

   (c) While interviewing the victims and those witnessed the incident on 12.3.99, it was gathered that the victim Muniasamy did not tease the girls as alleged and reported but was simply talking to them.

   (d) The FIR indicates that since Muniasamy beat up Parthiban the latter beat up Mutthu, the father of former, on 16.3.99. But our investigation reveals that Muniasamy did not beat up Parthiban but only showed his displeasure through facial expression over the fact that he was beaten up and humiliated in public by the latter on 13.3.99. Parthiban who then tried to assault the former did not tolerate even this. In fact, what happened was that since Parthiban was not allowed to assault Muniasamy with the timely intervention of friends of latter, he along with his caste men rushed to the house of Muniasamy and attacked his father Mutthu.

2. *Money and Muscle Power*: Once the case was registered under POA Act and the police arrested the accused, the accused came forward for a compromise, promising that nothing of that sort would be repeated in future. When the victims did not yield to this pressure, the accused used their money and muscle power. According to the statement of the victims and witnesses, it is clear that to stop them going to the Court, they were first lured by possible monitory benefits. When that failed, they were threatened with dire consequences and also suggesting the possibility of loosing all support from those whom they were depending on for their livelihood.
3. *Tampering with Evidences*: Though *protecting offenders by tampering with evidences* is an offence under section 3(2) (vi) of the POA Act, Mr. Karuppaiah Thevar, who was a resident of the same village, a known advocate and an influential person in the AIADMK party and whom the victims approached for help and advice, asked them to sign some documents which the advocate claimed required for punishing the accused. The innocent victims, not knowing what kind of documents they were signing and what would be its consequences, signed them all. Actually these documents were in favour the accused. The documents declared that the victims were not interested in taking up the case further but willing to go for a compromise. The advocate used these documents in the Court and the case was subsequently acquitted. By the time the victims realised what had happened to their case, it was too late to take any decision in their own interest.
4. *Lack of Will of Police*: Despite the fact that the police man was a witness to the whole incident as it was the police who came to the spot and rescued the victim and took him to the police station and also filed FIR, he did not stand as witness to the victim and refrained from taking the case to its logical end. Had he been so, he would not have allowed the victims to sign such documents used for acquitting the case. In a way the police joined hands with the accused covertly. Though this was an offence on the part of the police under Section 4 of the POA Act, the police, as usual, is left free.

Case No. 11

Offence: Threat to life and discriminatory remarks for apprehending the caste Hindus indulged in illegal fishing; *Crime No.* 27/98, Mr. Alagan Vs. M. Gurupatham, Offence under POA Act: 3(1)(x); *Victim*: Mr. Alagan, S/o. Arumugam, Chakhandi Village, Sivagangai District.

Victim's Views

1. *Could you tell about the POA Act case you had filed?*

We were four – Jawahar, Muniyandi, Sekar and myself – in charge of protecting a *Kanmai* (lake) and preventing illegal fishing over there. One day, we caught a person who indulged in illegal fishing. He belonged to Ambalaharar caste i.e., Valayar caste (Backward Caste). His name was Murugan. When we were going back to the village along with the person we caught, his entire village people came running towards us. They snatched away the fish that we took possession of, and started beating us. I was beaten. We then reported the matter to the taluka office. But the police, accepting money from the accused, did not take any action against them. Our village then decided to register a case under the POA Act. We did so. Police inquiry was conducted and subsequently the matter was referred to the Special Court. Our witnesses were strong and gave evidences in Court properly. But the accused party requested us for a compromise. We also could not oppose them that easily. We then agreed. The case was closed after getting a written promise from the accused that they would not indulge in such activities in future. Moreover, we received Rs. 6500/- from the Government after the charge sheet was laid.

2. *Do you need this law?*

It is definitely needed. Without this law, poor people like us cannot live here even with minimum dignity. The police in general accept bribe from the accused and work in their favour. Only a few support our case. But this law is very much needed and has to be strongly implemented. If this law is withdrawn, we shall be pushed back into the old days of slavery.

Case Highlights

Context

The victims decided to file a case under the POA Act only when their effort to punish the guilty by informing the incident to the taluka office and the police had failed.

Police Attitude

The police refused to perform their lawful duty, since they had already accepted money from the accused for helping the latter escape the due legal punishment.

Factors Responsible for the Acquittal

The accused requested the victim for a compromise. Owing to their socio-economic vulnerability, and being a minority, the victim had no option but to accept the 'offer' of the compromise.

The victims also did not feel disappointed since they were paid Rs. 6500/- from the Government as compensation, and the accused were also forced by the police to give in writing that they would not repeat such an act in future.

Recommendation

The POA Act is very much needed and useful for the helpless victims and therefore requires to be implemented vigorously.

Case No. 12

Offence: False allegation of having dashed against a caste Hindu and in response the latter catching him by the collar and attempting to assault him with footwear besides discriminatory and derogatory remarks; *Crime No.* 3/91: N. Veerachamy Vs. C. Vinayaham; *Offence under* PCR Act: 7(1)(d); *Victim*: Mr. N. Veerachamy, S/o Mr. Narayanan, Ilayangudi village, Ramanathapuram District.

The Incident (as per the FIR)

The victim Mr. N. Veerachamy was an employee in the welding section of Shri Mangalam Nidhyakalyani Spin Mill when the incident under reference took place. On 27.3.91 at about 6.30 in the evening Veerachamy came out from the Mill's main gate and was walking towards south on the main road. At that time another employee of the same Mill, Mr. Vinayaham, S/o. Mr. Chinnathambi Thevar, residing at Parur village, Orikottai (post), Ramanathapuram (District) was standing on the eastern side of the main road, near St. Francis High School.

The accused Vinayaham caught Veerachami by the collar and abused him in discriminatory and derogatory terms. He abused, "You degraded Pallan caste mother fuckers. How dare, you went ahead rubbing my body. How dare, you feel so proud of yourself. Is it because you are also an employee in this mill." He also attempted to beat Veerachamy with his footwear. Chandiran, S/o. Udayan, Maari, S/o. Nahan and S.V. Mani, S/o. Veerapathiran Pillai, who were there with the victim, were the witnesses to the incident. They intervened and advised Vinayaham to go away from the place. Due to this incident, Veerachamy felt terribly insulted and humiliated. Therefore, he approached the PCR Police Station, Ramanathapuram and submitted a petition seeking justice. Accordingly, with the above information, an FIR was prepared and a case was registered under section 7(1)(d), PCR Act on 28.3.91 at 18.30 hours. Mr. K. Irulandi, S.I. who registered the case sent the original copy of FIR along with the petition of the victim to the Special Court, Madurai, and to other senior officers concerned for necessary action.

Victim's Views

1. *Could you brief about the case you had filed under the PCR Act?*

I am an employee in a spin Mill. One day when I was going to the Mill, one Mr. *Chinnachamy Thevar* deliberately dashed against me. When I asked him as to why he did so, he started abusing me in the name of my caste in a very derogatory manner. So, I filed a case under the PCR Act at the PCR police station, Ramanathapuram. Subsequently, this case was referred to the

Court. But in the Court the witness, while explaining how the incident took place, said something different from what actually had happened. The witness said so because the accused bribed them. Moreover, one of the witnesses was an upper caste person, who did not want to antagonize his fellow upper caste person, did not give evidence properly. Since the witnesses did not depose the case properly, the case got acquitted.

2. *Do you think the POA Act is needed for the protection of the SCs?*

It is definitely needed. Though my case ended in acquittal, now the Thevar caste people know the implication of fighting with us. They are now afraid that we might file cases against them under the POA Act.

Case Highlights

The victim filed a case under the PCR Act since the incident took place in public place, and the victim was hopeful that all those who had viewed the dispute would give evidence as witnesses.

Regarding factors that lead to the acquittal of the case, mention may be made to the following two factors:

1. The witnesses turned hostile by accepting money from the accused.
2. One of the witnesses was a caste Hindu who did not want to antagonize his fellow caste men and therefore did not give evidence properly in the Court.

The suggested recommendation was that the PCR and POA Acts should continue as they act as deterrent whenever the caste Hindus indulge in violence against the SCs.

Case No. 13

Offence: Discriminatory and derogatory remarks against a SC government employee; Crime No: *6/91: Balakrishnan Vs. Subramaniam; Offence under PCR Act:7(1)(d); Victim*: Mr. Balakrishnan, Rameshwaram, Ramanathapuram District.

Victim's Views

1. *Could you tell about the POA case that you had filed?*

I am an employee in the Toll Tax Office, Rameshwaram. I filed a case against Mr. Sivasubramaniyam. One day I went to meet Mr. Radhakrishnan, my superior in the office, asking for the joining report. Sivasubramanian, who was sitting nearby, said to Radhakrishnan immediately, "You are giving all papers to these fellows who change forms every now and then like the *Thennali Raman*. But if we ask, you don't give us any papers. You have been supporting these *Pallan* mother fuckers and Paryan mother fuckers". It was for these derogatory remarks that I filed a case. But since the police did not send proper documents to the Court, the case got acquitted.

2. *Do you think the POA Act is needed?*

Yes, it is needed. But the concerned officials should implement the Act properly. It is a security for government employees like me.

Case Highlights

The context in which the case was registered under the PCR Act may be explained in the following two points:

1. The victim was an educated government employee and was well aware of the PCR Act, and the fact that the discriminatory remarks made by the accused was very much an offence under this Act. However, instead of filing a case under the PCR Act, he only complained to his immediate superior in the office.
2. The matter turned out to be a case under the PCR Act only after about 5 months when the matter was finally referred to the police concerned.

Regarding the attitude of the police towards the victims, it may be noted that the police did not send necessary documents to the Court in support of the case under reference.

According to the researcher the following are the Honourable Special Court's reasons for acquitting the case under reference and the researcher's comments on the same:

1. Though the incident of discriminatory and derogatory remarks against the victim took place on 04-01-1991, a formal complaint to this effect was made only on 19-06-1991. This delay of over five months was one of the important reasons for acquitting the case.

   But the honourable Judge would very well understand that despite the fact that the victim could directly approach the PCR Police Station, Ramanathapuram for the discrimination meted out to him, he, as a government employee, only approached his departmental head for necessary action against the accused. But the department seemed to have taken about 5 months to realise that it was a case of caste discrimination and therefore to be dealt with by the concerned police officials. The fact is that the incident was formally reported as soon it took place. The delay in reaching the police was not due to the victim, but others viz, the victim's department officials and the police who handled the case. How can the victim be made responsible for the delay? What is the punishment prescribed by the Court for those responsible for the delay? Nothing.
2. Another reason for acquitting case is that though the complaint was first lodged with the officer under whom the victim was an employee, the officer was not brought to the Court for trial. But it is more than obvious that the task of producing all witnesses is the lawful duty of the police officials who charge-sheeted the case. It was the fault of the police who did not care to produce the witness at the Court for trial. What is the Court's pronouncement against the police who neglected their lawful duty? Nothing.
3. The Court acquitted case also for the reason that it did not consider the evidences given by the third witness reliable in view of the fact that: (a) the third witness had an enmity with the accused who, as his superior officer in the same department, had once warned him for having come to the office drunk, and (b) the third witness was not only the victim's co-employee in the same department, but also his neighbour, residing next to his residence.

But nowhere in the POA Act, it is stated that witness should not be a co-employee or a neighbour. In fact, in a case like this, none other than those who are very close to the victim would come forward to be the witness especially in view of the possible dire consequences. Then, why should the Court doubt the reliability of the evidence given by the witness under reference?

4. Yet another reason for acquitting the case was that in the FIR only one discriminatory remark had been recorded. But during trial the witness mentioned about two such remarks. Therefore, there were discrepancies in the number of discriminatory remarks made.

However, the fact that the discriminatory remark "parathayoli" is there in the FIR, and the same was avowed during the trial as well. It cannot be ignored. The second remark that came to light during the trial is nothing but additional information. How can this be considered a reason for acquitting the case?

Case No. 14

Offence: Discrimination and harassment at work place (government school); *Crime No.*72/99: Mr. K. Pandyan Vs. Veluchamy; Offence under POA Act:3(1)(x)

Views of Witness (Mr. Muthu from Aruppukottai)

1. *Could you, as a witness to Pandian's case, tell me about the case and what happened after you made your statement in the Court of law?*

This was the case of ill-treatment and harassment meted out by the school Headmaster, Mr. Veluchamy to Mr. Pandian who worked in the SNTR school, Aruppukottai. The school authority did not provide Pandian even with minimum facilities such as table, chair and drinking water at his work place. He complained to the District Collector and the District Educational Officer. Then the school authority responded positively, but other forms of harassment and discriminatory practices continued. This situation forced him to register a complaint under the POA Act. I was one of the witnesses in this case.

As required, I gave evidence in the Special Court as a witness. But the person typing my statement typed the matter differently, twisting the case in favour of the accused. Later, they came for my signature on the 'twisted statement'. When I asked them to read out the statement, I found the statement to be different from what I had stated in the Court. I then refused to sign the statement. The Magistrate asked the reason for my refusal. I explained what had happened. He accordingly asked the persons concerned to make necessary changes in the statement. I then signed the statement. The point is, such things happen even within the Court itself, and that too in the presence of the Magistrate.

There is no security for the Dalit victims and for their documents and statements even in the police stations. When Pandian gave a petition, the police did not accept it as it was. They first prepared a statement the way they wanted and then made an FIR on the basis of that statement.

2. *When neither the police nor the Court seem to be taking the PCR/POA cases seriously, do you think the laws like the POA Act will be of any use to the Dalits?*

The Act is of no use to Dalits since it is not implemented properly. If it is implemented properly, I shall not say so.

Views of an Advocate Associated with the Case

1. *As a common man and a student of law, what are your comments on the use and abuse of the POA Act with particular reference to the case of Pandian Vs. Veluchamy which you had closely followed up?*

Pandian was the only SC person working in the SNTR School. Others were mostly belonging to Backward Castes. Prior to his promotion as librarian, there were many instances of mishandling of and malpractices in accounts, particularly in matters of scholarships given to the SC students. After he became the Librarian, he came to know about the malpractices. He started opposing them such like. This is how the problem began.

Then the school authority tried covertly two options: either to make him endorse such practices or get him transferred to some other school. There was a healthy social relation among all other staff, but he was selectively isolated and looked down upon. Even the peons used to treat him differently. To bring disgrace to his credibility, the teachers used to tell their students not to go to the library. But on the other hand, they started charging him as if he did not help the students coming to the library. Knowing no way of stopping the misuse of scholarship money by the school employees, he started telling students to be vigilant as to how much money they sign for and how much they actually get in hand. This angered all the school-staff, particularly the Headmaster. To teach him a lesson, they, one day, removed his chair and another day they removed his table. They then overtly started telling that his work was of no value to anyone. They went on harassing him in overt and covert forms in all possible ways. He tolerated all these.

By hiding the daily attendance register one day the staff went to the extent of not recognizing his attendance in the school. For one full month he could not sign the register even though he had been going to the school regularly. Subsequently, he petitioned to the District Educational Officer and others stating that he was not allowed to sign the attendance register. However, the Headmaster paid him salary for that month. But he covertly made some changes in the Pandian's service record, curbing his career promotion. Pandian was neither transferred, nor allowed to work in the school peacefully.

It was in this context, he filed a PCR case. We also joined him. But the police refused to accept his case. We protested against this attitude of the police. Then FIR was filed. It took more than a month for us to make the police file an FIR under the PCR Act. The only reason for the police refusing to register our case was that we did not have money. If we had given Rs. 1000/- to the police, our case would have been filed on the very day.

The police officials in charge of implementing the PCR/POA Acts have made these laws as means of generating additional income for themselves. Whenever a victim goes to the police station, the police collect around Rs. 1000/- to file a case. Later, they collect around Rs. 5,000/- from the accused to do the needful to acquit the case or for a compromise. It is a day-to-day reality practised overtly while dealing with the PCR/POA cases. To help the accused, the police invariably make wrong entries and statements in the FIR. In return, they extract a lump sum money from the accused. The police misuse the law, but they will say that the Dalit misuse the law. This is totally untrue.

If we look into the Court side, atrocities against Dalits is more severe here than in the police stations. I know that we should not comment on the judgement of the Magistrate. But how many witness does he want to prove or disprove a particular case – one or two or five? It is understood that the victim would not say anything against his own interest and would obviously say what was reported in the FIR. The first witness, the police, also gave evidence as per the FIR. The witness who came with the victim also deposed the facts correctly. How many more witness do we need to prove the case? Yet the case was acquitted.

But what happened in the Court was that when the witness made his oral statement as asked by the Magistrate, his statement was typed differently, twisting the case in favour of the accused. When the witness wanted to know what was being typed as his statement, the Magistrate himself asked the witness as to who instigated him to counter-check his statement. This incident reflects that such practice of twisting the witnesses' statements and typing it in such a way as to help the accused has been in practice for a long time. This also reflects the Magistrate's concern for the accused. The Magistrate is supposed to be impartial and concerned so as to ensure justice to the victims.

I express this anguish as a student of law. The Court is meant for *Dharma* and justice, and the Judge is for ensuring these ideals. If the Judge himself overtly favours the accused, how can we say that the Court is meant for upholding justice and how can the POA Act be implemented effectively. Such attitude of the Judges of Special Courts results in acquittals of most of the POA cases, and this, in turn, gives an impression to the public that the SC and ST people unnecessarily file cases under the PCR and POA Act; that most of these cases are false ones and that is why most of them get acquitted. But in reality, this is not true. Why should we then file cases under these laws and what is the use of these laws? At least in some cases the Court should convict the accused, and let the people see the offenders behind the bars, undergoing punishment. If the Court can not do this, what is its use and why should it be there at all?

2. *Do you mean to say that these laws are of no use to the Dalits?*

These laws are good, but are not implemented properly. Out of 100 cases, even if 10 to 20 cases end in conviction, the impact and use of these laws will be felt by the people. But it is not so. If it is a civil or criminal cases, will there be such judgements? We are not against compromise. If the accused realises his mistake and apologises, there is nothing wrong in going for a compromise. Such cases in fact constitute the majority cases ending in acquittal. But such cases of compromise are alleged to be false cases. It is not true.

The Act (POA) is very good. It needs to be there. But mere presence of these laws will not uproot caste discrimination and untouchability. In most of the villages around here, there is separate glass system for the Dalits. In tea stalls, they have to sit on the floor, while others are provided with benches. When we take up such issues, the police say, "don't create problems; adjust with the existing system".

3. *It is generally alleged that the Dalits file false cases against the non-Dalits. What are your comments?*

None of us does so. There may be one or two rare cases. This also I am not sure of.

NGO's Views

Mr. Shanmugavel, Secretary, Thiyagi Imanual Peravai, Paramakudi, Ramanathapuram District.

1. *What is you opinion on what happened during the trial of the Pandian's case with particular reference to the statement made by one of the witnesses?*

While typing the witness's declaration in the Court in favour of the victim, the typist twisted the case in such a way as to help the accused escape punishment. If a typist can change the fate of the case without the knowledge of the victim and that too within the Court, how can we hope to achieve justice with the help of the POA Act. The primary aim of this Act is to protect the SCs from atrocities. But from the experiences of those Dalits who appealed to this Act seeking justice, it may be said that the magnitude of harassment and humiliation experienced and the financial hardship faced in the process of seeking justice through the POA Act is in no way less, if not more, than the atrocities committed against them.

Case Highlights

Context

1. Though the victim wanted to resolve the problem of discrimination and ill-treatment meted out to him through other means, he was forced to take refuge in the POA Act as the last option since his all other attempts had failed.
2. NGOs which and individuals with law background who came forward to help suggested to file a case under the POA Act.

Police Attitude

1. The police initially refused to file an FIR for the case under reference.
2. The FIR was filed only after a month-long protest by the complainant along with a few NGOs.
3. The main reason for the delay in registering the case was that the complainants did not give Rs. 1000/- to the police as usually expected.
4. The police used to collect upto Rs. 5000/- from the accused either to get the case acquitted or to go for a compromise.

Acquittal Factors and Recommendations

1. Refer to the researcher's views.

2. The Court is not free from caste prejudice. The Magistrate seems to be more concerned with the accused rather than the victims.
3. In the present case, an attempt was made in the Court itself to defeat the case by way of twisting the witness's statement in favour of the accused with the help of none other than the typist of the Court. All such practices do happen with the knowledge of all the staff in the Court. The Judge is also aware of it.
4. The biased attitude of the Judges towards the SCs is one of few important reasons for the most PCR/POA cases ending in acquittal.
5. The SC's main intention is not always, to punish the accused unless it is a case of loss of lives and valuable properties. Once the accused has realized his mistake and willing to apologize for the same, SCs are always willing to compromise. But agreeing for a compromise does not mean the cases are false as it is often concluded.
6. Though the law is good, neither the police nor the Court want to implement it earnestly, and thus there is hardly any conviction.
7. In the process of seeking justice through the POA Act, one undergoes more harassment and humiliation than the actual offences committed against them.
8. The POA Act has not helped the Dalits much, since it has not been able to bring any change in the discriminatory attitude of the caste Hindus.

Other Case Highlights

1. Untouchability and caste discrimination are observed even in the school and that too by none other than the Headmaster himself.
2. In the case under reference, the Headmaster resorted to discriminating the person more overtly when the latter refused to be party to his corrupt practices.
3. Not providing him any chair or table and water were some of the ill-treatment meted out to him, besides the

discriminatory altitude of the entire school staff including the peon. He was also not allowed to sign in the daily attendance register.

4. The service record of the victim was covertly tampered with a view to curbing his career promotion.

After careful examination of the various documents he could gather and comparing them with the views expressed by the individual concerned, the researcher made the following observations:

Though the incident of verbal abuse against the victim took place on 18.6.98, a case to this effect was registered only on 23.1.99. This delay of about six months on the part of the victim and his subsequent consultation with the NGOs like the *People Watch* have unfortunately given room for the Honourable Special Court to presume that the case was not a genuine, but a false and concocted one.

The Honourable Court, unfortunately 'could not' probe into the details of discriminations and harassment meted out to the victim till that incident of verbal abuse took place which pushed the victim to the edge of his tolerance. The Honourable Court also 'could not see' the victim's genuine efforts to find amicable solutions to the problems he faced and the charges levelled against him by the school authority through other means such as writing to the higher government officials of the school system. When most of his problems remained unresolved and were also growing in magnitude, he had no option but to consult NGOs like the *People Watch*. With neither money nor muscle power, individual victims like Pandyan would obviously need the support of NGOs to seek justice formally through legal provisions like the POA Act. Going through this tiresome process obviously took the victim more than six months. Owing to the delay and taking the support of NGOs, which are known to be the agents of justice, which have all the times stood for judicial activism and whose credibility and commitment to the national cause are beyond doubt, the Honourable Court doubted the genuineness of the case and went to the extent of labelling it as false and concocted. In fact, it was in this context that the Justice Krishna Iyer Committee had suggested that the Scheduled Caste

Welfare Associations should be associated at every stage of the case as a purely official body to tackle these legal problems adequately. The SC and ST Commission has also noted that Voluntary Organizations and committed individuals can act as mediators in inter-caste disputes (Government of India, 1990:39).

Another major reason for which the Honourable Court acquitted the case is that the police officials including the Inspectors and DSP, who investigated and charge-sheeted the case, did not submit to the Court certain documents vital to the decision of the case. Having been socially discriminated, economically dependent and marginalised, and ignorant of even the minimum procedures to be followed in any case of caste discrimination and atrocities, the Scheduled Caste victims like Pandyan have none other than the police to secure them justice. But if the police themselves refrain even from performing their lawful duties, where would these victims go for justice? Moreover, when there is a provision in the POA Act itself to punish the police officials who do not perform their duties in a manner they ought to have, why did not the Honourable Court punish the police? Why should it let the accused go unpunished? Why did not it give order for further probing into all related issues and take the case to its logical end? Why should the Court choose to acquit the case?

Case No. 15

Offence: Discriminatory and derogatory remarks and attempt of physical assault in response to a case of attempt of murder filed earlier; *Crime No*.11/92: M. Kalimuthan Vs. R. Mutthuchamy Chettiyar; Offence under PCR Act: 7(1)(d); *Victim:* Mr. Kalimutthan, S/o. Mr. Muniyandi, Vettikulam, Mayilurani, Ramanathapuram District.

Victim's Views

1. *Could you narrate the incident for which you filed a case under the PCR Act?*

Mr. Mutthuchamy Chettiyar had attempted to murder me in the past when I was busy irrigating my land. I then filed a complaint at the police station, Thiruppalangudi. But the police took money from the accused and did not initiate any action. After one month, Mutthuchamy Chettiyar once again came to me when I was standing at the *Vettukulam* bus stop. He abused me, "you, degraded Pallan caste fellow. How dare, you filed a case against me? What could you now do to me filing a case against me? Could you suck my penis?" He came over to beat me. Then only I lodged a complaint at the PCR police station, Ramanathapuram.

2. *How did you loose the case in the Court?*

The high caste people dominate our village. Being afraid of dire consequences from these dominant caste people, our witnesses did not depose the case properly. That is why; we lost the case in the Court.

3. *What is your opinion on the need of the PCR and POA Acts?*

Because of these laws, the caste Hindus are little hesitant to engage in conflict with us. In the absence of such laws, there will be none to protect our interests.

Case Highlights

Since the local police did not take any action against the accused as pleaded earlier, and the accused in turn not only threatened but also abused the complainant in discriminatory and derogatory terms, the victim was in a way forced to file a case under the PCR Act.

Having accepted money from the accused, the police were polite and helpful only to the accused, not to the victim.

Being afraid of dire consequences and belonging to the minority group in the village, the victim and his witnesses themselves contradicted their own plea for justice saying that there was no such incident at all.

Researcher's Views on Judgement

The Honourable Special Court, Madurai, acquitted the case under reference mainly on the ground that the victim said in the

Court that he was not abused in the name of his caste, and there was no such incident at all as claimed in his FIR. But what is to be noted with due respect to the Court is that had there been no such incident, how could and why would the victim file such a case at all? And why should the victim contradict his own statement recorded in his petition and subsequently in the FIR? Such a drastic change on the victim's part would not have occurred, had he not been forced to say or do so by the accused.

While interviewing the victim, it was found that he had been threatened by the accused. He was told that he would be killed if he would give evidence in the Court in favour of his case.

Moreover, as practised and required, not only the police but also the Special Public prosecutor verify the validity of each and every case filed under the PCR/POA Acts. A minimum of 25 per cent out of the due financial compensation is given to the victim only when the case is charge-sheeted. The case is charge-sheeted only when there is truth in it. The Honourable Court acquitting the case indeed puts at stake the credibility of the police officials and others who investigated and charge-sheeted the case.

It would have been in the interest of the victim, had the Honourable Court probed the case further as to why the victim turned against his own plea for justice. It could have ordered to find out whether or not there was anyone forcing him to speak against his own case, in the Court and to take the blame on himself.

Moreover, the fact that the victim himself had turned against his own complaint suggests that he had been forced to do so. And it is often found difficult for the victims to prove his innocence in view of his vulnerable situations. Therefore a case of this kind should have been registered also under Section 12 of the Act which puts the responsibility of proving innocence on the accused. Of the six PCR cases examined here, including the present one, not even a single case had been registered under Section 12 of the PCR Act which is also an offence under the PCR Act.

Recommendations

In view of the fact that the victims themselves contradicted their own statement regarding the nature of discriminations registered in the FIR, on the basis of which the accused was charge sheeted, and the validity of the case was further verified by the SPP, one is obviously left with no option but to conclude that the victim had been forced to take the blame on himself. Therefore, instead of acquitting the case, the Honourable Court could have ordered a fresh investigation as to why the victim turned hostile against his own case.

Summary

From the foregoing analysis, which is primarily based on the views of the victims and/or their witnesses of the 15 acquitted cases examined, the following conclusions may be drawn regarding: (a) the context in which the victim approached the police and filed cases under PCR/POA Act, (b) attitude of the police towards such victims, (c) factors responsible for the acquittal of the cases under study, and (d) recommendations for effective and earnest implementation of these laws.

The Context

The victims (SCs) – being mostly illiterate and therefore ignorant of their constitutional rights and safeguards, particularly, the special laws such as the PCR and POA Acts, being economically poor and therefore depend on the non-SC community members who are known for practising untouchability and indulging in violent crimes against them, and being numerically less in each village and thus depending on the caste Hindus for their safety and security – never dared going to the police station to lodge complaints under the PCR/POA Act against caste Hindus. They did so only when the threat to their lives, property and dignity persisted.

All the acquitted cases chosen for the present study were of such nature. The SC victims filed cases under these laws only when their women are raped and murdered (Case No. 1 and 2), when their beloved ones get killed (Case No. 3), when their land is grabbed (Case No. 4), when they are denied access to common path which is linked to their basic livelihood (Case No. 5 and 6), and deprived of minimum wage which is again related to their basic livelihood (Case No. 7), when even their minimum means of livelihood is jeopardized (Case No. 8), when they are prevented from exercising their due rights in the religions festivals (Case No. 9), or when targeted just for their school going boys talking to their fellow school going girls belonging to non-SCs (Case No. 10), or when threatened of dire consequences for performing the duly agreed upon duty (Case No. 11), and when faced with threat to life (Case No. 15). It may, however, be noted that those SC government employees living in urban or semi-urban areas did not spare even the discriminatory and derogatory remarks made against them, and they resorted to filing cases under these laws (Case No. 13) and harassment at work place (Case No. 14). Of all the 15 cases studied only in two cases (Case Nos. 2 and 14), the NGOs had played a role in bringing justice to the victims. In most other cases the victims had filed cases on their own, putting themselves and their families at risk.

Attitude of the Police

The police in general did not give due importance to the complaints made by the SC victims, even when it was a case of serious criminal offence. Under some pretext or the other the police in most cases failed to arrest the accused as required by the POA Act. In one of the cases, the victims had to physically catch the accused and hand him over to the police. The complainants often had to resort to public protest and sought the help of NGOs and local leaders to get their grievances registered under the PCR/POA Act. Even when it was a clear case to be registered under the POA Act, the police registered it under the PCR Act with a view to helping the accused. In a few cases the police had demanded money from both the victims to register and pursue the case and the accused to escape punishment due under the laws.

Instead of supporting the victims, the police often threatened them with dire consequences from the accused. They discouraged the SC victims to register case under the special laws indicating the difficulties in pursuing the case. There had been instances where counter cases being filed against the victims who insisted on pursuing their cases. Unless they were local leaders or representatives of any political party or committee, the SC victims in general felt afraid of going to the police fearing harassment. The victims in general expressed that the police was more concerned about protecting the accused.

Factors Responsible for Acquittal

The accused in general adopted different strategies to get the cases against them acquitted. With their money power, the accused influenced the concerned police officials who helped them escape punishment due under the special laws. With their money power, they influenced also the victims and their witnesses either to go for a compromise before filing the FIR, or to refrain either from giving evidence in the Court, or from pursuing the case any further, or to give evidence in such a way that would result in acquittal. When money power failed, the accused used their muscle power. They threatened the victims of dire consequences. As fellow caste men, the caste Hindu witnesses often took the side of the accused, and refrained from giving evidence in the Court of law in favour of the victims. In some cases even the trusted advocates belonging to caste Hindus deceived the victims by making them sign some documents, as if these were necessary for punishing the accused, and later using them to defeat the case.

Having been economically dependent on either the accused or his fellow caste people to earn their living, the SC victims in most cases were forced to refrain from pursuing their case to its logical end. The victims' inability or unwillingness to give the expected money to the police was also found to be one of the reasons for the police not registering the case. They in most cases were ready to compromise with the accused as soon as the latter said "sorry" to them, which the former could never even think of earlier in their villages. In some instances, the victims gave up the case once they got the first instalment of monetary compensation due under the law. They did so owing to the fact that they would have to face the accused on a day-to-day basis in their village and that they would need their support even in future for their socio-economic sustenance. Due to threat of dire consequences from the accused, in one of the cases, the victim himself gave evidence negating what he had reported in the FIR, which ultimately lead to the acquittal of the case. The fact that the victims and their witnesses, in most cases, had to go to the Court more than once not only put them into a lot of financial hardship but also discouraged them from pursuing the case further. Such a situation also leads to acquittal.

The police too had played their part to acquit a number of cases. The police who are supposed to be the guardians of the SC victims expected and accepted money from the victims to pursue their cases. They demanded money also from the accused to help them minimize or escape punishment due under the PCR Act and POA Act. By taking bribe from the accused in some cases, the police tutored the victims and their witness in such a way that lead to the acquittal of the case. The police willfully neglected their duty of sending necessary documents to the special Court. And in some cases, though the necessary documents were sent, they were not sent in time which led to the acquittal of cases. Delay in reporting the case to the police concerned had often been referred to as one of the factors giving room for doubting the validity of the case. Since the benefit of such doubt is always given to the accused, most of such cases ended in acquittal. The failure of the police in performing their lawful duties not only as officer-in-charge of registering, investigating and charge-sheeting (in consultation with the special public prosecutor) the PCR/POA Act cases but also as one of the main witnesses of such cases had often been used as one of the reasons for acquitting the case. As per the POA Act, the Honourable Court should have prosecuted such police officers and ordered further investigation of the case instead of acquitting the cases.

Looking at the kind of judgments given even for cases of *murder,* and *rape with murder,* it was expressed that even the Judges were not free from caste prejudice. As evident from one of the cases, not only the victims but also all the accused claimed that the Magistrate was influenced by them through money, political connection and caste sentiments to give judgment in their favour.

Recommendations

The victims and their witnesses doubted and questioned the credibility of the police and others who played decisive roles in the process of prosecution. They questioned the impartiality of the police department and the judiciary being dominated by the non-SC/ST officials, particularly, the Backward Caste Hindus. They therefore recommended that at least 50 per cent of the officials in the police department and judiciary which deal with the PCR and POA Act cases should have or come from the SC/ST background. In view of the fact that even the government employees, like the Village Administrative Officer, who is supposed to honour the laws of the nation and whom the villagers approach on a day-to-day basis for a variety of reasons, showed utter disregard for these special laws, the SC victims did not have the confidence that the special laws would protect them. They therefore recommended that the SCs should be helped to live together in large number in separate settlements, away from the caste Hindus. The other recommendations include the following:

The police officials not performing their lawful duties may be identified and due action be taken against them. Whenever doubt arises regarding the validity of the case due to the kind of role played by the police, the Honourable Court may institute another police inquiry instead of acquitting the case. The Court may order due action against those police officials who have failed to perform their lawful duties, and due to which the case could not be proved beyond doubt in the Court of law.

When the victim himself gives evidences negating what he had reported in the FIR, the Court, instead of acquitting the case, may order one more trial to find out whether or not the victim had been forced to do so. Most importantly, the NGOs, which are the only source of support to the SC victims, should be recognized as witnesses for the victims, instead of labelling them as organizations instigating victims to seek protection under the POA Act.

In view of the fact that in none of the PCR cases the police used Section 12 of the PCR Act, which makes the accused responsible for proving his innocence, the Honourable Court may give direction to the police department to use Section 12 of the PCR Act wherever needed. After all, the Court knows well that in most cases of untouchability and atrocities, the victims are not only economically weak compared to the accused but also economically dependent on the caste Hindus who commit atrocities. And therefore the need for such direction from the Court becomes indispensable.

5

Implementation of Special Laws

Experiences of Police, NGOs and Others

The present chapter is devoted to verify further the main findings emerged in the previous chapter, particularly, with regard to the various factors responsible for acquittal of cases registered under the Protection of Civil Rights Act 1955 (PCR Act) and the SCs and STs (Prevention of Atrocities) Act, 1989 (POA Act), and the use and abuse of these laws. For this purpose, as stated in chapter one, the views of two Inspectors General of Police (IGP) – one from Tamil Nadu and the other from Maharashtra – who were in charge of implementation and monitoring of these special laws in their respective States have been taken into consideration. Though the areas of study, the chosen three districts, fall in Tamil Nadu, the views of IGP (PCR), Maharashtra have also been taken into consideration so as to understand whether or not there is uniformity in their views on the issues. After all, both were in charge of implementing the same laws, and the same rules and regulations governed both their actions and decisions. For the same purpose, the views of a Deputy Superintendent of Police (DSP), who was the officer at the district level in charge of investigating the POA Act cases registered in Ramanathapuram district, and also the views of a Special Public Prosecutor, who represented the interests of the

Scheduled Caste victims in the Special Court of law have been taken into consideration. The views of a student of law, who was about to complete his law degree and who showed a keen interest in ensuring justice to SC victims through the special laws, have also been considered in the context. In addition, the views of few NGOs associated with some of the chosen PCR and POA Act cases have been taken into consideration. The views of a few common men and the experiences of Research Assistants involved in data collection for the present study have added strength to the understanding of the issue.

The ideas shared by the respondents interviewed were tape-recorded. This chapter presents the transcribed and translated (from Tamil to English) version of the respondents' responses/statements in *direct speech*. Though it is important to read the entire text of the transcribed version of the responses so as to comprehend the magnitude of the issues addressed, the most important points emerged in each interview have been listed at the end of each case under the sub-title "Highlights of the Responses". This is hoped to help the readers grasp the thrust of each interview.

Views of IGP (PCR/HR/CID), Chennai

When the researcher visited the State level Head Office of the IGP (PCR/HR/CID), Chennai, Mr. Shyam Sundar, IPS was heading the Office. I had an informal discussion with him for a few minutes. Though I had planned for an interview in depth, it could not materialize since he was, by that time, transferred to other department. During my second visit to this office one Mr. C. Balasubramaniyan, IPS was heading the Office. The following are his views, which he expressed in response to number of questions put to him on November 16, 2001. In this section, the data collected from the IGP through a questionnaire have also been used wherever necessary.

1. *Why has there been a high rate of acquittal in PCR and POA Act cases?*

The victims have to follow their cases and cooperate with the investigating officers right from giving a complaint at the police station up to the level of investigation. Though charge sheet is laid in time, there is delay in conducting the trial in the Court due to many cases pending trial at the courts. And in this process of delay, the victims' anger against the accused goes down. The victims also yield to the pressures of the accused. The pressure is exercised either by coercion or bribe or by inducement of meeting the victims' financial needs. The victims get part (one-fourth) of the compensation once the charge sheet is laid. Three-fourth of the amount is kept with the department. Since most of these cases end in acquittal, the victims do not get their full compensation. Instead, they get similar consideration (cash compensation) from the accused. Instead of going to jail, the accused prefer paying some compensation money to the complainant and opting for a compromise. So the main witnesses i.e. the complainant and others, turning hostile is the root cause for most of the cases ending in acquittal.

2. *Why do the victims turn hostile?*

It is because of their vulnerable condition; their deplorable situation.

3. *Does that mean the victims do not get due support from the police?*

No. It is not so. The victims have to defend their case in the Court. The policemen are not from one, but from all communities. They are therefore for all communities. The police represent a mixed caste group. How can we expect them to be this way or that way? One or two per cent of the police may side either with the politicians or with their own communities. Not all.

4. *What have been the contexts in which the victims usually seek police protection and register cases under the PCR Act and/or POA Act, and their experiences in the process?**

As per the information provided by the IGP, about 40 per cent of victims go to police stations to register complaints only

* Answer to this question is based on information obtained from the IGP(PCR), Chennai through a questionnaire. The filled-in questionnaire was received on 30.2.2002 (IGP's letter No:C.No.B2/605/2001 dated 25.2.2002). The researcher's interpretation of the data has also been presented for this question.

when they have the support of their fellow caste people, though about 30 per cent of them do it even without such support. About 10 per cent of them go to police station only when they have the support of NGOs, and about 20 per cent do so on instigation by the caste Hindu enemies of the accused.

According to the IGP, it is for punishing the offenders, 40 per cent of the victims seek protection under these special laws. It is further noted that while 20 per cent of victims seek protection under these laws mainly to avoid further loss to them, 25 per cent of them do so to receive compensation due for the loss suffered. And only 10 per cent of them register cases under these laws with an intention of threatening the caste Hindus who try to exploit them in every possible way.

The IGP had recorded his views also on other related issues, particularly with regard to how the police treated the victims when the latter approached them to either register a case or for protection. The IGP had noted that "on an average in about 30 per cent of cases, the victims are threatened in overt and covert forms by the police, and thereby discouraged them from filing cases under these special laws."

With regard to the police adhering to all steps necessary to punish the offenders under the PCR and POA Acts, the IGP had noted in the questionnaire that out of the annually total number of registered cases, on an average, in about 75 per cent cases necessary steps had been followed properly, and in about 25 per cent of cases it had not been. This means that the scope for acquittal would have been very high in the remaining 25 per cent cases. Further, he had noted that out of the total number of acquitted cases, every year as high as 75 per cent of cases ended in acquittal due to the kinds of role the police played, either directly or indirectly, in the process of settling the registered cases. In about 25 per cent of acquitted cases, the police's overt persuasion of both the victims and the accused to opt for a compromise had been responsible for the acquittal. Another 25 per cent of cases seemed to have ended in acquittal as a result of the victims' inability either to produce the witnesses in Court in the required time or to depose the case properly. Their inability was mainly due to their fear of dire consequences from the accused. About 15 per cent of cases seemed to have ended in acquittal due to the victims' economic backwardness and their dependence on the caste Hindus. All these factors seemed to have curtailed victims' ability to take their cases to its logical end.

These data are indicative of the fact that the mere existence of such laws alone cannot ensure protection to the SCs and STs. The SCs and STs need the support of their fellow caste people and NGOs to avail the benefit of these laws. Yet, it is no less true, without these laws it would be difficult for the victims to protect themselves from the caste Hindu offenders.

5. *It is reported that the police wrongly orient the victims regarding what they should or should not be telling in the Court to defend themselves often leading to the acquittal of the case. Do you agree?*

This is called tutoring the witness. Whether the police tutor the witness properly or not, it is the duty of the affected persons to depose in the Court as to what exactly happened at the time of assault. If they forget or not prepared to depose the truth, how can we, the police, be responsible?

6. *When the SCs are in minority and often threatened with dire consequences, how will they depose the case without the support of the police?*

Now you are coming to the point. The only way to resolve this problem is that wherever the SCs and STs are in minority, the government should ask them to settle in those places where their communities are strong (in majority). Only then, their problem will be solved permanently. Taking advantage of the SCs' numerical vulnerability (being minority), the caste Hindus are up in arms and assault them, destroy their properties, and set their houses on fire. For example, take any village; the SCs are not more than 10 families. They do not own lands, and work mostly as agriculture coolies (wage labourers). They are dependent on the Caste Hindus. They go and beg their masters, caste Hindus, for food. In such a situation, what kind of respect can they enjoy in the village. The Government should help these SC families to shift to the nearby place/village where their own community people are in large number. In such places, nobody can attack them.

7. *Is it true that any incident of atrocity on the SCs should be reported to the police within 24 hours of the incident, otherwise the case becomes invalid?*

No! Not at all. It may take some time for the victims to reach the police station to report the incident. Now all police stations have been instructed that as soon as an incident of atrocity on a SC person is reported, they have to file a case. Going to the spot and sending memos will follow afterwards. Earlier, there was a lethargic attitude on the part of the police. They used to say, "You (SC victim) may go back now. There is no SI here to file your case". But, now it is not possible. Because the victims immediately give a telegram; some even send a fax message. They send fax messages everywhere, even to the Chief Minister. So everybody will be apprehended. Failure to register a case will amount to a serious offence. There are orders even to suspend such officers. In every forum, the Director General of Police (DGP) gives instructions, "If there is a complaint, register a case". "Don't refuse to register a case". Registration is done freely.

8. *It is said that most of the cases registered under the PCR and POA Acts are false. Is it true?*

It is easy to say so. Not all the cases are true. At the same time, not all the cases are false. The false or the exaggerated cases are 33 to 35 per cent. The remaining 67 to 65 per cent of cases are exactly true and genuine.

9. *There was a case in which a woman (SCs) was raped and murdered. The matter was taken to the police. But the police refused to take any action for a week. Why such an attitude?*

Then, such police officers should be punished. The matter ought to have been brought to the notice of the senior police officer, and the senior officer ought to have taken up investigation, and pinned down those accused.

10. *It is said that the politicians intervene and cover up such matters. Is it true, and if so, what to do?*

Who are the politicians? They are, first, ordinary citizens. If a police officer is honest, upright, above everything, he need not fear for any politician.

11. *It is generally argued that since the Indian Penal Code (IPC) has scope for dealing with caste related discriminations and violence, there is no need for special laws such as the PCR and POA Acts. Do you agree with this?*

IPC is related to certain offences, whereas there are many new types of atrocities that Lord Macaulay never even thought of. He never foresaw that these types of offences could also take place in India. He drafted the IPC considering those offences, which normally take place. He never dreamt of provisions given in the POA Act. That is why, the Government of India thought of this new Act. Initially, the PCR Act came into operation. This was the mildest possible Act in the country. That is why later they passed a very powerful Act with lots of stringent provisions i.e. the SCs and STs (Prevention of Atrocities) Act, 1989. If someone abuses a SC person by his caste name, what provisions do the IPC has to punish him? If one is forced to carry the night soil, what section of IPC can be used? Which IPC section deals with forced cleaning of solid or non-solid waste? Rape case is dealt with under Section 376 of IPC. If we register a rape case under this section, there is no financial compensation for the SC victims. It is only in the POA Act, that compensation is provided.

12. *There have been occasions in the recent past when the police delayed investigation. Why should the police do so?*

You are talking about the past. If the police refuse to accept the complaint and if the victims inform me, I will immediately suspend the concerned police officer in the PCR Unit. This is an open threat given to my own subordinate officers. If the complainant gives a petition (regarding the atrocity), it should be treated as a complaint, and not as a petition, and accordingly, the case has to be registered and investigated. If it is true, proceed; if false, refer it. You may ask about the present-day procedures that I have initiated. We have been prompt in sending messages to all the PCR Unit officers. We have been very vocal and overt in sending messages. We have also written to a few PCR Units questioning why they had not arrested the accused in certain specified cases.

13. *When a complaint is made at the police station, what should the police first do? Should they first investigate the case and then arrest the accused, or first arrest the accused and then begin the investigation process?*

There is no question of verifying first the complaint given by the complainant. The complaint should be registered as a case. And along with the complainant, the investigating officer or his team should visit the spot, study the problem and undertake further investigation. This is the method we have adopted. This is the legal requirement. When our field officers enquire, we emphasise the point that they should arrest the accused first. Later on, they may release the accused if the case was found false in the investigation.

At the same time, if the complainant has registered a false case, I have ordered not to spare him. Such a fellow should be treated as a rowdy. He should be under watch. Whenever he misbehaves, the police will take him in custody. Once in one or two months, the police are asked to round up all the antisocial elements. In such attempts, these fellows will also be arrested. I have no mercy for such fellows. One should be impartial.

14. *Don't you think your instruction to subordinate police officials to take action against false complainants, will further encourage those police officials who often do not like to register case under these Acts, and who generally discourage and also threaten the complainants not to register cases?*

If you tell me one case where the police behaved so, I shall take action against such police officers. If an accused has to be booked, I tell them to book. I don't care for the intervention of any politician.

15. *Today in many villages untouchability and caste discrimination are practised. Is it a part of your duty to find out on your own whether or not such practices exist, and accordingly, take action, or is it only when someone complains of such practices, you take action?*

There are two ways of doing it. One is getting the complaint and taking action, and the other is taking suo-muto action. The police are competent to take action as they see things on their own. For example, here is a letter informing me of the double tumbler system in Samayanallur. As soon as I got this letter, I have directed the local SDO, Samayanallur, and my own DYSP, PCR Unit, Madurai to organize a raid and take appropriate action against those observing double tumbler system. The other one is called suo-muto complaint. For example, whenever the double tumbler system is in operation in hotels or tea stalls, our own team of police officers along with the local police go there in the morning hours when the hotel is in full swing and trap the hotel fellows observing double tumbler system. If our policemen see with their own eyes the practice of double tumbler system, they will register a suo-muto case. They need not expect a formal complaint from the affected people. This is a part of our activities.

16. *Why have the police not been able to arrest caste violence completely?*

If people are like me in each and every police station, they will take appropriate action. But people are not so. Our society is like that. So, the entire police force of Tamil Nadu cannot be involved in enforcing this Act. But we have got a specialised agency, viz., the PCR Unit. We have 34 PCR Units in Tamil Nadu. In each of these Units, there is one Inspector and also a Sub-Inspector. There is a DYSP for every two to three districts. There are eleven ranges in Tamil Nadu. I have 7 DYSPs. To start with, let these 7 DYSPs investigate those cases registered under their jurisdictions. Let me stream line their investigations. Let me process these cases. Then I will have the confidence that my officers are involved in the investigation, and so I can take the responsibility. If I get four more DYSPs, we will have our DYSPs in all the eleven ranges. And with this, the entire enforcement department will be there with me.

But my opinion is not the opinion of the present Direct General of Police (DGP). He differs from my views. He says that one IGP cannot review all the cases of 34 PCR Units. Instead, he says that the SP of every district can do, and the DIG of every range can do this. The Government obviously heeds only his views, not mine. I am talking about practicability. I speak what is practically possible. There is CID for Civil Supplies. Why this department has to function independently? Why cannot this be closed down and this responsibility be vested in the hands of local police? This is not done because it has a specific purpose, and so they do not want to give up their power to the local police. Similarly, the PCR office is also specialised agency with a specific purpose. So it has to function independently, directly under the Central Government. But the State Police force feels that this power should also be with them.

17. *Why do you propose such an arrangement? Is it because you feel that the police in general are more concerned with other cases, not much concerned with the PCR/POA Act cases?*

Yes. Even if it is a rate's net, it has to be an independent net. If you go and ask the PCR police any help, they shall at least have the consolation of being approached. In a general police station, the police would think, "Oh, the complainant is giving a complaint against a person who is above me in this sub-division (police), who is known to me and who also belongs to my caste". He would therefore hesitate to register the case. But in the case of specialised agency, it may not be so.

In such specialised agency (PCR Unit), when there are two top-level positions such as IGP and ADGP, one should be given either to a SC or ST person. I would say that now more than the Brahmins, it is the non-Brahmins who commit inhuman crimes against the SCs. They are the people practising untouchability. They are the people who discriminate them. In view of this, I suggest that in the remaining one position a Brahmin be appointed, not the non-Brahmin middle level caste person.

18. *It is often said that the PCR police stations at the district level do not even have the minimum facility such as vehicle. Do you agree with this?*

It is a very important point. I can ensure this facility only when it is brought under my control. Vehicle cannot be provided immediately, because it is under the control of SP (manpower). Presently, vehicles, their maintenance and manpower are under the control of the SP. I have nothing. I am not controlling them though I get the pay and allowance, and I get funds from the Government for the maintenance of these vehicles.

19. *We observed that the PCR Unit in Ramanathapuram is operating from a vehicle-shed. What is your comment on it?*

If it is so, what does it reflect? Is the SP doing his job efficiently? Any police official negating his duties should also be prosecuted under SC and ST law. "In fact, we sent a proposal stating that the entire PCR wings should be attached to us and operate separately and independently. Entire amount we are contributing. In a way, they are spending our money" (IGP office staff said). There are differences of opinion. The Government should initiate an open forum, and debate on these matters. If I were given a chance in such a forum, I would express everything openly. I am willing to express even in front of senior officials and national leaders as to how they have failed in controlling atrocities on the SCs and STs. No leader has so far taken up the practice of untouchability as a serious offence, nor have they been vocal in punishing such offenders. When all other departments function separately, why the PCR Wing alone should not function so? It is because of this, that I cannot control or command even a sub-inspector at the local level. They respond only to the SP.

20. *It is said that the SP does not spare due time to deal with the PCR or POA Act cases. Is it true?*

Yes, because the Sub-Divisional Officer has many other responsibilities and work; he cannot give due importance to PCR cases. The SP finds it difficult to spare even five minutes in a month for the PCR cases. As a result, he is unable to review the cases in depth and unable to finalise any proceedings. He just asks the DYSP, "Do you register cases under the PCR Act? You alone deal with these cases, all right". But we are not like that. We, our officers, review each and every case in depth. In this month alone 80 cases have been reported. I will review these 80 cases personally. But my DGP thinks that I, as IGP, alone cannot do this. But, I can.

We have our differences. So, there should be a uniform stand on these matters. The Government has to realise this and issue a uniform instruction that only the specialised agency called the Human Rights and Social Justice or the Protection of Civil Rights Unit should investigate caste related cases of violence and untouchability.

21. *One of the DYSPs said that the POA Act is needed to protect the SCs. But it cannot be, rather should not be, implemented strictly since it will result in more violence against the SCs. What is your comment on this observation of a police officer in charge of implementing the Act?*

Jesus has said, "all your views are not necessarily my views, and all my views are not necessarily your views". That DYSP's views may be his personal views. He did not take into consideration what is widely practised in the country. If you had probed further you could well understand that he was not from one of the affected castes (SCs or STs). He might be from other communities. If I know what community (caste) the DYSP belongs to, I can say as to why he said so. If the DYSP is not himself a SC person, it is likely that he does not understand the problems of SCs, and that is why he said so regarding the use of POA Act.

I therefore suggest that 50 per cent of the officials who are in charge of investigation, preparing charge sheet and conducting the prosecution or trial, should come from the downtrodden communities (SCs and STs). Then only, the downtrodden would have adequate protection and get justice. Otherwise there is no salvation for them.

22. *The POA Act is centrally funded and managed, and there are also Special Courts to try these cases. Similarly do you think there should be special police stations different from the existing PCR police stations, with more power and independence?*

Not necessary. The existing 34 police stations/PCR Units (in Tamil Nadu) are sufficient. (Every district has got a PCR Unit).

23. *Since the SPs and DYSPs are not there exclusively for implementing PCR and POA Acts, they may not even respond to your directions? What will you do then?*

Yes. I, as IGP (PCR), cannot control even the Sub-Inspector of a local police station, because the SP posts them, and the DIG posts the SP. They are not my choice. They have got their own whims and fancies. Moreover, their posting in the given sub-division is often through political influence. So they listen only to their local masters. Implementation of PCR and POA Acts should not be pushed into in the hands of police who are already burdened with general cases. Similarly, my posting here is the discretion of the Government. Just because I am not suitable for a particular post, I am posted here. Luckily, it is a God-sent message for me that I have to serve the downtrodden. I feel elated for being posted here. Others may not feel so and shall view it as a punishment. I felt, as soon as I was posted here, that I have got a chance to serve the downtrodden. I have to protect them. But I may not be allowed to continue for long. For them (the SPs and DYSPs) the DGP is everything. Though this may so happen, I will not give up. I will chase them. Otherwise I, myself, may put up a case at a higher level indicating the lack of interest shown by the police on matters pertaining to the protection of the SCs and STs. I shall not hesitate to issue orders against such police officers. Inaction cannot be accepted. Even if 50 per cent police officers are spirited and committed like me, untouchability will not be there; atrocity cannot be there. Whichever village I visited, the practice of untouchability has been stopped.

24. *What is your opinion on the Dalits' self-defense initiatives?*

For self-defence, the Dalits should have courage even to attack the offenders. No one will go to the one who resorts to retaliation. Take for example, a local rowdy. No one goes near him, even though he is a SC person. No one would dare challenging him. But in the case of a meek Harijan, even a small boy passing by the street shall call him by his caste in a contemptuous manner. If there is a dog in a ground, all the 10 boys standing around it will throw stone on it. If there is no dog at all, there is no scope for these boys to throw stone on it. So, I suggest that in whichever village caste discrimination is in practice, all the SCs of that village should be shifted to other places or villages where their fellow caste members are large in number.

25. *What are your suggestions?*

The Government of India gives up to Rs. 5,00,000/- (rupees five lakhs) with 50 per cent subsidy to help the SCs construct their own houses. Instead of this, even with Rs.1,00,000/- a house can be built for a SC person. Not separate houses, but block-houses, having a 100-metre length and with due space for building staircases. In this way, housing them all in one building can bring 300 to 400 families together. They can lead a secured life in one place. Nobody can attack them. In villages, we have constructed *Samathuvapuram* (a housing scheme meant to ensure social equality among different caste groups by providing houses to them all in one place). In this scheme, independent houses have been provided to both SC and Backward Caste (BC) families who can maintain these houses. But if there are well-to-do SC families in the same village, the one or two BC families residing in the *Samathuvapuram* may, over a period of time, sell off their houses to the well-to-do SC families of the village. They prefer to go back to their earlier village premises. In that case, the *Samathuvapuram* will turn out to be another colony, exclusively of 'Harijans'. So, though the SCs may live in the *Samathuvapuram* houses comfortably, they may still live only with their own caste members and may still have to continue with their despicable unclean traditional occupations. So, first we have to stop them doing such unclean traditional occupations. They should be engaged in dignified work.

If a cow dies, let the non-SC people of the village manage it. If some one dies among the non-SCs, let them bury the dead. Why should the SCs be bothered? Let us all do these works. Each one has to do his/her own work as per their requirement. Did Gandhi not do all works on his own? Did he not clean his bathroom? If not today, one-day a change will come. This change will come only when the SCs and STs are educated to defend themselves collectively against those who perpetuate atrocities on them; only when they realise that such mass collective comes under general exception.

The only suggestion and a solution, as I said earlier, is that in whichever village there is no security for the SCs, in whichever village there is caste discrimination, and in whichever village there is practice of untouchability, the Government should buy all the lands and other properties including the houses of the SCs of that village and resettle them all at another village or nearby town where their caste members are large in number, and where they will be respected and their labour will be honoured. For example, take the case of *Pathinettu Petti* (18 villages) in which only the SCs are living. Let any *Thevar* caste people (BCs) dare attacking them. If any one goes there to attack, he cannot come back safe and unhurt because the SCs over there are in a sizeable majority. They themselves are a courageous people. This is my theory.

Suggestions of IGP (PCR) (as recorded in the questionnaire)

There should be a special committee for creating awareness among both the beneficiaries and implementing authorities of these laws as to how it can be better used and enforced.

As soon as a complaint is lodged, the victims should be given a receipt acknowledging it, and register a case as per the rules. Then, the police should conduct on the spot enquiry.

Monetary and other forms of relief should be made available to the victims at the earliest.

Highlights of the Responses

1. The police have to be neutral, even though they may hail from different caste background. One or two per cent of them may support their fellow caste people while dealing with PCR/POA Act cases. Not all.
2. For no conviction or delay in conviction, or for more cases ending in acquittal, the police alone cannot be blamed. It depends on the extent to which the victims cooperate with the police in the investigation process. It also depends on the victims' willingness to pursue the case to its logical end. The

delay in the conviction process is also due to the huge number of cases pending trial in Special Courts.

3. The victims are unable to pursue the case mainly due to their economic backwardness, their dependence on the caste Hindus (the accused) for food and security, and their insignificant numerical strength in the village *vis-a-vis* the better economic status, political and bureaucratic status and connections and numerical preponderance of the accused.
4. The accused often prefer settlement outside the Court to escape harassment and legal punishments, including imprisonment and the humiliation of facing trial in the Court. They even come forward to pay some amount of compensation to the victims. The victims are also forced to agree to such modes of settlement since they cannot overtly antagonise the accused caste Hindus of their own or nearby villages owing to their dependence on them for economic and physical security.
5. Many cases of PCR and POA Acts end in acquittal owing to the witnesses turning hostile. "Witnesses turning hostile" is not the choice of the witnesses, but an option they are forced to adopt in view of their economic and social vulnerability, particularly in the rural areas.
6. The mere presence of the PCR Act and POA Act does not mean that they will be enforced as desired. While 30 per cent of the victims of caste violence prefer going to the police stations and register cases against the accused on their own, about 40 per cent of them do so only when they have the support of their fellow caste people. While about 10 per cent of the victims register cases under these laws only when they have the support of NGOs, about 20 per cent of them do so out of instigation by the caste Hindu enemies of the accused.
7. According to the IGP (PCR), about 40 per cent of victims register cases under these laws mainly for punishing the accused, while about 20 per cent of them do so mainly to avoid further loss to them. While about 25 per cent do so mainly to receive financial compensation for the loss suffered, about 10 per cent of victims resort to this option with an intention of teaching a lesson to the accused.

8. In the opinion of the IGP in about 30 per cent of cases, the victims, who go to the local police station to register complaints under the PCR or POA Acts, are threatened in overt and covert forms by the police and discouraged.
9. Though in majority of the cases (75%), the police follow all necessary steps – to ensure justice to the victims right from filing the case to till the case reaching the Special Court, in about 25 per cent of cases it is not followed. By so doing, the police indeed leave enough scope for these 25 per cent of cases ending in acquittal.
10. Out of the number of acquitted cases, the kinds of role the police played, either directly or indirectly, have been responsible for as high as 75 per cent of cases ending in acquittal.
11. According to the IGP, most of the acquitted cases are not false cases. The false cases may account only for 33 to 35 per cent, and the remaining 65 to 67 per cent, cases are exactly true and genuine ones.
12. Any police officer refusing to register the complaints of victims should be punished.
13. The police officers, if they are honest and upright, can effectively deal with the politicians coming in their way.
14. If a complainant submits a petition regarding an atrocity, the petition has to be treated as a complaint, and not as a petition. Accordingly, a case has to be registered under appropriate sections of the PCR/POA Acts and investigated.
15. Once a complaint is lodged under the PCR/POA Act, the accused has to be arrested. He or she may be released if the case is found false.
16. If the complainant has registered a false case, he or she has to be taken into task and subjected to severe punishment.
17. The PCR police stations are not only to deal with cases formally registered, but are also to undertake suo-muto actions. The PCR police officials are supposed to identify on their own the violators of these laws and prosecute them as per the PCR/POA Act.
18. In the present administrative set up even the IGP (PCR/HR) cannot have any control even over the SI of a local police

station who works and acts under the direct control of the local SP.

19. Government may build block houses (multi-storeyed building) at much cheaper a rate and bring together more SC families at one place under one roof. Such an arrangement will help them protect themselves from the caste Hindus and others.

Recommendations of the IGP (PCR)

1. The PCR police station should function in a manner the CID for Civil Supplies functions. PCR/POA Act cases should be investigated only by PCR police officials appointed exclusively for the purpose.
2. Presently, at the district level the SP concerned does streamlining of the processes of investigation of PCR/POA cases registered in the district. In view of the enormous amount of other cases that the SP is required to look into, the investigation of these cases should be entrusted with the DYSP of the concerned PCR/HR police station in the district. Streamlining of all such cases throughout the State (Tamil Nadu) should be left exclusively to the IGP (PCR, HR) with no or minimum interference from the IGP of the State. The IGP (PCR) should be allowed to function independently with more exclusive powers.
3. Of the two top police officials – IGP and ADGP – who together presently manage the PCR/HR Unit of the State, at least one should always be from Scheduled Caste or Scheduled Tribe background to ensure just and fair treatment to the cases processed.
4. Among the police officials investigating the PCR and POA cases, at least 50 per cent should be from the SC/ST communities; otherwise the investigation process may not be just and fair.
5. District level PCR police stations are not adequately equipped with necessary infrastructure facilities such as proper office and vehicles, though there is periodical financial allocation form the PCR office for such purposes. The PCR police stations should have a proper office,

vehicles and other necessary infrastructure facilities exclusively under its control.

6. The SC people should refrain from performing defiling, unpaid or underpaid occupations such as sweeping, scavenging, disposing of dead cattle etc. They should be accommodated in more dignified jobs. The Government should initiate this process.
7. The Government may set-up special committees to create awareness among the police and civilians, particularly the SCs, so that the special laws (PCR and POA Acts) are better understood, used and implemented earnestly.
8. As long as the SCs live in villages in a small number, they will not be able to protect themselves against atrocities and exploitations of the caste Hindus. All SC families living in villages without any security mechanism should be shifted to villages where their fellow caste members are in a large number, and where there is very limited or no scope for the caste Hindus to exploit them.
9. Another suggestion is that such SC families may be shifted to urban areas.
10. The Government should initiate discussion and find out loop-holes if any in the process of implementation of the two special laws and send a uniform order stating that cases registered under the PCR and POA Acts should be handled only by the specialized agency like the PCR/HR Units. This would avoid duplication, improve efficiency and ensure speedy justice to the victims.

Views of IGP (PCR), Maharashtra

Mr. T.K. Choudhary, who had served in Maharashtra as the IGP (PCR) for four and half years (since 1992) was the ADGP (CID), Mumbai, at the time of this interview. The following are his responses to some of the questions posed.

1. *Could you please share your views on the PCR and POA Acts in general?*

In 1955 the Government of India passed the Protection of Civil Rights Act. Six years later, the police created a post of

Deputy Inspector General (DIG) (PCR) to oversee the implementation of this Act. The Government of India later felt that the provisions of PCR Act were not forceful enough to prevent human right violations committed against the SCs and STs. Moreover, the PCR Act did not have provisions to deal with the problems of the Scheduled Tribes. So the Government then promulgated another Act known as "the SCs and STs (Prevention of Atrocities) Act, 1989" (POA Act) with more stringent penal provisions covering many forms of atrocities. The conviction rate in the PCR Act was very minimal, because certain enabling provisions were not there, either in the Cr.P.C. or in the PCR Act itself. So the PCR Act branch came into being and it was activated after the POA Act came into force.

In 1992, I was posted there. I spent a maximum of four and a half year in the PCR office as DIG. We were for the first time involved in implementing this law. Maharashtra is one of the States with the maximum number of cases registered under these laws, mainly because, compared to other States, the SCs in Maharashtra are quiet educated and aware of their rights. They are also economically well-off, though majority of them depend on menial, agricultural and traditional works.

The PCR office was given the responsibility of visiting each and every place of offence. But the staff were not enough. We were finding it difficult to undertake such a task. Therefore the staff just used to make cursory visits. They were to ensure that the police stations promptly registered the cases and investigated the cases absolutely on merit, and also to oversee the investigation of registered cases and follow up prosecution of the accused. They started taking interests. The PCR branch was given more man-power.

2. *Could you brief the administrative structure of the PCR office in the State?*

The PCR office was started with a position of DIG (PCR), which was later on upgraded to IGP (PCR) in my time itself. On top is the IGP (PCR) with the support of a SP and others, followed by four regional level PCR offices, each headed by a SP with necessary supporting staff, and under these are the divisional level PCR offices, each consisting of two to three divisions and headed by a DYSP. Below this level there is district level PCR Mobile Squads, each headed by an Inspector.

3. *While the PCR cases are to be investigated by an Inspector, the atrocity cases by DYSP. Can the Inspector (PCR) bring pressure on the DYSP to investigate the atrocity cases earnestly?*

Yes. There is anomaly. The atrocity cases are to be investigated only by the DYSP. But we have taken up the matter with the Government stating that we do not have enough DYSPs to investigate all atrocity cases and that we cannot spend so much of time. We have requested the Government of India to allow us to get atrocity cases investigated by Inspectors. The PCR Inspectors themselves do not investigate PCR cases, but mainly monitor the investigation of PCR cases. Any Inspector can investigate PCR cases. Now we do not have enough DYSPs to investigate atrocity cases. But sometimes the PCR Inspectors monitor the investigation done by the DYSPs and report their observations to superior officers, so that the SPs and DYSPs come into the picture. This is how the anomaly is taken care of.

4. *Is it true that the local police do not pay adequate attention to PCR cases as they are primarily intended to take care of law and order and that they do not have enough time for PCR/POA cases?*

Yes, it is true that because of law and order pressure, not only PCR investigation, but also all other investigations suffer. There are too many law and order and security problems.

5. *What are your suggestions for this?*

Our Chief Minister is very keen on having separate investigation agencies, which would not be involved in maintenance of law and order. Both these agencies – PCR/POA Act office and of the law and order – should be separate, so that they may work exclusively for that agency and carry out investigation in a proper manner.

I had some time ago proposed that the PCR branch itself should investigate PCR cases as they are not involved in resolving law and order problems. They (PCR branches) should be strengthened and every district should have a DYSP (as the head of PCR office). And they should investigate not only PCR/POA Act cases but also cases of human right violations. The DYSP (PCR) is a person apart from the local police and he is the best person to handle it. So far, the Government has made them (DYSPs) nodal officers for investigating cases of human right violation. But they do not have adequate staff. There is only one Inspector in the district PCR Unit. But there are so many local police stations in the district. He cannot go to every police station and investigate cases. (So he has to depend on the local police).

6. *You were the IGP (PCR) for over four years, and you worked under the Director General of Police (DGP). Were there any instances in which the DGP came in your way of investigating any PCR/POA Act case?*

As a system, there should be no problem. The DGP is the head of the State police force, and various branches are under him. Officers report their problems to him. Some times, difference of opinion may occur. But this is between two individuals. It so happened in my case in 1993. When I was handling a case of human sacrifice of a Dalit youth in Osmanabad district, the then DGP did not agree with my investigation. The Additional DGP also did not agree with me and with my investigation. But it was my firm opinion that it was a murder case of a Dalit youth and that it was a case of human sacrifice. I personally wanted to investigate the case. I tried to convince them. In the meantime, the case was handed over to CID. The CID then reduced the murder section, and filed a charge sheet under section 304A against only one person. And all the Government functionaries were discharged from their liabilities. But then one social worker filed a private complaint in the Court of law for which I was required to a give a statement. I stuck to my gun and gave the true statement before the Court of law. I also submitted whatever document I had with me. This incident took place in 1993 and even now the case is pending in the Session Court where I am required to depose the case myself.

7. *In the light of the case you narrated, do you think that there is a need for the IGP (PCR) to function independently by-passing the DGP, and if so, is there a way to do so?*

It is not necessary, because it was a singular incident. Normally all our DGPs and ADGPs (law and order) are very much concerned about the violation of human rights and protecting the rights of the SCs and STs. But there are certain elements in the IPS also which might have feudal attitude. It cannot be ruled out. Feudal elements are there in all services. We also have some. The DGP comes in the way of the IGP's investigation (PCR). Probably as a head of the police department, he feels that the prestige of the police department is involved when some one does not do a proper investigation. Though the PCR wing is separate from the law and order department, it is part of the police department and, therefore, the blame will largely come upon the police department. That is what the feeling of the police (law and order). But I do not agree with them. In fact, individually, I had myself proposed that the PCR department should be brought directly under the Home Department of the State, and the confidential report of the IGP (PCR) be written by the Home Department. So that, the DGP (law and order) and other officers do not put any blame on them. So the IGP(PCR) should be independent. He should report to Home Department and liaison with Human Rights Commission and SC and ST commission.

8. *When the PCR and POA Acts are Central legislations, why should its implementation be left wholly to the State Governments?*

Ultimately, the implementation of Criminal law is the State Government's responsibility. So, the task of supervision of these laws cannot be made over to the Central Government, but it can be with the Home Department.

9. *Do you think, asking the IGP(PCR) to write the confidential report (CRs) of the DYSP in charge of investigating POA Act cases will make the DYSP more accountable for earnest investigation of POA Act cases?*

It is not possible, because there are too many DYSPs – almost 300 to 400 – in our State. He will then have to write CRs for 400 DYSPs. Reasonably as senior Officers, the SP or Police Commissioner of the district can evaluate their performance.

And most of our senior officers are well aware of the rights of the minorities and SCs and STs. Only a few, might be resenting against these laws mainly due to the privilege of "reservation" that is available for the SCs and STs.

10. *Some of the officers (law or order) genuinely say that it is difficult for them to devote enough time for the PCR cases. Do you agree with it?*

My contention is that the PCR police officers themselves should investigate PCR cases. Their machinery should be strengthened and Inspectors should be allowed to investigate (POA Act cases) and they will report to their DYSPs at the divisional level and their SPs at Regional level. Their IGP will scrutinize each and every case; if not by the IGP, at least by the SP. They should scrutinize the prosecution, so that the investigations are not neglected.

11. *Do you agree, there is caste prejudice among the police in general and the PCR police in particular, and thus effective implementation of the PCR and POA Acts is at stake?*

Caste prejudice in the police department was never there. Recently, I have noticed some resentment among open category officers against reservation. But I can tell you for certain that no police officers in the State (Maharashtra) follow or preach untouchability. That is ruled out. Even economic exploitation is not done by police officers. In very rare cases, you may find this. We have always treated such police officers with special harshness. We have registered number of cases against them under the PCR and POA Acts. Not that we spared them. At the same time I can say that caste prejudices in the present time are on the increase.

12. *There have been instances in Tamil Nadu in which even the accused have confessed that by paying Rs. 500/- to the investigating officers – be it DYSP or Inspector, the accused can end the case. What is the situation in Maharashtra?*

It is a case of blatant corruption. Corruption can be in any case: it can be in PCR case or it can be in any other case.

Corruption has to be tackled at a different level. But here the complainants are mostly poor people. They are not influential. But the accused are normally influential people. That is why they commit atrocities. No poor open category man will do that. It is always the *Jamindars,* the feudal lords and persons who are influential and persons who want to exploit the SCs and STs. They are always the accused. No doubt about it. That is why, even if you give the task of investigation to the PCR branch, the accused might influence the PCR police officers as well. So, these are the hazards of service. There may be good work done by large number of officers and bad work done by a couple of officers. But, I have noticed, that even the Scheduled Caste officers themselves are not very strict about the investigation. This is my observation. They do not take care either.

13. *Do you agree that there should be special reservation in the police force investigating PCR and POA Act cases to ensure fare and earnest investigation?*

No. I don't think it is necessary. As I told you, I belong to an open category. I risked my career in supporting and firmly investigating the murder of the SC person. But the SC persons in the village did not support me. The *Kotval* (police constable) turned hostile. Another SC officer backed out and reversed the statement. And one Muslim officer and an open category officer stood by their statements. And a person who filed a private complaint in support of the cause of the SC person was a Brahmin.

14. *Was it because the SC police constable was under pressure and faced a threat to life?*

It is possible in a village, but it is not possible in a city. It is not possible against a police officer.

15. *What in your opinion, are the major factors responsible for high rate of acquittal in PCR and POA Act cases?*

Conviction is very rare in most of the cases in India. Conviction even in violent cases has gone down. The same thing is happening even in PCR/POA cases. The main cause for this is that the witnesses turn hostile. This might be due to pressure from the accused, or there might be corruption or some temptation on their behalf. Or they might not be interested in getting involved in any such thing, and might forget the matter. The SC person in the village knows that he has to stay in the village and earn his living in the village. When has no alternative, why to earn enmity of others. That is the attitude of the SC victims.

16. *Do you think that the police are also a part of this pressure in any way?*

The police may not be a party to it, but they are not doing anything tangible to single out the person.

17. *Apart from witnesses turning hostile, are there other reasons for the acquittal of PCR/POA cases?*

Some of the provisions of our Evidences Act are very strict. It is therefore very difficult to prove any offence especially when there are no witnesses. The law depends too much on eye-witnesses. In large number of PCR cases – be it a case of rape of SC woman or not allowing SCs to fetch water from common well, two single persons are involved: the accused and the complainant. And there are no witnesses. Such cases often end in acquittal.

18. *Can delayed reporting be a cause for acquittal?*

It should not be a cause, because the persons staying in remote villages will take time and energy to walk up to the police station; especially when he may not have any money to reach the police station. So, in PCR cases normally delay in reporting should be condoned. But at the same time, the provisions of PCR/POA Acts for punishing those who resort to caste based abuses is openly misused by the SC persons, especially by the educated.

19. *Do you think that cases of caste abuse coming from villages are also of the same type?*

Most of the caste abuse cases are from towns and cities. You will not find a case of caste abuse in villages. The cases registered in extreme rural places are mostly related to untouchability and economic exploitations.

20. *What could be the approximate percentage of PCR/POA cases ending in acquittal due to the police not performing their lawful duty?*

I would say, the police are very strict, so the non-performance of their role is not the cause of acquittal. I would not be able to give you exact figure, may be around 50 per cent.

21. *Is the judiciary in Maharashtra free from caste prejudices and corrupt practices?*

It may be possible. There is a possibility. But I do not wish to comment on the judiciary. As I told you, all agencies have elements, which are prejudiced.

22. *What according to you, is the percentage of true and false cases reported under the PCR and POA Acts?*

Well, the true cases are true cases and the false cases are false cases. In the eyes of the law, when the complainant files an FIR, the law trusts that FIR, unless otherwise proved wrong. If the witnesses say, "No, it is not true what the complainant says", then the case fails. Otherwise, most of the cases are not false cases. Even if the SC person lodges a false case, it is the duty of the police to come to a conclusion on the basis of merit. And the mentality of the accused person should also be found out – whether he has such a habit or not, and what is his mental state. If he is a teacher in a school, he may not be inclined to atrocities, compared to a person who is having landed property.

23. *Instead of designating the existing Session Courts as Special Courts, do you think exclusive Special Courts are needed for the trial of PCR/POA Act cases?*

Yes. "Exclusive Special Courts" is our recommendation to the State government. When I was IGP (PCR) it was recommended that an exclusive Special Court in each district should be earmarked for the trial of PCR/POA Act cases.

24. *Are all the charge-sheeted cases true cases?*

Police is a prosecuting agency. We cannot say it is a false case once it is charge sheeted.

25. *What is the role of the Special Public Prosecutor?*

The Public Prosecutor's role is very limited. In the investigation, if it is a merited, the Public Prosecutor also needs to make a merited presentation before the Court of law. He presents the case in the Court of law on behalf of the police.

26. *For a case to end in conviction what are the essential steps that the investigating police officer has to take?*

There are inbuilt provisions. He has to collect proper evidence. Truthful or merited investigation should be carried out. Expedite the investigation. Bring the accused before the Court of law, and the matters are then left to the Court. Everything depends on the deposition of witnesses in the Court of law. Just telling the police what was being witnessed is not relevant, because we can only help the police in investigation.

27. *Is it the duty of the police to guard the witnesses going to Court to give evidence particularly when there is threat to their lives?*

There is a provision in the POA Act Rules to give protection to the witnesses. They can be carried in the police jeep to present before the Court of law. In Maharashtra we follow it.

Highlights of Responses

1. In Maharashtra, the PCR office has a more elaborate structure. On the top is the IGP (PCR) with a support of a SP and others, followed by four regional level PCR offices, each headed by a SP with necessary supporting staff, and under these are the divisional level PCR offices each consisting of two to three divisions and headed by a DYSP. Below this are the district level PCR Mobile Squads, each headed by an Inspector.
2. The DYSPs are there neither in required numbers, nor do they have enough time to do justice to the cases registered under the POA Act.

3. The PCR Inspectors themselves are not investigating PCR cases, but mainly monitoring the investigation of PCR cases. Any Inspector can investigate PCR cases.
4. The local police have to attend to a number of law and order issues, and because of that they do not pay enough attention to PCR/POA cases.
5. Only the PCR branch should investigate all PCR/POA Act cases. Since the PCR police are not involved in law and order problems, they can dedicate themselves to earnestly investigate PCR/POA Act cases
6. The PCR office should investigate not only PCR/POA Act cases, but also cases of human rights violations.
7. The district level PCR branches should be strengthened. Every district level PCR office should have a DYSP as its head.
8. The PCR Inspectors should report to their DYSPs at the Divisional level and their SPs at the Regional level. Their IGP (PCR) will scrutinize each and every case, at least at the regional level. They should scrutinize the prosecution.
9. As a system there should be no problem between the IGP (PCR) and the DGP above him. But sometime the DGP does intervene in the investigation carried out by the IGP (PCR), which greatly affects the credibility of the IGP and the investigation he carried out.
10. Normally, all our DGPs and ADGPs (law and order) are very much concerned about the human rights violation against the SCs and STs and feel the need for protecting them. However, there are certain feudal elements in IPS also. It cannot be ruled out.
11. Though most of the senior police officers are aware of the rights of the minorities and SCs and STs, a few of them are resentful of these laws on the ground of reservation policy of the Government.
12. Caste prejudice in the police department of Maharashtra was never there. Recently, I have noticed some resentment among open category officers against reservation. We have registered number of cases against police officers also under the PCR and POA Acts. Not that, we spared them. At the same time, caste prejudices are presently on the increase.

13. Corruption is a problem in PCR cases as it is elsewhere. It has to be tackled at a different level. ....Even if you give the investigation to the PCR branch, the accused, being influential, might influence the PCR police officers as well.
14. I have noticed, the Scheduled Caste officers themselves are not very strict in investigating PCR cases. So, I don't think reservation for the SCs and STs in the PCR/POA police force will work to ensure fare and earnest investigation.
15. The Scheduled Caste officers' not supporting SC/ST cases is possible due to the socio-economic pressure on them. But this may be possible only in villages, not in a city and, that too, on a police officer.
16. The main cause for the high rate of acquittal in PCR/POA Act cases is "witnesses turning hostile". This might be due to pressure from the accused or some temptation on the part of the witnesses or corruption. It might also be due to lack of willingness of the witnesses to get involved in such cases. The fact that they have no alternative means of economic support, and they have to live in the same village even in future to earn their living from the caste Hindus do not encourage them to enter into enmity with others.
17. Many PCR/POA Act cases get acquitted because some of the provisions of our Evidence Act depend too much on eyewitnesses. In a large number of cases, single persons are involved: the victim and the accused. It is therefore difficult to prove the charges without witnesses.
18. Delayed reporting cannot be a cause for acquittal, because the persons staying in remote villages will take time to walk up to the police station; many times he may not have money to reach the police station. So, in PCR/POA Act cases normally the delay should be condoned.
19. About 50 per cent cases registered under the PCR/POA Act end in acquittal due to the police's non-performance of the role that they are expected to.
20. Corrupt practices in the judiciary of Maharashtra are a possibility. As stated earlier, all agencies have elements, which are prejudiced and corrupt.
21. Most of the registered cases are not false cases. Even if the SC person lodges a false case, it is the duty of the police to come to a conclusion on the basis of merit.

22. Once a case is charge sheeted, the police cannot say it to be a false case.
23. Exclusive Special Courts should be there for each district for the trial of PCR/POA Act cases.
24. There is a provision in the POA Act to give protection to the witnesses. They can be taken in the police jeep to be produced before the Court of law. In Maharashtra we follow it.
25. Individually, I had myself proposed that the PCR department should be brought directly under the Home Department of the State, and that the confidential report of the IGP (PCR) be written by the Home Department. The IGP should be independent and he should report to Home Department. He should liaison with the Human Rights Commission and SCs and STs Commission.
26. The task of supervising the implementation of the two special laws cannot be left to the Central Government; it should come to the Home Department of the State.

Views of Deputy Superintendent of Police (DYSP)

The DYSP is the investigation officer for the POA Act. The following are the responses of the DYSP, Ramanathapuram district to some of the questions posed.

1. *What is your opinion on the implementation and the uses and abuses of the POA Act?*

Abusing Dalits in the name of their caste is not a common practice. This happens in certain situations. It happens when the non-Dalits become emotional or angry and when they are in a drunken state. But in villages, the POA Act is used as a weapon; even such emotional outbursts are not spared, and cases are filed. We, the police officers, are aware that whoever does not take proper action, whoever is against this Act, whoever delays the case can also be taken into task as provided in Section 5 of the POA Act*. In the entire world, no Act has such a provision. So, whether the complaint is true or false, we immediately prepare the charge sheet. But what happens at the last stage? They talk it

* But the correct section is: Section 4.

out in the village itself and go for a compromise, since they have to face each other everyday. The accused pleads with the victim as to why he filed a case against him instead of settling the matter through discussion. There is better awareness among the SCs these days.

Recently, there was a case of college students. One of the SC students had filed a case against some students under the POA Act stating that while he was travelling in the bus some students selectively identified him and started beating him knowing his SC background. But when we enquired, we found that out of the 24 accused students one was a Scheduled Caste student himself. When we enquired the witness, they said, "Sir, there is no problem of this kind". We found that there was enmity among the students in the past. When asked the petitioner as to why he considered it to be a case of caste discrimination, he said, "Sir, these students humiliated me like this earlier also. Since they did this to me for the second time, I gave this complaint to stop them doing the same again". When I said, "It is a serious case and it can ruin the career of these students, he replied, "If so, you may leave other students and file a case only against that boy".

This district is better. It is difficult to work as an officer in the PCR Unit of Salem district. It is a curse working in such an office. When a complaint is lodged in the PCR Cell, we do the preliminary investigation and only then FIR is filed. When we call the concerned members to the police station for inquiry, influential local leaders of both groups do not let these people come to the station on their own. The leaders stop them and negotiate for compromise. They do not even let us know how the incident took place. The respective caste leaders settle all the issues. They are always present in front of the police station. If we register the case that is also a problem; if we don't, that is also a problem. About 200 people come together and sit on a *dharna*. If the case is false, the other party (non-Dalits) also resort to protest. Such protests take place very often in Salem. The Dalits will also write petition to the Collector stating that the police did not take action properly. Some districts are peaceful. In some districts, the leaders use it as a business without investment.

Education is important. Things have improved to the extent of 80 per cent. Separate glass system in tea stall is no more possible, although in one or two places it is still practised. The SC leaders are not ready to expose such practices. When we go there to enquire, none comes forward to acknowledge such practice. Those who give this information to us do not want to be identified. How can we take action?

2. *Do you attempt to identify such practices in villages?*
   Yes, we do.

3. *You say only about 40 per cent of the cases are true and the rest all false cases. Are these 40 per cent of cases taken seriously and the accused are convicted?*

No, because in most of the cases the parties come to a compromise. If it is an IPC case, there is no problem. But POA case is not like that. It generates enmity between castes. We do not have a system that says that the SCs can live on their own and others can live on their own. Even the POA Act does not say so. After all they have to face each other everyday in their village. They have to live in the same village even in future. Whenever a complaint is lodged against the non-SCs, they say to the SCs: "What sort of a person you are? Why did you go to the police for this problem when we have lived like brothers?" In turn the SC person says: "No, no! He only told me to do so. No problem. It just happened. We can sort it out between ourselves". After all, man is a social animal.

4. *Do you think that this Act has generated a sense of fear among the non-SCs?*

Yes. Because of this Act, there is fear among the non-SCs and the scope for atrocities also is limited. This fear is very much there. It is there amongst both the literates and illiterates. It is enough to maintain this fear. If we go strictly by this Act, it will only aggravate the situation and result in more and more problems. Nowhere in the world there is community-wise law like this. I know this because I have been in PCR unit. If we implement this law strictly as we do in the case of other laws, there will only be conflicts and problems in the society. We cannot solve such problems by strictly implementing these laws.

5. *Suppose we withdraw this law, do you think that caste related conflicts could be effectively dealt with?*

Once a severely wounded snake went to a Muniver (saint) and said, "Swamiji, you told me that I should not bite anyone whatever may happen to me. See what has happened to me. I have been beaten severely". In response the saint said, "yes, I told you not to bite anyone, but I never told you not to threaten them by hissing". Like this, the SCs should use the POA Act as a means to threaten the non-Dalits who are likely to discriminate against and commit atrocities on them. If we do not have this law, what had happened to the snake will happen to the Dalits. Though it is said that we cannot change people through law, and though proper punishment is not given to the accused by strictly implementing this law, the fear of being booked under this law in itself prevents the non-Dalits from committing atrocities on the Dalits. Even if we strictly follow the Act and punish the accused, this will only increase the enmity between these caste groups. But this Act is needed.

6. *A common man says: "what is so big about this law. We have seen these laws. If we give Rs. 500/- to the police, everything will be over". What is your opinion on such comments?*

It is not so. Everybody knows its implications. Moreover, such information you should gather from responsible people. Statement from lower-level staff will be different from those given by higher-level staff. We cannot pass judgment on the basis of statements from lower-level staff.

7. *You say, this law will create problem in society if we implement it strictly. Shall we then stop enforcing it?*

No. We have to implement the Act. But we can't be very strict. If we do so, there will be problems in the society. At the same time we cannot nullify the need of it. We just have to keep it going. Ignoring our caste, religious background, it is said, we are all equals before law. But this kind of a law (POA Act) will only create conflicts between castes. Any one, even the SCs and STs, who seriously think about the need of this law, will come to this conclusion only. The other side may also feel the same way. So, it is wrong to withdraw this law completely. It is also wrong to think of implementing it strictly. We have to keep this law as the base and use it in the manner we try to kill a snake with the help of the stick without getting the stick broken.

8. *You have law, but you don't implement it. Will it not encourage the violators of such laws?*

There is a difference between the general law and this law. That is why we can't implement this law strictly. If we implement this law strictly, everyone will become very conscious of what caste the other person belongs to. The people of all castes work at all places – be it industry or farming. Fearing possible legal action under this law, the employers will be sceptical and scared of employing the SCs. These employers say: "I can not employ you (SCs), I am sorry. I don't mind keeping my industry closed". There have been such incidents in Selam. Once in Selam there was a case registered under the POA Act against the manager of TADCO (Tamil Nadu Agriculture Development Corporation). The petitioner had stated, "I went with 10 other members to the manager to get a loan. But the manager not only refused to give loan but also said, "If we give loan to your caste fellows, this is what happens. You don't repay the loan, and we cannot give you loan". At the most, the manager would have said, "You see, so far we have given loan to so many people belonging to your caste. Nobody has repaid it so far. We have been pressurised by our top-level officers and also served memos for being unable to collect back the loan amount. How do you expect us to give you loan?" This is what the manager would have said. But the petitioner twisted this into a case. How can we arrest such a senior level officer? This is too atrocious. But these things do not happen in Ramanathapuram town though these are common in Selam, Coimbatore and even in Thindukkal towns.

At this stage it is worth noting the views expressed by another DYSP: The DYSP, in-service training, Madurai (Reserve Line Post) said: "Laws such as the PCR Act and POA Act are very much needed. We have not yet come to a stage where the protection of Dalits can be ensured without such laws". He further said: "Corruption is everywhere, and the police is not an exceptional case". Speedy laying of charge sheet and the trial of each PCR/POA Act case within 15 days are the two important things to be followed for successful implementation of these laws, he added.

Highlights of Responses

1. According to the DYSP, abusing the Dalits in the name of their castes was not to be treated as an offence under these special laws, since it happens only when the non-SCs become emotional or angry or in a drunken state. But there is nothing wrong in using the law to bring about a positive attitudinal change among these sections of people.
2. Whether the complaint was true or false, the police laid the charge sheet. Later, the DYSP also told that the police always carried out preliminary investigation to assess the validity of the cases before filing the FIR.
3. The DYSP did not consider the case that he quoted, i.e., the SC student's complaint against a few other caste students, to be a true case on the ground that one of the accused was a Dalit himself and the case was only an outcome of a past enmity between them. *But if one carefully looks at what the victim had said as reasons for his complaint, it is more than obvious that it was a clear case of an offence under the POA Act. The decision of the victim to withdraw the case after the police persuasion reflects nothing but his concern for the career of the accused. In no way this decision justifies the declaration of the case to be a false one.*
4. In view of the kind of problems that the police officers faced, particularly in districts like Salem, working in the PCR police station was considered to be a curse.
5. Though the practice of separate glass system was not allowed in most of the tea-stalls, it was still practised some places. The police could not eliminate this practice because the SCs, as claimed, were afraid of exposing individuals following such practices. *But this in no way justifies the continuation of such inhuman practices. The police can resort to suo-muto actions to end such practices.*

6. According to the DYSP only about 40 per cent of cases registered under the PCR/POA Act were true. But even these true cases did not end in conviction. In most cases both the victims and the accused opted for a compromise at the last stage of the case. The victims were happy once the accused said "sorry" to them, which was not possible otherwise. *But in reality the victims go for a compromise only when there is no other option possible. In most cases, the victims are forced to withdraw the case through overt and covert forms of coercive means.*
7. According to the DYSP, dealing with cases registered under IPC was not a problem for the police, but those registered under the POA Act was a problem since, it created enmity between the SCs and non-SCs and disrupted the healthy community living in the village.
   That is why, perhaps, the police prefer registering most of the POA Act cases under the IPC. This attitude of the police becomes all the more evident while looking at the copy of Summary of Penal Provisions that the researcher had collected from the PCR unit, Ramanathapuram. In this copy, *the police themselves have written in red ink the IPC sections 354 against 3(1)(xi) of POA Act which is meant for the offence of dishonouring* or *outraging the modesty of women by force, and the IPC section 376 against 3(1)(xii) of the POA Act which is meant for the offence of using one's position to exploit a woman sexually (see Annexure No.*3).
8. There is no system, which will help the SCs live away from the non-SCs. They have to live in their own village and interact with the caste Hindus living there who are dominant both in terms of their number and socio-economic status and on whom they depend on for their livelihood. It may, however, be noted that there is a provision under section 17(3) of the POA Act which permits the SCs to live separately.
9. The PCR and POA Acts have created a sense of fear among the non-SCs. It is enough to maintain this fear. These Acts cannot be implemented strictly as done in the case of other laws. If it is done so, it will only result in more caste conflicts.

10. Strict implementation of the POA Act will also reduce drastically the job opportunities for the SCs in private sectors as these employers would all the time feel that they cannot exercise any control over the SC employees owing to the fear of being booked under these laws.
11. In the absence of laws such as the PCR and the POA Acts, the SCs may be killed and they will have no security.

Views of the Special Public Prosecutor (SPP)

The following are the responses of the SPP, Special Court, Madurai to some of the questions posed.

1. *Why do maximum numbers of cases registered under the PCR/POA Act get acquitted?*
    1. The police dealing with these Acts in general are not adequately trained with regard to the application of various provisions of these Acts. They are not very familiar with the various sections and clauses under which the accused are to be booked, and the procedures to be followed at every stage of the case.
    2. Often, most of the cases are not properly registered i.e., not under the appropriate sections.
    3. The witness is often afraid of coming to the Court to give evidences owing to possible dire consequences from the accused/caste Hindus.
    4. The Police do not take the investigation task seriously.
    5. Though cases registered under the POA Act are to be investigated by no less than DYSP, it is often done by lower level police staff, and is done just for the sake of completing the formalities.
    6. The police generally do not accompany and give due support to the victims and their witnesses while going to the Court. This puts the victims in more vulnerable situations. They avoid extending such support under some pretext or the other. Often they say: "We have other duties as well".
    7. The travel and food allowances due to the victims and their witnesses to go and give witness in the Court are hardly accessible to them. Earlier, it was given in the

Court itself, and was therefore accessible to them easily; but now they have to go to the Collector's office to get it. This in itself costs them money: sometimes more than what is due to them. This also takes much of their time, and subject them to enormous harassment. Often, the victims and witnesses spend from their own pockets. This is also a reason why the witnesses do not come to the Court to give evidence.

8. Proper compensation is not given to the victims. This again is an important reason why the Scheduled Castes do not pursue their case to its logical end.

2. *What is your opinion on the relevance of PCR and POA Acts?*
   1. These Acts are very much needed for the protection of the Scheduled Castes/Scheduled Tribes. In the absence of such laws the Scheduled Castes/Scheduled Tribes will be put into more vulnerable situations, and subjected to more humiliation and atrocities.
   2. Only because of such laws, the non-Scheduled Caste people treat the Scheduled Castes with some respect. Therefore, these Acts are needed to be there.

3. *Do you, as the Special Public Prosecutor, get proper recognition in the Office?*

"I am a Special Public Prosecutor for 7 districts in Tamil Nadu to deal with cases registered under the PCR/POA Act. But I don't have an office. I don't have a clerk to assist me. I have not received any fee or remuneration in the last one and a half year of my appointment here. I sent bills, but never get paid. The response often given by the Government is, "lack of funds". Without getting paid, I find it difficult even to maintain myself".

4. *Your suggestions:*
   1. The police should be properly trained and guided to use these laws effectively.
   2. The TA/DA to the victims and their witness should be given in the Court itself. The Government has to take decision in this regard at the earliest.

3. The Special Public Prosecutor should be given due recognition by meeting at least his/her basic requirements like office, clerical assistance and the due remuneration in order to function effectively as the Special Public Prosecutor.

Views of an Advocate

1. *As an advocate, what are your comments on the uses and abuses of the POA Act with particular reference to the case of Pandian Vs. Veluchamy which you had closely followed up?*

Pandian was the only SC person working in the SNTR School. Others were mostly belonging to Backward Castes. Prior to his promotion to the post of the Librarian, there were many instances of mishandling of and malpractices in accounts, particularly in matters of scholarships given to the SC students. After he became the Librarian, he could understand such malpractices. He opposed such practices. This is how the problem started. Then the school authority decided covertly either to make him accede to such practices or to get him transferred to some other school. There was a healthy social relation among all other members of the staff, but he was selectively isolated and looked down upon. Even the peons used to treat him differently. To bring disgrace to his credibility, the teachers used to tell their students not to go to the library. They also started charging him as if he were not helping the students coming to the library. Knowing no way of stopping the misuse of scholarship money by the school employees, Pandian started telling students to be vigilant as to how much money they sign for and how much they actually get in hand. This enraged all the school staff particularly the Headmaster. To teach him a lesson, they removed his chair one day, and on another day, they took away his table too. They also overtly started talking that his work was of no value to anyone. They went on harassing him in all possible overt and covert forms. He tolerated all these.

But one day the staff went to the extent of not letting him sign the daily attendance register by hiding it. So, for one full month he could not sign the register, though he had been going to the school regularly. Subsequently, he sent a petition to District Educational Officers and others stating that he was not allowed to sign the attendance register. However, the Headmaster paid him his salary for that month. But he covertly made some changes in the Pandian's service record, so as to damage his prospect of promotion. Pandian was neither transferred, nor allowed to function in the school at peace.

It was in this context that Pandian filed a PCR case. We also joined him. But the police refused to accept his case. We protested against this attitude of the police. Then FIR was filed. It took more than a month for us to make the police to file an FIR under the PCR Act. The only reason for the police refusing to register our case was that we did not give them money. If we had given Rs. 1000/- to the police, our case would have been filed on the very day.

The police officials in charge of implementing the PCR/POA Act have made these laws as means of generating additional income for themselves. Whenever a victim goes to the police station, the police collect around Rs. 1000/- to file a case. Later, they collect around Rs. 5,000/- from the accused to do the needful either to get the case acquitted or for a compromise. It is a day-to-day reality practised overtly while dealing with the PCR/POA cases. To enable the accused, the police invariably make wrong entries and statements in the FIR. In return, they extract lot of money from the accused. The police misuse the law, but they will say that the Dalit misuse the law. This is totally untrue.

Atrocities committed against the Dalits are more severe in the courts than in the police stations. I know, we should not comment on the judgment of the Magistrate. But how many witnesses does he (Magistrate) need to prove or disprove a particular case – one or two or five? It is understood that no victim would say anything against his own interest and would obviously say what he had already reported in the FIR. The first witness, the police, also gave evidence as per the FIR. The witness who came with the victim also deposed the facts correctly. How many more witness do we need to prove the case? Yet the case was acquitted.

What happened in the Court during trial was that when the witness made his oral statement as required by the Magistrate, his statement was typed differently, twisting the case in favour of the accused. Later, when the witness wanted to know what was being typed as his statement, the Magistrate himself asked the witness as to who instigated him to counter-check his statement. This incident reflects that such practices of twisting witnesses' statements by the typist within the Court with a view to helping the accused has been in practice for a long time. This also reflects the Magistrate's concern for the accused; while he is supposed to be impartial and committed to ensure justice to the victims.

The Court is meant for *Dharma* and justice, and the Judge is there for upholding these ideals. If the Judge himself favours overtly the accused, how can we say that the Court is meant for justice, and how can the POA Act be implemented effectively? Such attitude of the Judges of Special Courts results in acquittal of most of the POA cases. This in turn gives an impression to the public that the SC and ST people unnecessarily file cases under the PCR and POA Act, and that most of these cases are false ones, and thus end in acquittal. But in reality, this is not true. Why should we then file cases under these laws and what is the use of these laws? At least in some cases the Court should convict the accused, and let the people see the offenders being punished and put behind the bars. If the Court cannot do this what is the use of the Court and why should it be there at all?

2. *Do you mean to say that these laws are of no use to the Dalits?*

These laws are good, but not implemented properly. Out of 100 cases, even if 10 to 20 cases end in conviction, the people will feel the impact and use of these laws. But it is not so. If it is a civil or criminal case, will there be such judgments? We are not against compromise. If the accused realises his mistake and apologises, there is nothing wrong in going for a compromise. But cases ending in compromise are also alleged to be false cases.

This Act (POA) is very good. It has to be there. But laws only on paper will not uproot caste discrimination and untouchability. In most of the villages around here, there is separate glass system for the Dalits. In tea stalls, they have to sit on the floor, while others are provided with benches. When we take up such issues, the police say: "Don't create problems; adjust with the existing system".

3. *It is generally alleged that the Dalits file false cases against the non-Dalits. What are your comments?*

None does so. There may be one or two rare cases. This also I am not sure.

Views of Research Assistants

The following are the views of the two Research Assistants (RA) who did the most difficult job of collecting data for this study from different stakeholders. These views are based on experiences they gained as 'untrained' social workers attached to NGOs that worked primarily among the SCs in villages. These views are also based on their experiences during data collection. The RAs had written down their views in Tamil, which the researcher has translated in to English as under:

Views of Research Assistant – 1

1. Though all the police officials concerned were aware of the fact that the research was for the Government of India, no police official, except one or two from Ramanathapuram PCR police station, attached any importance to this study. They only tried to impress upon us that they were the most powerful ones.
2. When we went to villages to record the views of the victims and witnesses, the caste Hindus, particularly the accused, did not allow us to have any access to the victims. They began to follow us wherever we went and pursued our movements very closely. They treated us as if we were their enemies. We therefore, had to interview the victims and their witnesses when they were in their fields outside their villages.
3. From our own experiences in villages, we can say that the socio-economic arrangement in villages is such that it is very much inimical to the Dalits' development and interest.
4. In view of the caste Hindus' antagonistic attitude towards us, we sought the help of the police concerned. But the

police said, "we can not do anything for getting the statements of the accused, and we cannot come behind you for this. When this happened with the RA(1), he informed the same to the researcher, who in turn, contacted the IGP (PCR), Chennai and sought his intervention in the matter. In response, the IGP said, "once the case got acquitted, the police have no right to call the accuse back to the police station to record their statement. Doing so would amount violation of their human rights. We cannot help you. You have to find your own ways of recording their views".

5. When we requested the police, particularly those from Sivagangai PCR police station, for certain data pertaining to a few cases under study, they made us make a number of visits to the station; in this way, we had to wait for more than a month. Yet we could not get the data we had asked for.
6. When we interviewed the victims, most of them said, "please do not talk about our case elsewhere. God would punish them (accused)". This only reflected how terrified they were. When they were in such a state of mind, how could we say that they filed false cases against the caste Hindus?
7. Though the police had been instrumental for the defeat of most of the cases under study, they did not come forward either to provide necessary documents or to get the statements of the accused as required. Had the police co-operated with us, the quality of our study would have been enriched further.
8. The Special Court at Madurai declined from giving us copies of judgments of the cases under study despite producing letter from the researcher and the Ministry of Social Justice and Empowerment, New Delhi. But we saw individuals collecting copies of judgments from the concerned staff of the Court without any official letter for the purpose.

Views of Research Assistant – 2

The RA (2) involved in the present study once met, as directed by the Statistical Inspector, PCR Police Station, Ramanathapuram, the Police Inspector, in charge of the police station at Parthibanur town to collect a few documents, such as FIR, pertaining to a case under study. The RA introduced himself and said that he had come there in connection with the study on the use and abuse of the PCR and POA Acts. In turn, the Inspector said snobbishly, "You are going to do a study. First of all, tell me. I am a *Thevar* (one of the dominant backward castes – Maravan caste), which caste do you belong to?" The RA felt extremely humiliated by this question. Having no other option, the RA replied to the Inspector's unwarranted, unprecedented and undesirable question, "I belong to the Scheduled Caste".

The RA felt all the more offended and shocked owing to the fact that he had to face caste discrimination at the hands of none other than the Police Inspector himself within the police station itself and that too when he had gone there as a RA of a research team involved in the evaluation of the implementation of the PCR and POA Acts. Though this discriminatory behaviour of the Police Inspector was very much an offence punishable under the PCR Act, the RA found himself helpless and could not resort to any legal action against him in view of the fact that he had to complete the task assigned to him by the researcher. He, however, shared the same with the researcher.

Based on the above and many other experiences of discriminations meted out to him earlier, the RA came to a conclusion that irrespective of their positions in the police departments, no police like to implement the PCR or POA Act earnestly, unless they belong to the SCs. Further, he raised a question, "When the policemen belong to the caste of the accused, which is true in most cases, how would they help the victims? How would they implement earnestly the PCR and POA Acts, which go against the interests of their caste people? As they have been, they would only help the accused escape the due punishment".

Therefore the RA suggested that "at least 50 per cent of the police officials who are directly involved at various levels in the implementation of these Acts, should be from the Scheduled Caste background, if at all we are serious about implementing these laws in their true spirits".

Views of NGO (1)

Mr. Shanmugavel, State Secretary, Thiyagi Imanual Peravai, which is an organisation of Dalit people in the town of Paramakudi, Ramanathapuram district. The following are his responses to various questions posed to him:

1. *This study is about the uses and abuses of the PCR and POA Acts. What is your opinion about the need of these Acts?*

Laws are meant to suppress disruptive elements. Indian society is a caste-based hierarchical society. It has two groups of castes: the ruling castes (caste Hindus) and the oppressed castes (Dalits). It has been part of the tradition of the former to treat the latter as slaves. In Tamil Nadu, those overtly involved in oppressing others are the Kallars, Maravars and Ahamudayars (the middle castes). Brahmins do not indulge in open violence against the oppressed castes.

These three castes oppress the Dalits in many ways to maintain their caste supremacy. When someone dies in their caste, they ask the people of oppressed castes to dig the burial ground to bury the deceased. If the Dalits disobey, they are beaten. This is a big human right violation. Protecting the human rights of all is the demand of the World Human Rights Organizations. The POA Act has been brought in only to protect these basic human rights. It is not against any groups as alleged. Another human right violation is that the Dalits do not have the right even to sit with others as equals. In front of the non-Dalits, they have to stand with folded hands, while others would be sitting. They have to adhere to this demeaning custom whenever they face or go in the vicinity of the ruling castes, even during funerals. When a member of the ruling caste dies, the members of a lower caste are asked to go from village to village to pass on the message of death. The latter have to do this job whatever be their state of health, engagements and priorities. Though the Dalits never like to perform this task, they are being forced to do. But when a Dalit dies, the ruling caste members do not even attend the funeral. One can never think of them doing similar service. The POA Act is only to protect the Dalits from such human rights violation, indignity and forced labour.

Another act of human rights violation practised in our villages is the custom of asking the Dalits to beat drums. In

Panakudi village, recently, there was a *mulapari* festival, celebrated by the entire village including the Dalits. In this festival, the Parayars (Dalits) of that village were asked, as usual, to beat the drums. Despite their unwillingness to perform that task, the Parayars were forced to perform. On this day, one of the caste Hindu members, using a loudspeaker, announced, "Now within 15 minutes the Parayars have to come here and beat the drums. If they don't perform at least by 8 o'-clock in the night, their houses will be burnt". All the neighbouring villages (Kuravakulam, Marakulam) heard this announcement. Yet, the Dalits did not lodge a police complaint fearing dire consequences. Their fear is not unrealistic, given the numerical preponderance of the caste Hindus, their violent nature and their enmity towards those Dalits asserting social dignity.

The above incident was brought to my knowledge, instead of approaching the local police station. I then immediately went to the police station. Subsequently, the person who made that announcement was brought to the police station. He promised that henceforth he would not do so. But the matter did not end there. The accused went back to the village and rushed to the Parayars' street with a sickle. He shouted at everyone asking for the person who informed the police. Everyone said, "no". He then asked them to swear in front of their village god. The Parayars then came running back to me and narrated what happened. We again went to the police station, and subsequently the person was brought back to the station. The entire Maravar caste people and the Parayars and other Dalits came to the station. There was a kind of panchayat meeting held at the police station itself. Then the person was asked to give in writing that he would not do the same again. He did so.

After three days, on November 3, 2000, the accused caste Hindu, with the support of fellow caste men, stole two electric motor pump-sets (used for irrigation purposes) belonging to two Parayar caste members who also owned cultivable lands. The loss of these electric motor pumps at a time when it was most needed for irrigating their paddy crops was indeed a loss of the most vital source of livelihood for most of the Parayars in the village. This was done in order to control the Dalits' economic independence and subvert their assertion for social dignity. If the Maravars can indulge in such activities, why should we not protest against them?

On 4th November 2000, the Dalits gave a petition to the police at Narikudi station requesting to register a case under the POA Act for tracing out the lost electric motors. Mr. Munusamy gave this complaint. But the police did not take any action. Then they came to me for help on 6th November. I wrote a petition addressed to the SP and asked them to meet him. They, along with a few educated people, met the SP. The SP endorsed their petition by signing and putting seal on it. Further, he asked them to approach the local police station. They did so. Only then the police filed an FIR on November 7th. However, this FIR was based only on the petition of 4th November, and not of 6th November. On the ground that the FIR was not based on the information provided in my petition of 6th November, the police officers, Murugan and Venkataraman, both belonging to the dominant caste, asked the victims to file an FIR afresh on the 7th November. The victims did so, not knowing how it would help the accused escape legal punishment. But why should the police do so? This only reflects that their loyalties towards their own caste is much more stronger than their commitment towards their profession and the protection of Dalits.

These police officers in any way take bribe from the caste Hindus as well. In fact, the Act has helped the police to make more money. We demanded that the police should first file an FIR stating that the electric pump motors had been stolen. We demanded that they should arrest the party (concerned accused). We insisted that we would otherwise resort to hunger strike and road blockade.

The general trend in the implementation the POA Act is the "delay in every necessary action". This is followed in almost all police stations. Besides, they generally favour the ruling caste members. This Act is not against any one, and not to oppress any caste groups. It has been introduced by the Central Government only to ensure Dalits their basic human rights. It is only to prevent atrocities committed against the Dalits. It only says, "Don't commit atrocities".

2. *Why most of the POA Act cases get acquitted in the Court? What are your views on this?*

All registered cases do not reach the Court. It is filtered in the police station itself. As soon as a case is filed, either an MLA or a district level secretary intervenes in the matter. In all political parties, the district level secretary position is always given to the ruling caste members, not to the Dalits. And all political parties are parties for strengthening the interests of their respective castes. Then how will they give district level position to the Dalits? None would like to work under a Dalit. This is in itself an atrocity. So the ruling political leaders intervene whenever a case is taken to police station. They persuade the police saying: "The person (accused) is our person (person belonging to our political party); he is a nice person, and he would not have done such things as alleged". In case where the FIR had already been filed, not knowing the political connection of the accused, the police, in turn, would say to the political leader, "What to do now? The FIR has already been filed. But, you don't worry, I will close the case while filing the charge sheet". The police promptly do the needful accepting money from the accused.

3. *What happens, when the case reaches the Court despite all these interventions?*

Most of the Judges in Court belong to the dominant castes. The advocates and judges themselves approach the accused and suggest what they should do. In Madurai Special Court, I came to discover, an internal understanding and also a top level order to this effect to close down all cases registered under the POA Act without taking due action (proper judgment). Looking into the kind of judgments delivered with regard the cases filed under the PCR and POA Acts, I have come to such a conclusion.

For example, in Aruppukottai town there is one STRN government school. One Mr. Pandian, a Dalit, was working over there as a clerk. Pandyan came to know that prior to his posting there, the school Head Master, with the help of his office clerk, was involved in appropriating students' money. But the Head Master could not continue his corrupt practices since the Dalit clerk refused to be a party to it. As a result, Pandyan was not given water to drink in the school. He was not provided even with the minimum requirements of a table and a chair. He was performing his duties as a clerk sitting beneath a tree in the school campus. We checked, and found it to be true. When we intervened and asked the Head Master as to why he did so, he asserted saying, "Yes, I shall do so". He said, he belonged to the ruling party. Then, Pandyan went to the PCR Unit, at Virudhunagar town and requested the police to register an FIR against the Head Master. For one month, the PCR Unit refused to file a case. Then we, representing such organizations as *Thiyagi Imanual Peravai* and *Puthiya Thamilagam,* went to the police station and pressurised them to file an FIR. Finally, the police filed an FIR and subsequently the charge sheet was also framed. As prescribed in the law, 1/4th of the compensation amount of Rs.6,250/= (out of Rs.25,000) was also given to the victim.

But surprisingly enough when the witness was giving evidence in the Court in support of this case, the typist of the Court typed something contradictory to what the witness had told the Judge. The typist would not have done such a thing unless she had already been instructed by the competent authority of the Court to do so. Otherwise how would she know what was actually to be typed to get that particular case acquitted? That means there was a clear-cut conspiracy hatched against the victim in the Court itself. Knowing the wrong reporting in the statement, the witness Mr. Mutthu (locally known as Auto Mutthu) refused to sign the statement. Then the Magistrate was approached, who, in turn, shouted at the clerk. A new statement was then prepared as reported by the witness. The purpose of the Act is to punish the guilty, but Government officers are functioning with an intention of protecting the guilty.

4. *Is this Act useful for the people, and if so, do you want this Act to be in force?*

In 1955 the PCR Act came into being. Owing to certain limitations of this Act, the POA was enacted in 1989. But we realise that even this Act has scope for the accused escaping due punishment. However, this Act is definitely needed. Ambedkar says, "The caste Hindus should feel that there is a knife straight above their head. Only then they will be afraid of troubling the Dalits. (Here the knife is referred to the POA Act). It is a different matter whether this knife is really used or not.

Under this Act, if an FIR is filed, the accused end up spending Rs. 6000 – 7000/- to protect his interest. This is definitely a big loss for him. He is automatically afraid of such a loss. Sometimes, they may even have to spend up to Rs. 10000/- to bail out the accused. According to this Act, nobody can be bailed out, but the police bail him or her out. How can the police violate the laws? The police may suggest to the accused that by paying Rs. 5000/- to them, they can go for anticipatory bail. The accused prefer this instead of spending over Rs. 7000/- to fight the case. But even this economic loss brings pressure and fear among the caste Hindus.

5. *Do the Dalits consider this Act as a protective device?*

The Dalits in general are not even aware of this Act. With regard to protecting people from diseases, the government approach is, "Prevention is better than cure", and accordingly, they conduct health awareness programmes. Why does not the Government follow a similar approach to making the Dalits aware of their protective laws and measures? It is sad that the Government has not taken up such a task as an important obligation. The law has not reached villages. But it is already alleged that the Dalit misuse this Act and file false cases. And except the Dalits, the people in general feel that this Act has to be withdrawn.

There are good people even among the Thevars (caste Hindus). Only those violating human rights should be booked under these laws. Good caste Hindus should not be booked under these laws. The Government is yet to demonstrate to the people the power and value of these laws. The SC people do go to the police saying: "please protect us and do justice". Though the POA Act has provisions to register all sorts of complaints of the Dalits, the police do not do so. Apart from the POA Act, the police can also book their grievances under IPC, which do not ensure them financial compensation. But the Dalit people in general do not know this. It is only when NGOs and other bodies intervene that atrocities against the Dalits get registered under the POA Act. Otherwise, the police use only IPC.

According to the law, the Government has to meet all his (victim) requirements such as TA and DA and ensure treatment to the affected. But the police never bother to extend any of these. The victim has to spend a lot of money and also run around leaving behind his usual daily work and sacrificing his daily wage. They also have to bribe heavily the police and others to make them take necessary actions. The victim also has to spend a lot of money in the Court. Whenever he goes to the Court, he has to spend from his pocket not only for himself but also for the witnesses. Even after all these, he loses the case. He ends up spending Rs.7000/- to 8,000/-. The money he gets after the case being charge sheeted is Rs.6000/-. But he ends up spending again Rs.2000/- to 3000/-. He feels, at the end of the day, dejected, and regret and repent for having filed a case under this Act. He even feels: "It is better that I remain meek even when I am abused, humiliated and beaten in the name of my caste, rather than filing a case under such laws and facing more harassment, humiliation and hardship".

6. *It is said that this Act is used against the interest of the ruling castes. Do you agree?*

If we look into the history, it is clear that the oppressed castes, whether Pallars or Parayas or Chakiliyars, do not antagonize or fight with the caste Hindus. They have always remained the most oppressed. They never ruled or oppressed others. Even today, they, out of fear, do not even report to the police about the atrocities of the caste Hindus. But the caste Hindus allege that the Dalits often register false cases against them under the POA Act. In this regard, I would like to share one thing. There was a *Thever* caste man from Puliyangudi village near Kariyapatti village. He brought a Pallar caste man to me. This Pallar man is like a slave to this Thevar. This Thevar wanted to punish another Thevar, his enemy. For this purpose, he forced his slave (Pallar caste man) to file a case against that Thevar under the POA Act. There have been a few such cases. And these are generally the false ones. In all such cases, the worst sufferers are the Dalits themselves. But if one looks at it critically, it can be understood that those responsible for the false cases are not the Dalits, but the caste Hindus. Moreover, in most cases the victims do not get the due compensation since the police close the case file before filing the charge sheet, which is mandatory for getting the one fourth of the due compensation. The police do so accepting money from the accused.

It is said that the DYSP is the officer in charge of investigating the cases registered under the POA Act. Instead of seriously investigating the registered cases, he closes the case files as soon as some one informs him that the case was false. When people like us intervene and ask, he says that he did conduct the inquiry and found the case to be false and therefore closed the file. Then we, for many reasons, give up the case at that level itself. But in some cases, we fought and made them register the case formally.

When the FIR file is closed, the police have to give us a receipt. This receipt we can produce in the Special Court within 7 days and institute another inquiry if we are not satisfied with the first one. But the reality is, neither the police give the receipt to the victims, nor are the victims aware of it and demand for it. Often, the victims do not get this receipt.

Recently, there was a girl from Muthenari village who worked at Thiruchuli near Narikudi town. One Mr. Pandi (foreman), a Thevar by caste, who came over there, started beating her asking as to why she was not doing her work properly? She was working for a Muslim man (owner). Regarding this incident, a complaint was lodged at the Thiruchuli police station and an FIR was filed. Immediately, the owner gave a considerable amount of money to the police concerned. Accepting this money, the police closed the case saying that it was found to be a false case. How atrocious was this act of the police? The police take money from the accused saying that it is better for them to pay the police a lump sum amount in advance and close the case, rather than spending so much money in facing the trial, besides subjecting themselves to judicial punishment. Bribing is very much prevalent at every stage of the case. This is one of the most important reasons for the POA Act not having any impacts.

7. *The evidences/witnesses have to be produced in the Court by the police. Is it done in time?*
   No.

8. *Do the police make an FIR as soon as an incident of atrocity is reported to them, and how to make them abide by the laws?*

No. They may take 3 to 4 days or even 10 days. Sometimes they even take a month to register an FIR. The police deliberately delay it with the intention of putting the blame on the victims themselves stating that the case was not brought to the notice of the police immediately. They delay this also to settle the matter through negotiations. The police, the ruling castes and the political leaders work in league with one another to do this unlawful act. This is in itself an atrocity against the Dalits. The Act says that those officers who do not investigate the case properly should also be punished. But when we are unable to punish even the offender who is an ordinary villager, how can we hope to punish the offenders who are the police officers. Where all do we have to go and how much money and other things we need to mobilise to do so? Punishing the police who violate the POA Act is practically not possible in view of their upper caste background and high-level political and bureaucratic connections, though the law has provisions for doing so.

This law is a good protective mechanism for the Dalits. But for this law, there is fear among the ruling castes. The caste Hindus now know that if they are booked under this law, they have to face lots of problems. Whether this law is implemented or not, it can be used by the Dalits as a weapon to threaten the oppressive ruling castes. If a case is filed under the IPC, nobody bothers. But if it is booked under POA Act, the accused is brought to the police station, at least to negotiate for a compromise.

9. *Do the police register the given complaints under appropriate sections?*

The victims may not know the various sections under which the offences committed against them have to be registered. But the police ought to know them. Cleverly, the police register most of the cases under 3 (1) (x), which is meant to punish only those non-SC/ST members who abuse in public the SCs/STs pointing to their social origin (castes) in a derogatory manner. Even the offence of assaults on women intending to dishonour her modesty which is to be registered under 3(1)(xi) is registered under 3(1)(x). This is done mainly to bring down the compensation amount due to the victim. The compensation for offences under 3(1)(x) is Rs.25,000/- only, whereas for offences under 3(1)(xi) it is Rs.50,000/-. So, registering cases under inappropriate sections brings more hardship and loss to the Dalits. Even when we write specifically the sections under which the case to be registered, in 90 per cent of cases the police do not honour it. They put often 3(1)(x) only. One reason for this is that even in the PCR Act, there is 3(1)(x) section. The police invariably follow the same section here as well.

10. *Has the Government provided required facilities to the PCR police stations and how the PCR Unit functions?*

In PCR Unit, nothing happens. The PCR police do only negotiations with the victims to withdraw the cases. No case is taken to the Court seriously. It only serves the purpose of showing statistics to the Government as to how many cases are reported every year under the PCR Act.

The PCR police officials do not enjoy due importance and facility in the police force. Recently, I had been to Ramanathapuram PCR Unit. Though it is supposed to be an office for one SI, one Inspector and 4 policemen, it operates from a small room. They have simply put two tables and few chairs inside their vehicle-shed. When I visited, I saw one Inspector and a SI sitting there. This is what they call, the PCR police station. By housing these PCR police officials in the car-shed with hardly any facility, the Government is only trying to fulfill certain formalities required by the law. The PCR police stations do not have proper place. There is only a telephone facility. There is no vehicle facility. The PCR Unit itself is treated as an enslaved unit. For an emergency, they need to borrow vehicle from other departments. They cannot take any immediate action. Owing to this, even when someone approaches them for immediate help, the police tend to say, "You may go now, we shall see tomorrow".

The PCR police officials do not go to the village to find out whether untouchability is practised there or not. Generally, when a villager gives a complaint, the police ask: "How much is the distance from here to your village. When we say "about 25 km", he asks for Rs.500/- under the pretext that his vehicle is not in order and therefore it has to be hired" or he would say that he does not have money also to buy petrol. When the victims manages to give him Rs.500/-, the police meet the accused and collect money from them also. When we go back to the police, they say, "There is no such incident of untouchability or atrocity. If you don't believe us, let this be investigated by the DYSP and only after his investigation FIR can be filed". In this manner, the police are only trying to delay the registration of the case.

11. *How useful is the provision of Special Court for the Dalits?*

Each district is supposed to have a Special Court as per the POA Act. But we have a Special Court in Madurai for eight districts. Suppose there is an atrocity in a far away place – Thirunelveli, how much of money do the victims have to spend meeting their travel and other expenses and doing the follow up from such a distant place? Though the Act has provisions of allowance for travel, food, medical care both for the victims and their witnesses, it is hardly implemented in any Court. So, the victims, after travelling to the Court once or twice, are forced indirectly to give up the case. In fact, it is a loss for the petitioner going through these tiresome legal procedures. Since the caste Hindus are, to some extent, afraid of this Act, the Dalits want to register cases under this Act. Otherwise, there is nothing special about the Special Court.

The Special Public Prosecutors (SPP) in the Special Court does not even have a decent table and chair though the Public Prosecutor for the general cases have single room and enjoy better facilities and treatment. The office of the SPP is not a safe place to keep any important documents. The office of the SPP itself looks like an oppressed place.

Initially, no one used to come to me. Whenever they came to me, they used to tell me, "The police do not take any action even after 3 or 4 days of filing a petition". Only then we intervene. Their petition is usually written very generally. The Dalits do not know how to write a petition. Only those who are part of NGOs and Associations write petitions properly. The police always try to find out some gaps in the petitions, and instead of registering them all under the POA Act, they convert every serious case as an ordinary case. The police are supposed to know from the victims in detail as to how the atrocity took place and who were all involved in the process, and file the FIR accordingly. But the police do not bother to register the case under the POA Act. Their aim is always to brush aside the case. They are not for punishing the accused. Only when we intervene and resort to protest and road blockades, they file the FIR. Even when we manage to register the case under the POA Act, the police close it down when they frame the charge sheet. In this way, those officers who are responsible for implementing this Act do not do their duty earnestly.

The Act is very good. But the implementing authorities – the police and even the Court – do not actually want to implement it. So most cases end in acquittal. Therefore the law is not of much use.

12. *If this law is of no use to the Dalits, why do the non-Dalits want it to be withdrawn?*

There is nothing to lose for the non-Dalits on account this law. You hardly see any non-Dalits being booked under this law or having changed his attitude towards the SCs. The non-Dalits oppose this law not because they meet with a check, but because it helps to control their supremacy over the Dalits and their discriminatory attitude towards the SCs. No doubt, there is merit in these laws. But unless those in charge of implementing them perform their duties earnestly, the laws cannot deliver the desired results. Only the Government can bring this change and this is the duty of the Government.

Highlights of Responses

1. The PCR and POA Acts are only for protecting the basic human rights of the Dalits as articulated by the Human Rights Organizations. They are not for suppressing the rights of any caste or community as alleged.
2. In Tamil Nadu, those overtly involved in oppressing others are basically three ruling or dominant castes viz., Marvars, Kallars and Ahamudayars, not the Brahmins.
3. These dominant backward castes force the Dalits to carry on their unpaid or underpaid traditional duties to maintain their caste superiority. Those challenging such unjust demands are met with dire consequences.

4. With the view to maintaining their caste supremacy, the dominant castes resort to even stealing the assets of Dalits and thereby make them economically dependent.
5. Despite blatant violation of their basic human rights and dignity, the Dalits do not take up the matter with the police, fearing dire consequences from the accused. They fear because they are not only economically dependent on the caste Hindus, but also numerically the minority in villages.
6. The POA Act is a good protective mechanism for the Dalits. It is due to this law, there is now fear among the caste Hindus who would otherwise not hesitate to attack and oppress the Dalits the way they want.
7. Though most of the Dalits are not even aware of these laws, and among those who are aware of them do not have the courage to use them, the caste Hindus allege that the Dalits misuse these laws by filing false cases.
8. If at all there were false cases, those might be the ones, which were forced upon the Dalits by one caste Hindu against another. The worst sufferers in all these cases are the Dalits, and the root cause of all such cases is the caste Hindus.
9. The Police have not been sincere when it comes to the case of caste discrimination or atrocity against Dalits. In general, they never consider these issues seriously and often do not register such cases.
10. The Dalit victims have to have the support of NGOs and fellow caste leaders to get their cases registered under the PCR or POA Act.
11. Most of the police personnel coming from the backward caste background in general support their fellow caste people accused of crimes against Dalits in the following ways:
    - They either delay or do not register the case at all. Even if a case is registered, they do not investigate the case properly. Instead, they only threaten the complainant and mislead them.
    - Though required, the police seldom give receipt to the victim after registering his case. Not knowing its importance, the victim often fails to collect the receipt from the police after filing the FIR.

- The Police always try to find out some gaps in the petitions and convert every serious case due to be registered under the POA Act into an ordinary case and thereby enable the accused to escape due punishment.
- The Police register cases under inappropriate sections and lessen the severity of the case. By doing so, the accused is protected from severe punishment and the victims do not get the due compensation.
- They close the FIR just at the instance of anyone telling them that the case under reference is a false one, without really verifying the case in detail.
- Though it is the duty of police, they do not bother to produce the witnesses before the Court in time.
- They extract money from the victims to pursue the case, and from the accused to acquit or settle the case out of Court. Bribing is prevalent at every stage of the case.
- The police and the accused caste Hindus work in league with each other for delaying the registration of cases under the POA Act.
- They overtly promise the accused that they would charge sheet the case in such a way that the case would automatically be acquitted.

12. Though the POA Act has provisions to punish the police who do not perform their lawful duties and violate the provisions of the Act, it is practically not possible since most of them belong to the caste Hindus and politically connected.
13. Though each district is supposed to have a Special Court, in the case of southern Tamil Nadu there is only one Special Court (at Madurai) for seven districts. Due to this, the victims and their witnesses, in particular, who are mostly economically poor are subjected to enormous financial hardship and physical harassment, besides the anxiety they undergo in the process.
14. Even the Court is not free from caste prejudice. Being members of upper castes, most of the judges and advocates themselves approach the accused and suggest as to what should they do to get their cases acquitted.

Recommendations

1. The PCR police stations do not often have the minimum infrastructure facilities such as a proper office room and vehicles, and money to maintain them. The Government, by giving no importance to these police stations, only seems to be fulfilling the mandatory requirements. Thus due importance is to be given to these police stations by providing at least the basic necessities such as proper office and vehicle.
2. Though the POA Act has the provisions of allowance for food, travel and medical care both for the victims and their witnesses, it is hardly implemented. The victims themselves meet all these expenses. Therefore, filing a case under the POA Act is often considered a financial loss for the victim. Therefore, due allowances should be easily accessible and made available timely to the victims and their witnesses.
3. The Special Public Prosecutor (Madurai) in charge of scrutinizing the POA Act cases did not even have a decent table and chair in his office. Therefore such officers may be provided with necessary infrastructure facilities.
4. There were instances in which the provisions of the POA Act were violated within the Court itself by the staff themselves. This puts the credibility of the Court at stake. This is a serious matter to be attended on a priority basis. Judges and Court staff may be sensitised on issues concerning the Dalits.
5. The Dalits in general are not even aware of the POA Act. The government has not made a sincere effort in letting the people in general and the Dalits in particular know these Acts and their various provisions. Therefore, the Government may initiate special programmes to make people aware of such laws and their uses.
6. The Government is yet to demonstrate to the people the power and benefit of the POA Act, since there has hardly been any conviction under this Act. So the act may be implemented earnestly, and the guilty punished without delay.

Views of NGO (2)

Mr. Gyanaprabu, President, Ambedkar-Immaual Mandram (NGO). The following are his responses to various questions posed to him:

1. *Why and how do the cases registered under the PCR and POA Acts often get acquitted?*

The SCs' economic backwardness drives them not only against their caste interest, but also against their individual interests. Meenakshipuram *"rape with murder"* case failed because of the internal fight among those who took up the case with regard to the sharing the money given as compensation as per the provisions of the POA Act. One of the witnesses turned against the other, as he was not sure of getting his share of the compensation money. He therefore accepted bribe and favoured the accused. That is why the case failed. The victim's husband ran away with the compensation money. Why should others spend their money and go to the Court several times? The SC people are not aware that according to the Act the witnesses are entitled for TA and food allowances. The Police also do not share this information with the victims in this regard.

2. *Why most of the cases registered under the PCR/POA Acts turned out to be false?*

Most of the cases registered under these laws are not false cases as alleged. They cannot be false, since the POA Act is directly under the control of the Deputy Superintendent of Police (DYSP), and thus the cases registered under this Act are supposed to be investigated by the DYSP. In case there be any error or misreporting in the FIR, the DYSP is supposed to identify them and correct them at the investigation stage itself. If there is no merit in the case, the FIR cannot stand. Then, how can the registered cases be false cases?

Moreover, the Dalits cannot afford going to the police. They resort to this means only when they are really met with atrocities and discrimination. Many a time, they go to the police only when there was no hope of punishing the accused in any manner and only when there was no hope of countering any further attack.

They seek justice through this Act when all other possibilities are ruled out.

In most cases, the police themselves help the accused escape punishment sanctioned under the Act. They change sections and reduce the severity of the cases accepting bribe, say up to Rs. 10,000/- from the ruling caste/accused. The police themselves approach the APP (Assistant Public Prosecutor) and DYSP and plead saying, "Sir, nothing of that sort happened as reported. It is all false".

The police are responsible for most of the cases ending in acquittals. Even now, many police stations do not register cases under the POA Act deliberately. The entire case is in the hands of police. If they want, they can punish the accused.

Most of the cases filed by the people of Arundhadhiar caste (one of the SCs) end up in acquittal as these people can not take each case to its logical end owing to their economic backwardness and lack of muscle powers which are most essential to pursue any such cases. They cannot afford filing cases against the caste Hindus as they are mostly landless and depend entirely on the caste Hindus for their livelihood. However, the Pallars and Parayars are relatively stronger and are not afraid of any dire consequences since they are not only landowners but also large in number and better organised.

Wherever the Dalits and Dalit organisations are strong, the PCR and POA Acts are better implemented. In other places, the Dalits cannot bring pressure on the police to implement these Acts.

The POA Act is very useful. The ruling dominant caste people are afraid of attacking the Dalits because of this Act. The Act has developed a sense of fear in the minds of the caste Hindus.

Views of NGO (3)

Mr. Sundarajan, President, Arundhadhiyar Association, Periya Vallikulam. The following are his responses to various questions posed to him:

1. *As a person who took up the case, could you narrate the incident of atrocity meted out to Mr. Palpandi?*

A few caste Hindus took Palpandi, a member of Chakiliyar caste (Arundhadhiar), to a nearby town for a political meeting. But after the meeting they left him there without giving him even bus fare. Somehow, Palpandi came back to his village. He then asked the Caste Hindus as to why they did so. Just for this reason, the caste Hindus abused him, *Yennada Chakiliya payala, chattham botu pesure* (how dare you – Chakiliyan – low caste fellow talking in loud voice). Palpandi was then tied up with a street lamp-post and beaten up by the entire village people. Instead of Palpandi and his people, the Caste Hindus first gave information to the police saying that Palpandi abused everyone indiscriminately after having been heavily drunk, and due to which they had to tie him up with the lamp-post. Those who beat him up belonged to the same political party whose political meeting Palpandi was taken to attend. After this complaint by the Caste Hindus, the police came to the spot on the same day and untied him and took him to the police station. A few members including myself, and those who beat him up were asked to come to the police station. The police asked me, a leader of the Arundhadiyar caste as to how he would like to resolve the case.

At the police station, the police suggested, "This is a problem of your village and therefore better to settle it within the village amicably. After all tomorrow you all have to face each other". The police then asked my opinion. I replied, "More than mine, the opinion of the victims who had been beaten in the most inhuman manner and made unconscious should be taken into consideration. Moreover, whatever the law says in such cases, you please follow the same". In response, the accused caste Hindus present there, threatened me in front of police officer, saying, "In our village we have already taken a decision. You tell all your caste fellows". After this threat, there was no scope for me to say anything more, because in almost all villages the Chakiliyars are at the bottom even economically. They entirely depend on the caste Hindus for livelihood. They are ignorant and afraid of others. They do not have the courage to protest against the caste Hindus, and therefore often remain timid.

Owing to this atrocity, Palpandi was bed ridden for 34 days. The concerned DYSP instead of punishing the accused filed a case against the victim (Palpandi) himself. Then the DYSP met me and asked to withdraw the case on the ground that there would be none to stand as witness for the victims. The case was first filed under IPC. We, as leaders, demanded to register the case under POA Act. The police, instead of taking immediate action indirectly supported the accused caste Hindus. The caste Hindus were therefore not afraid of any possible police action against them. The police in a way suggested the accused the ways and means of escaping due legal action against them.

Since we kept on protesting, the police finally filed the case under the POA Act. The victim got Rs. 6000/- as compensation. But the accused was left unpunished. Though the victims sought to protest against such crimes, they could not express it due to threat of dire consequences of loosing their daily wage, employment and other means of livelihood and also of subjecting their family members to the risk of their life itself.

The PCR Act is nothing. The caste Hindus are never afraid of it. But the POA Act is relatively a better legal protection since it drags the accused caste Hindus to the police station and the Court. However, this act is not protecting us fully since the police feel more for the caste Hindus. They scare the victims saying that they would no more give them jobs and wages, but all possible hardship to their family whenever the latter would insist on registering a case under the POA Act. The police, as said before, suggest ways for the caste Hindus to escape legal actions. Even in this computer age, untouchability is so much rampant in villages. The officers are also against us. The society is also against us. Our caste people are in fact going backward.

2. *Do the Dalit police officers take prompt action against the accused?*

The Dalit officers can of course take action. But the caste Hindus often accuse their action of bias. The caste Hindus often get them transferred to other police stations. Moreover, their immediate higher-level officers do not let them perform their lawful duties. They are harassed in very many ways in the police station itself.

Though the Act has provisions for punishing the guilty, they have not been applied effectively and earnestly. The Government may claim that the Dalits have all facilities and legal protections. But actually these are not implemented properly and the Dalits have not benefited from them. Though the Government officers are aware of this fact, they pretend as if they were unaware of this reality. They indeed do not have the concern for the development of the Dalits. Even after 50 years of independence, these Acts have not been of much use to the Dalits. Among the Dalits, only those few who can manage their own economic needs, can assert their self-respect and dignity. But their own people discourage even these individuals since such assertion would antagonize caste Hindus who in turn would render many others jobless. Not many have benefited from these laws in villages.

3. *It is alleged that the Dalits misuse these Acts by filing false cases against the caste Hindus. Do you agree?*

This accusation is based on false assumption. First of all, do the Dalits have the courage to use and misuse these Acts? The reality is that they do not even open their mouth when inhuman atrocities are committed against them. The fact is that the caste Hindus do not much like these laws in favour of Dalits. The caste Hindus feel that it is because of such laws that they are sometimes taken to the police station and also to the Court. They therefore do not like this law to continue. The Dalits neither have the courage to misuse the law nor are allowed to do so. The Act is like an unsharpened knife. It is a good Act. It has created fear to some extent in the minds of the caste Hindus. If this Act is withdrawn, then the Dalits will be doomed. The POA Act is a weapon, which can be used for self-defense.

The basic problem faced by the Dalits is their economic dependence on the caste Hindus. Once they are made economically independent, the caste Hindus will also come to know, over a period of time, the worth of the Dalits. If the Dalits are mindful of their self-respect and dignity at this stage, their family will suffer. But there is no escape. The benefits of all the efforts of Government are in fact eaten away by the middlemen. If the Dalits get these economic benefits and become economically independent, the scope for committing atrocities on Dalits will be very much lessened.

Highlights of Responses

1. The Dalits/SCs were used by the caste Hindus for their political interests and ignored later on.
2. As a strategy to escape legal action, the caste Hindus, who had beaten the Dalits, informed the police first as if the Dalits had beaten them.
3. The police, who had come to the spot and witnessed the crimes committed against the Dalits, filed a case against the victims instead of punishing the accused.
4. The police did so to compel the victim to withdraw the POA Act case filed against the accused.
5. NGOs and SC leaders had to resort to pressuring the police to register the case under the POA Act.
6. By not taking immediate action, the police indirectly supported the accused. They also suggested to the accused ways of escaping punishment under the POA Act.
7. The POA Act is more powerful than the PCR Act.
8. The SC police officers can take prompt action against the accused. But they are not allowed to take such action. Their actions are often labeled as biased.
9. Though the SCs have laws to protect their interests, these laws have not been implemented earnestly.
10. Only those SCs who can manage their economic needs on their own can use these laws and assert their self-respect and dignity.
11. The SCs have no courage to misuse these laws as alleged, and they are also not allowed to do so.
12. The POA Act is like a weapon, which can be used for self-defense.
13. The basic problem with the SCs is their dependence on the caste Hindus for their livelihood. In such a condition if they assert their self-respect and dignity, their family will also suffer.

Views of a Common Man (1)

Mr. Subbaiah, Maraiyur, Narikudi Union, Virudhunagar District.

1. *Could you share your experiences with regard to the use and abuse of the PCR/POA Act?*

There are number of practices of untouchability in our village (Maraiyur). Out of the 48 Panchayats of Narikudi Union in the Virudhunagar district, in about 98 per cent of villages untouchability is practised. I can prove and show to anyone interested. In our village *thundu glass* (separate glass) system is observed in tea stalls even today. The Pallars have been provided with separate glasses. The same system is observed for the Parayar and Chakkiliyar caste people. We have been prevented from wearing slippers while walking through our village areas. Even when they carry a heavy load of water pots, our women have to go round the village. They have no access to walk through our village streets. We do not have the freedom to fetch water from the mini-well dug in the nearby river. We have to stand away from the well and use only the *ahappai* (a big serving spoon made out of coconut shell with a long bamboo handle) to scoop up water from the well, whereas the caste Hindu women can directly fetch water from the mini-well using either their tumblers or mugs. We have no access to enter into our village temple. To put an end to all these practices of discrimination, we filed a case under the PCR Act.

The police officers concerned came to the spot and conducted inquiry. But the caste Hindus of the village, using their money and muscle powers, prevented the police from taking any drastic action due under the law. Though the tea-stalls remained closed for three days, it was reopened on the fourth day onwards, the status quo was maintained. The only result of going to the police is that I am harassed, threatened and pressurized to leave the village. When I went to the SI requesting to give protection to my life, he said, "you are educated and your plea is valid. But if we take action against the caste Hindus, they would attack most of your caste people who depend on them even for their basic needs such as food. The caste Hindus are economically powerful, politically influential and have the support of Government officials at higher levels. In such a situation, if we take action against them, it will only affect your interests. How can we take action against them?" No action, since then.

2. *What are your comments on the need of such laws?*

Though these laws are very useful in protecting the interests of the SCs, making use of them is difficult and also costly. The custodians of these laws do not have the will to implement it. And those trying to seek protection under these laws are harassed, faced with dire consequences. And they have to spend lot of money from their pockets. I wasted so much of money trying to take the case to its logical end. I have become like a beggar. I am now left with no money to carry on the case further. If I had filed the case under the POA Act, at least I would have got some amount of financial compensation. The POA Act is better than the PCR Act.

To implement this law effectively by the police, the political leaders should extend their support. On the contrary, the political leaders belonging to the caste Hindus themselves commit worst forms of atrocities against the SCs. Even when the local police take right action, the senior police officials under the influence of the political leaders twist the entire case upside-down as desired by the accused. And the case is ultimately acquitted.

The allegation that the SCs misuse these laws is totally false. If they have developed such courage to harass the caste Hindus by misusing these laws, they, in fact, do not need such laws. But this is not the present situation. Those believing so, may come to me and I shall show how the caste Hindus commit atrocities against the SCs. The SCs in our areas do not even have the courage to use this law in any way.

Yet this law is a must. It is with the help of this law, the SCs are able to protect themselves to some extent. Unless the SCs are made economically independent, they cannot develop the courage to use such protective laws to protect themselves from the oppressive caste Hindus.

Highlights of Responses

1. In about 98 per cent of villages of the 48 Panchayat Unions of Virudhunagar District, untouchability is practised. Such practices include separate cup/glass system in tea-stalls, denial of access to common path, common well and entry into the village temple.
2. The end result of filing cases under the special laws for justice is harassment, threat to their stay in the village and their very life itself.
3. The police advised the victim not to pursue the case filed under the PCR Act. The police argued that such a move would affect the victims' interest further, since the Dalits often depend on the caste Hindus both for their livelihood and physical protection. Though the PCR and POA Acts are good, it is difficult to use them, since it costs lots of money, which the victims cannot afford.
4. POA Act is better than the PCR Act.
5. To implement these laws effectively the political leaders should refrain from interfering.
6. The SCs misusing the POA Act is a false allegation. If they had developed such courage, these laws would not even be needed.

Views of a Common Man (2)

Mr. Periyasamy Thevar, Karisalkulam village, Virudhunagar district.

Periyasamy Thevar belonged to one of the dominant backward castes known as Maravar, popularly known as Thevar in Tamil Nadu. The following are the direct English translation of his responses in Tamil to a few questions on the use and abuse of PCR and POA Acts.*

---

* To make his responses presentable, most of the filthy words and abusive phrases that he had used to express his anger towards the SCs and the two special Acts on the one hand and towards the police implementing these Acts on the other have been avoided here.

1. *You are aware of the PCR Act. What is your opinion on the Act?*

The PCR Act is nothing. There is nothing great about it. It is nothing but an eyewash by the Government to woo the Dalits and to keep them merely as vote banks. What can the Government do to us with these laws?

2. *It is said that the Dalits file cases under these Acts against the caste Hindus mainly to threaten the latter. Is it true?*

Whenever we (the caste Hindus)) fight among ourselves, we immediately abuse each other as *son of Pallan/Parayan/ Chalakiliyan*. We also abuse each other commenting on each other's dress saying *you have dressed up like the Pallan/Parayan/ Chakkilyan*. While abusing our women, we say, *you look like a Para chirukki/Palla chirukki* (This means that women of these castes are immoral or loose character easily available for the upper caste men's lust for sex). We use these phrases as abusive words without any hesitation as we are so used to it. Just for using these words these Pallan caste fellows register case against us under these Acts and drag us to the police station.

As far as I know, in the Virudhunagar Special PCR police station alone, there may be about 2000 petitions (PCR Cases) against us. But we finish such cases bribing the police concerned with just Rs.500/-.(Earlier, if we take stick to fight, they (SCs) also do the same. If we take *aruval* (Sackle), they also do the same). But if we abuse them in the name of their caste, we just have to spend Rs.500/-. And the SCs cannot do anything to us with their laws. In fact, other laws are more powerful.

When we go on procession under the banner of *Thevar Peravai* (Thevar Association), we abuse them (SCs) saying that the Pallans and Parayans are children of bastards and prostitutes, and we challenge them to confront us. None can do anything to us. The SP (Superintendent of Police) himself stands for our protection when we go in vans and lorries in large numbers to Pasumpon (the birth place of their leader Mr. Muthuramalngam) to celebrate the birth anniversary of our leader. What could the police pluck? They just talk big of the SC/ST Act. No Act can pluck anything from us.

3. *Your leaders have been trying to remove this Act. Why?*

That is for political reasons, and to somehow get the votes of all our castes (of caste Hindus, particularly of the Thevars). Our fellows do not even know what the SC/ST Act is, because no FIR is filed under this Act. You may ask whether a single FIR is lodged under this Act in Vinudhunagar district. It (the PCR Wing of the police) is like the liquor prohibition department. They (police) come in their vehicle to collect their *maamool* (bribe). We are not at all affected by this Act. But even then, this Act has to be removed. Like the Muslims having separate laws, the Pallans, Parayans and Chalakiliyans also have an Act. Such Acts should not be there.

4. *You are a well-known person in this area. You know the happenings in the country. Please tell me whether untouchability is still practised?*

Eagle is always eagle and crow is always crow. These two cannot be equals. Can Tiger and Cat be equals? These people (SCs) simply make noise in the crowd. Can they come to our village with slippers? Can they first of all sit and have tea in our tea stalls? Can they first of all have tea in our village? Can they have tea in glass instead of *Château* (coconut shell)? In this Virudhnagar district, can you walk with slippers identifying your self as Pallan or Parayan or Chalakiliyan? Can you go there with towel on your shoulder? If our people come to know that you are a Dalit SC person, your pant and shirt will be removed; they will beat you, abuse you saying *"Yennada Pallapayale, yennada Parapayale, yennada Chakkiliya punda mayane"* (all abuses). What can you do? What case? Let them give the case to the police. We will give Rs. 500/- to the police and the case will be withdrawn. After all, that S.I. (Sub-Inspector) has to work there. Why we have our own MLAs? Why then we have our MPs? What for our officers are there?

These laws, whether they exist or not, make no difference to us. These Acts are there for the police just to go around and collect money and eat. Actually, we are not at all afraid of these laws. Even for them (SC/ST), these are of no use. These are just eyewash; meant to get their votes. For getting the SC/ST votes political leaders like Nehru, Indira Gandhi, Rajiv Gandhi and Kamarajar kept telling them that there are special laws, which they extend for every 10 years, 11 years. Vajpayee (Prime Minister) also did the same. They say that they belong to RSS, this and that. From Advani to all MPs say that they do not like the SCs. But after getting our votes, they give preference only to SCs. This Karunanidhi also does the same.

5. *They (Dalits) say that they need such laws? What is your opinion on this?*

Let them ask whatever they want. Who gives them? They shout for reservation. Who is going to hear them? Which Government is going to listen to them? No government will listen to them. Sometimes, the Government simply allows them to organise a fast, organise a procession and also sends a few CID persons as they send to our meetings. That is all. These Pallans, now I say, cannot improve even after 100 years. They have to remain like (abuses here) our slippers only. Definitely, the SCs are our slaves only. Let any Government come to power, let them also enact another law, let even military rule come, all these do not matter to us. We have decided to keep them the way they are. We have money. We have strength. We have all MLAs. So the Pallans and Parayans have to remain like this only. These SC/ST Act cannot be useful even to *'pluck our hair'*. It may be a big thing for them. They can give petition in the police stations saying that have been abused as Pallan, Parayan and Chalakiliyan. They can give in writing. That is all. Indeed, we are happy that the fact that we abused them is being recorded. Which S.I. has arrested us so far? For this, there is DYSP also (abuses here).

Let me now abuse the SCs. We abuse them using loud speakers when we go on a procession every year for the *Pasumpon Muthuramalinga Thevar Guru Pujai.* Be it IG or DIG – they all stand for our security. Let these sons of..... (abuses) come and arrest us. Has the Government not heard that we abuse the SCs? Has the SP not heard of it or have not all those police standing in line heard of it? Have the reserve police not heard of it? They bring 2000 to 4000 police. Last time Kalaignar Karunanidhi (Chief Minister of Tamil Nadu) sent police even in aeroplane for our security. We went all the way abusing them (SCs). We stopped at every village and abused the SCs over there using our loud speakers. We challenged them saying, *you bastard*

Pallans. Which policemen questioned us? They (Police) only chased them (SCs) off. Can they chase our van or us? Can't they book us under the SC/ST Act? We have also made video recording of the whole procession. Let them book us under this Act, at least by using these video taps. They will not do that. So, there is absolutely no loss or problem to us due to this law.

You seem to be a good person. So you can ask about Thevars. We indulge in murder. We indulge in rape and looting and do anything we like. If the police can question us, we will uproot this Thevar Varkam (race) itself.

Highlights of Responses

1. The common man under reference does not seem to have any respect or regard for the PCR and POA Acts and for the police department in-charge of implementing these Acts.
2. He abused and challenged the police right from the level of Inspector General to simple police constable and claimed that his caste people are so powerful that none can book them under these Acts.
3. Whatever evidence the police department or the SCs may have, they cannot arrest his caste people under these laws.
4. To him, these laws cost nothing more than Rs.500/-, which is the usual bribe amount given to the police the moment an FIR is lodged against them under these laws.
5. He said the police officers, MLAs and MPs of his caste were there to support them in this regard.
6. The PCR wing of the police department is there only to collect bribe.
7. He very overtly expressed that the Thevar caste people will continue to keep the SCs under their feet.
8. The SCs have to serve them as slaves and the Scheduled Caste women are meant for them.
9. The PCR Act and the POA Act are nothing but an eyewash strategy adopted by different political parties to secure Dalit votes.
10. He claimed that these laws were of no use even to the SCs.
11. The Thevar caste people will continue to indulge in murdering and looting of SCs and raping the SC women. None could do any thing to them.

12. The Thevars are not at all afraid of these Acts and the police cannot challenge their dominance.

Summary

Though the conclusions emerged from the views of each respondent have already been presented under the sub title "Highlights of responses", the following are the consolidated summary of this chapter having for its focus on the views of police officials and others who play a pivotal role either in implementing or in preventing the implementation of the special laws, PCR Act and POA Act, effectively.

Mere presence of special laws alone cannot ensure protection to the SCs/Dalits in villages. The Dalits should have the required knowledge, capacity and courage to use these laws. The success of each case depends on the victims' cooperation with the police in the investigation process and their willingness to pursue the case to its logical end. But given their vulnerability arising out of their insignificant numerical strength in villages and their total economic dependence on the caste Hindus who are, in most cases, the accused, it is certainly difficult for the Dalits/SCs to muster up courage to invoke protection of these laws. With most of the witnesses turning hostile and thereby engendering the acquittal of those cases merely increase no doubt the vulnerability of the victims and their witnesses. It is in this regard the IGP (PCR), Chennai concluded that as long as the Dalits/SCs are economically poor and dependent on the caste Hindus for their livelihood, and as long as they live in small numbers in each village, they cannot protect themselves and assert their self-respect and dignity. It is therefore recommended that the numerically insignificant SC families in villages be shifted to those villages where their fellow caste members are in large numbers, and where there is no or a very limited scope for exploitation by the caste Hindus. The SC families may also be shifted to urban areas. The SC people may be educated to refrain from performing defiling, unpaid for or underpaid occupations such as sweeping, scavenging, disposing of dead cattle etc. They should be accommodated in more dignified jobs. The Government should initiate this process.

While some police officers considered working in PCR police station as blessing, others considered it as a curse in view of the kind of problems they had to face. While some police officers felt that the PCR and POA Acts had created a sense of fear among the non-SCs, and it was enough to maintain this fear to protect the SCs, others urged the need of its earnest implementation. Though the police in general claimed that they played a neutral role despite belonging to a different caste background, they are considered responsible, in one way or the other, for the acquittal of about 75 per cent of the PCR/POA Act cases, as maintained by the IGP (PCR), Chennai.

With regard to the percentage of false and true cases, different police officials gave different figures. According to the IGP (PCR), Chennai, out of the total number of reported cases, only about 33 to 35 per cent were false cases and the remaining 67 to 65 per cent cases were true cases, whereas the DYSP, Ramanathapuram asserted that as high as 60 per cent of cases were false cases and only about 40 per cent of cases were true. What may also be noted is the fact that neither the Dalits/SCs nor the police officials at the lower level were fully aware of the special provisions of these two special laws, particularly of the POA Act and their uses. The Government should make earnest efforts to create awareness among people in general and among the concerned officials in particular about these laws. More specifically, the police should be properly trained and guided to use these laws effectively.

In some of the Panchayat Unions of Virudhunagar district, practice of untouchability was prevalent in most of the villages. Such practices included separate cup/glass system in tea-stalls, denial of access to common path, common well and entry into the village temple. Despite such blatant violation of their basic human rights and dignity, the SCs did not take up the matter with the police fearing dire consequences from the accused and harassment by the police. Some of them even remarked that the end result of going to the police for justice was nothing but harassment and threat to their stay in the village and to their life itself. However, most of the victims and NGOs were of the view that in the absence of special laws such as the PCR and the POA

Acts, the SCs would have no security and their people might get killed on a day-to-day basis.

With regard to the importance and recognition given to those implementing these special laws, it is learnt that the district level PCR police stations were not equipped with necessary infrastructure facilities such as proper office and vehicles. Such offices did not even have a vehicle under their exclusive control to be of support to the SCs faced with threat and dire consequences in remote villages. The Special Public Prosecutor, who plays a crucial role in every PCR/POA Act case, said that his office does not have even the minimum necessities such as chairs and tables, and he was also not paid the due remuneration for months together.

With regard to the power of the two special laws, most of the victims said that the laws were of immense support to protect their dignity and human rights. While the State level police officials said that the laws were very useful and necessary ones, the district level officers said that they were draconian laws and thus their strict implementation would be difficult. The caste Hindu accused have different things to say. According to a common man, the caste Hindus were not afraid of the special laws; they had respect neither for the two special laws nor for the police officials implementing them. To him, the PCR wing of the police department was there only to collect money both from the accused and the victims. Regarding the reaction of the accused, the police argued that the accused often preferred out of Court settlement to avoid punishments and to escape the humiliation of facing trial in the Court. The victims often had to agree to such settlement owing to the fact that they depended on the accused and their fellow caste people for economic and physical security.

From the points of views of NGOs and other common men, even the Special Courts did not seem to be free from caste prejudice. They held that being the members of upper castes, most of the judges and advocates helped the accused covertly to escape punishment due under the laws. Though the POA Act has provisions for punishing the policemen and officers who fail to perform their lawful duties, the Honourable Court, instead of invoking those provisions of the special laws and punishing the police, often acquit the case. And the economically backward and dependent victims can neither challenge such policemen, nor pursue the case further.

In the present administrative structure of the office of PCR/HR, Chennai even its IGP does not have any control over the policemen of the local police station as having been put under the direct control of the local SP (law and order). At present, the SP (law and order) of the concerned district does the streamlining of investigation of the PCR/POA cases registered in the district. In view of enormous amount of other cases that the SP needs to look into, the investigation of PCR/POA cases may be entrusted exclusively to the concerned DYSP in the district. Streamlining of all such cases throughout Tamil Nadu should be left exclusively to the IGP (PCR/HR) at the state level with no or minimum interference from the DGP of the State. The IGP (PCR/HR) should be allowed to function independently with more exclusive powers. The PCR police station should function in a similar way the CID (civil supply) functions

To ensure just and fair treatment of every PCR/POA Act case, at least 50 per cent of the police officials investigating those cases should be from the SC/ST communities. Most importantly, of the two top police officials – IGP and ADGP who manage the PCR/HR Unit of the State, at least one should be from either Scheduled Caste or from Scheduled Tribe background.

Though the POA Act has provisions for allowance for food, travel and medical care both for the victims and their witnesses, it is hardly implemented. The TA/DA to the victims and their witness may be given in the Court itself. The Government has to take decision in this regard at the earliest.

In view of certain incidents where the provisions of the POA Act were violated within the Court by its own staff, the credibility of the Honourable Court has come to be doubted. Therefore the Court staff and others concerned including the Judges/Magistrates may be more sensitised to ensure justice to the Dalit victims and to win their confidence.

6

Legal Protection to Dalits

Contesting Views

This chapter primarily consolidates the findings emerged in chapters four and five, and arrives at logical conclusions with regard to: (1) the context in which the Dalits are generally subjected to caste discriminations and atrocities, and the context in which they seek protection and justice under the PCR and POA Acts; (2) the attitude of the police towards such victims; and (3) the various factors responsible for acquittal of most of the PCR and POA Act cases. The method adopted for arriving at logical conclusions is "content analysis" of the findings of chapter four, which focused on identifying the gaps in the prosecution process from the points of views of the victims and witnesses of the chosen 15 acquitted cases, and chapter five which focused on identifying the acquittal factors from the points of views of police and the Special Public Prosecutor, who are directly responsible for implementing these laws, and others. It may be noted that wherever a part of the text of previous chapters is reproduced here, the relevant page numbers have been mentioned then and there, with a view to enabling readers to refer back to the previous chapters.

(1) The Context

Before understanding the term *context,* which refers to the situation in which the Dalit victims resort to police protection and intervention and seek justice under the PCR and POA Acts from the points of views of victims, police and others, it is necessary to reiterate the point that to seek protection under the special laws, the victim or someone on behalf of the victim has to report the incident of caste discrimination or atrocity to the police concerned. But the reality, as noted earlier, is that most of such incidents go unreported owing to the victim's vulnerable socio-economic conditions. Therefore, the *context* examined here pertains only to the experiences of the victims and others related to the reported cases, and more specifically, to the experiences of those related to the chosen fifteen acquitted cases.

With regard to the context in which Dalit victims seek or do not seek police protection particularly under the special laws, chapter four concluded as follows:

> "The victims (SCs) – being mostly illiterate and ignorant of their constitutional rights and safeguards, particularly, the special laws such as the PCR Act and POA Act, being economically poor and therefore depend on those non-SC and ST community members who constitute most of those indulging in violent crimes against them and also practising untouchability, and being scattered over few families in each village and thus forced to depend on the caste Hindus for their safety and security – would never dare going to the police station to lodge complaints against caste Hindus under the PCR/POA Act, unless they are forced to do so" (p.124-5).

The above observation is indicative of not only the reasons for most Dalits not taking their complaint to the police, but also the factors that are to be taken into consideration while attempting to understand the *context.* More specifically the attempt here is to understand the context in terms of: (a) the nature of atrocity committed against the Dalits, and (b) the kind of support the Dalit victims wield to seek police protection under the special laws. Obviously, the Dalit victims – who are in most cases vulnerable both socially and economically – would seek police protection under the special laws only when the gravity of losses suffered and humiliation faced is much higher and beyond their tolerance level, and only when there is enough support for the same from fellow caste people and/or from NGOs and other sources.

To begin with, the context under reference may be understood by way of examining the chosen fifteen acquitted cases in terms of the nature of atrocities committed and indignities inflicted that lead the Dalit victims to seek protection under the special laws. Table 6.1, which is the result of a content analysis of information provided in Table 1 (Chapter 1), may be looked at for the purpose. In Table 6.1, the chosen 15 acquitted cases have been grouped into 8 categories on the basis of nature and magnitude of atrocities committed.

Table 6.1

Nature of Atrocities Committed Against the Chosen 15 Dalits Cases

S. No.	*Particulars*	*Case Numbers**	*Number of cases*
1	Dalit women raped and murdered, Dalit man murdered (loss of lives and dignity)	1, 2 & 3	3
2	Physical assault and threat to life	10 & 11	2
3	Land encroached (loss of livelihood)	4	1
4	Threat to government job and humiliation	14	1
5	Denial of rightful wage and occupation	7 & 8	2
6	Threat to livelihood and dignity with the denial of access to common path within and outside village premises	6 & 5	2
7	Public humiliation to Dalit government servant, and threat to life	12, 13 & 15	3
8	Denial of right to participate in religious festivals	9	1

*The case number is based on number given in Table 2.6 in Chapter 2.

As indicated in the table, the nature of atrocities is found to be not only extreme and serious but also inhuman. The atrocities ranges from *rape with murder* and *murder* to *threat to life, public humiliation* and *verbal abuses.* For instance the two cases of *rape with murder* (case No. 1 and 2) and one case of murder (case

No. 3) are cases of *loss of lives and dignity*. Case numbers 10 and 11 are no less serious as these are cases of *physical assault* and *threat to life*. Most other cases are primarily cases of *threat to livelihood and dignity,* and *public humiliation.* There was also a case of *threat to government job* and *harassment at work place* (case No. 14). Government job was not only prestigious but also the main source of income for Dalits, which no Dalit would give up. Denial of right to participate in religious festivals (case No. 9) was another major case, which the Dalit victims decided to address legally. Such offence was viewed as disrespect to their caste as a whole. On the whole Table 6.1 indicates that the nature and magnitude of losses suffered and humiliation experienced by the Dalit are such that none would be able to tolerate these. And therefore none would refrain from going to police seeking protection under the special laws.

The cases of public humiliation as indicated in the Table were taken very seriously in the study area. Though most of the victims of cases studied did not have the courage to take up such cases to the police, they were found to be very conscious of their self-respect and dignity. To take up cases to the police they often needed the support of more knowledgeable fellow caste members and NGOs. On the whole, Table 6.1 indicates that Dalits go to police and seek legal protection only for certain kinds of offences, particularly when the crimes committed, the losses suffered and humiliation experienced were of serious nature, against their self-respect and dignity, and also beyond their tolerance level.

To understand the *context* further, it is important to know as to what happens to many other cases of offences brought to the police for necessary action. Do all such cases get registered, charge sheeted and tried in the courts or not? The often-articulated answer to this vital question is "No". Such response raises number of questions: Is it because the offences brought to the police are not offences as per the special laws? Or is it because the police do not perceive them as offences though as per the law they are? Or is it because most of these cases are false?

Not so surprisingly, the very police who are in charge of implementing these laws do not consider certain offences such as discriminatory and derogatory remarks/abuses against Dalits as offences even though the special laws do consider them so. According to the Deputy Superintendent of Police (DYSP), the officer-in-charge of investigating POA Act cases in the district of Ramanathapuram:

> "Abusing Dalits in the name of their caste is not a common practice. This happens in certain situations: when the non-Dalits become emotional or angry and when they are in a drunken state. But in villages, the POA Act is used as a weapon; even such emotional outburst are not spared and cases are filed" (p. 160).

The above statement reveals in no uncertain terms that according to the DYSP abusing Dalits in the name of their caste is not an offence, though the POA Act perceives it so, and the abused also consider it as an insult and against their self respect and dignity. If the senior police officer like the DYSP himself does not consider *abusing Dalits in the name of their castes* as an offence, how and why would his subordinate police officers, who do the registration of most of the cases, consider it so? And if such were the understanding among the police, how would any Dalit have the courage to approach the police to register cases against those non-Dalits making derogatory remarks and committing atrocities against them?

At this stage, it is necessary to understand the *context* also in terms of the kind of support the victims wielded both from within and from outside their villages. Such support might have been either from their fellow caste people and leaders or from NGOs and other means, which would have helped them seek justice under the special laws. It may be recalled that out of the 15 cases examined for the present study, only in about 20 per cent cases (three cases: case No. 2, 10 and 14), the NGOs had played a major role in seeking protection under the special laws. In most other cases (about 80% of cases), the victims had approached the police on their own. Moreover, most of the offences studied here had taken place only in those villages which constituted a very less Dalit population and which were also located in an area predominantly inhabited by the dominant Backward Castes, and therefore there was hardly any scope for any Dalit from other villages coming forward to help the victims.

According to an approximate estimate of the IGP (PCR), on an average about 40 per cent Dalit victims approached the police to register cases under the special laws because they had the support of fellow caste people, and about 30 per cent of victims did so without such support. None of the two categories of victims, who together constituted about 70 per cent, had the support of NGOs to register their cases. The victims' lack of access to NGOs' support is further validated with the IGP's another observation: "only about 10 per cent victims got NGOs' support to struggle for their cause" (p.132-3).

Moreover, the Deputy Secretary to Government, Department of Adi Dravidar and Tribal Welfare, Tamil Nadu Ms. Sivagamy, I.A.S. said, "the NGOs often do not take up such issue (caste conflicts), but work mostly on other issues such as child labour, minimum wage etc." (p.135).

Even the Social Work profession, which trains professionals to work in NGOs, has not yet recognised such a problem as an issue of concern for the profession, and as an issue needing professional intervention (Ramaiah, 1998: 124-46). Despite the fact that even the Justice Krishna Iyer Committee had suggested that not only voluntary organizations (NGOs) but also Scheduled Caste Welfare Associations should be associated at every stage of a case of atrocity against Dalits purely as official body (Government of India, 1990: 7), the police do not recognise such organisations. It is due to such realities in the rural area, most of the victims of cases studied here had to struggle on their own through the tiresome investigation and trial processes without any support either from NGOs or from fellow caste people. And they had to go through such processes only to get defeated finally in the Court of law.

The IGP's yet another important observation was that about 20 per cent of cases reported under these special laws represent those cases where the Dalits were instigated and used by one non-Dalit against another (p.133). Though the percentage of such cases seems to be much lesser, particularly in view of some of the observations made by the victims and NGOs as discussed in Chapters 4 and 5, the fact to be reiterated here is that such cases were neither registered, nor charge-sheeted when registered. Moreover, no SC person, given his lack of economic, bureaucratic, and political supports, would ever dare filing false cases against the non-SCs, whom they depend on not only for their socio-economic sustenance, but also for physical security. What is also to be noted is that even in such instigated cases, the worst affected would be often the SC persons who are used by the non-SCs as scapegoats.

The above analysis makes one point further clear that mere presence of laws alone cannot protect the SCs. Presence of laws does not mean they would come to the rescue of the victims or the victims could easily make use of them. The police have a major role in making these laws accessible to the needy victims.

(2) The Police's Attitude towards Dalit Victims

It is evident from the views expressed in the previous chapters that (a) most of the incidents of caste discriminations and practices of untouchability remained unreported mainly due to the victims being scared of possible dire consequences from the accused, and the police's callous attitudes towards them; (b) majority of the cases taken to the police were not even registered but settled out of Court through negotiations between the concerned victims and accused, 'facilitated' by the police; (c) in India on an average about 24 per cent of the cases reported under the POA Act (during 1993-99) were closed after preliminary investigation, doubting the validity of these cases (referred cases); (d) though as high as about 76 per cent cases reported under the POA Act (during 1993-99) were considered true in the eyes of the police and accordingly, charge-sheeted (Table 2.4) and subsequently sent to courts for trial, yet most of the charge-sheeted cases (89.95% on an average during 1993-99) ended in acquittal, and (e) in this entire process beginning from the time an incident of offence was brought to the knowledge of the police and till the time the Court concerned made its final pronouncement on the matter, the victims are subjected to immense hardships of various nature, resulting in extreme form of anxiety in their minds. All these speak volumes of the plight of SC victims seeking justice under the special laws through the help of the police.

Victims' Views on Police Attitude

For an objective comparison of the views of victims and their witnesses with that of the police and others regarding the police attitude towards Dalit victims, the relevant major findings of chapter four may first be recalled (p. 125-6). On the whole these findings indicate that the responses of police towards them had neither been cordial nor encouraging.

1. The police in general did not give due importance to the complaints brought by the SC victims, even when it was a case of serious criminal offence.
2. Under some pretext or the other the police in most cases failed to arrest the accused as required by the POA Act. In one of the cases, the victims had to physically catch the accused and handed him over to the police.
3. The complainants often had to resort to public protest and sought the help of NGOs and local leaders to get their grievances registered under the PCR/POA Act.
4. Even when it was a case to be registered under the POA Act, the police registered it under the PCR Act with a view to helping the accused.
5. The police demanded money both from the victims for registering and pursuing the case, and from the accused for escaping punishment due under the laws.
6. Instead of supporting the victims, the police threatened them of dire consequences from the accused and discouraged them, indicating the difficulties in pursuing the case. They even filed counter cases against the victims who insisted on pursuing their cases.
7. Unless they were local leaders or representatives of any political party or committee, the SC victims in general felt afraid of going to the police, as the latter had often harassed them. They in general expressed that the police would cheat them.

The Police's Views on Police Attitude

Regarding the responses of the police towards the Dalits/SCs seeking protection under these special laws, the IGP (PCR/HR/CID), Chennai said as follows:

Though the police involved in the process of implementing special laws and investigating cases under these laws are from different caste background, they have to play a neutral role (p.144). However, he has also said, "... on an average in about 30 per cent cases, the victims are threatened in overt and covert forms and thereby discouraged from filing cases under these special laws" (p. 133).

The fact that the IGP said, "If people are like me in each and every police station, they will take appropriate action. But people are not so" (p. 138). "Even if 50 per cent of police officers are spirited and committed like me, untouchability can not exist; atrocity can not be there" (p.142). This observation of the IGP indicates clearly that even 50 per cent of the concerned police officers are not spirited and committed to implement these special laws earnestly, and that is why, perhaps, untouchability and atrocities continue unabated even now. It is only because of this perhaps, the IGP also said that out of the total number of acquitted cases, those ending in acquittal due to the 'kind of roles' the concerned police played constituted as high as 75 per cent (p.133).

The police's attitude towards the Dalit victims is evident also from their opinion on the extent of true and false cases registered under these special laws. It is interesting and revealing to know that the top level police officials dealing with PCR and POA Act cases differ from each other drastically in their opinion on this issue. According to the IGP (PCR), Chennai:

> "....out of the total number of reported cases, only about 33 to 35 per were false cases and the remaining 67 to 65 per cent cases were exactly true and genuine (p.135) whereas in the opinion of DYSP, Ramanathapuram as high as 60 per cent cases were false cases and only about 40 per cent cases were true (p. 162). But according to the then IGP (PCR) Maharashtra, most of the cases registered under the PCR/POA Act were true cases (p.156).

Though the caste Hindus alleged that the SCs misused the laws by filing false cases against them, the SC victims argued that the police in general refused to register their cases, and that they had to resort to protest, taking the support of NGOs and fellow caste leaders to get their cases registered under the special laws.

What may be recalled is the fact that most of the SCs were not even aware of these laws, and those being aware did not even have the courage to use them. Their fear is based on the fact that there were instances in which the police instead of supporting the victim filed counter cases against them taking money from the accused. These filed realities overtly endorse the observation of the IGP (PCR) Chennai and Maharashtra that "most of the cases" registered under the PCR/POA Act were true cases.

NGOs' Views on Police Attitude

Regarding the role of the police, one of the NGO representatives said as follows:

> "They (police) take money from the victims to pursue the case, and from the accused to acquit or settle the case out of Court. Bribing is prevalent at every stage of the case" (p.188).

It is worth recalling here a statement made by a police constable at the PCR Unit, Sivagangai town when the researcher was there to have a discussion with the Inspector over there. The constable said, "Sir, the *Thevars* (one of the Backward Castes known as *Maravar*) here are not at all bothered about these laws (PCR and POA Acts). They are not afraid of these laws". Another NGO representative stated:

> "In most cases, the police themselves enable the accused to escape punishment due under the Act. They change sections and thereby reduce the severity of the cases accepting bribe. The police themselves approach the APP...and plead for the accused" (p.191).

These statements are very much in agreement with the statement made by the IGP on the issue of the kinds of roles played by the police (refer the foregoing pages).

Others' Views on Police Attitude

The "Others' Views" represents here the views of the two Research Assistants and of common men. Referring to a case under study one of the Research Assistants involved in the process of data collection made the following points:

1. NGOs and SC leaders had to resort to protest to force the police register cases under the POA Act.
2. By not taking immediate action, the police indirectly supported the accused. They also suggested the accused ways to escape punishment due under the law.
3. Though the policeman came to the spot and witnessed the crime committed against the SC person, he filed a counter case against the victims instead of registering a case against the offender. By doing so, they forced the victim to withdraw the case (p.195).

Another Research Assistant (RA) who approached the Police Inspector at a local police station at Parthibanur town had a humiliating experience. When the RA met the concerned Inspector and requested for certain documents as directed by the Statistical Inspector, PCR Police station, Ramanathapuram the Inspector responded snobbishly:

> "You, you are going to do a study. First of all, tell me. I am a Thevar (by caste). Which caste do you belong to?"

The RA felt extremely humiliated. Yet, he replied to this unwarranted and undesirable question saying: "I belong to Scheduled Caste" (p.174).

Moreover, as stated before, when the DYSP himself did not consider the abusing of SCs in the name of their castes in discriminatory and derogatory terms as an offence under the PCR/POA Act, how and why would/should his subordinate police officials consider so? Therefore, it is more than obvious that the DYSP and most of his junior police officials did not give any importance to such cases, and would have also done everything possible to end such cases in acquittal. They would have referred most of such cases as false and invalid, and subsequently closed them all. Such an act on the part of the police is, at the first instance, in violation not only of the PCR/POA Act but also of basic human rights of these communities as citizens of India. The DYSP further said that though the practice of separate class system for the SCs in tea stalls is eliminated to a large extent, it is still practiced in some villages. It cannot be eliminated completely because the SC leaders are afraid of exposing those practising it (p. 162).

The point here is: If the SCs were afraid of exposing those practising untouchability in village tea stalls, it only reflects that the police in that area did not give them enough support and confidence to do so. If the police had taken prompt and proper action against the accused even once in that area trusting the information provided by the victims or assessing the validly of the complaint given, the offenders would have learnt a lesson. But the police, for reasons best known to them, seldom did so. And for the same reasons they seemed to be suspecting and doubting the validity of every case reported.

While discussing about the responses of the police towards the SCs seeking protection under the special laws, a common man belonging to caste Hindu (Maravar) said:

> "The PCR/POA Act is nothing but an eyewash to woo the SCs and to keep them merely as vote banks. With these Acts, the police could not do anything to the offenders" (p.198).

> "When we go on a procession under the banner of *Thevar Association,* we abuse them (SCs) saying that "the Pallans and Parayans (SCs) are children of bastards and prostitutes. None could do anything to us. The Superintendent of Police (SP) himself stands for our protection when we go to celebrate the birth anniversary of our leader. What could the police pluck from us?" (p.199).

> "Our fellows do not even know what the SC/ST Act is, because, no FIR is filed under this Act. They (police) come in their vehicle to collect their *maamool* (bribe). This law not at all affects us. But even then, this Act has to be removed"(p.199-200).

> "These people (SCs) simply make noise in the crowd. Can they come to our village with slippers? ...Can they have tea in glass instead of *cheratai* (coconut shell)".

> "In this Virudhunagar district, can you walk with slippers identifying yourself as Pallan or Parayan or Chakiliyan? Can you go there with towel on your shoulder? If our people come to know that you are a SC person, your pant and shirt will be removed; they will beat you and abuse you.... What can you do? What case?

> Let them give the case to the police. We will give Rs. 500/- to the police and the case will be withdrawn (meaning the police having accepted bribe would force the victim to withdraw the case). After all, the S.I. (Sub-Inspector) has to work there. Why do we have our own MLAs? Why have we our own MPs? What for our officers are there?" (p.200)

Regarding the police response or attitude, the common man further said:

> "These laws, whether they exist or not, make no difference to us. These laws are there just for the police to go around and collect money and eat" (p.200).

While sharing his experience in participating in the procession led by the Thevar Association, the common man said:

> "We went all the way abusing them (SCs). We stopped at every village and abused the SCs over there using our loud speakers. We challenged them saying 'You bastard Pallans'. Which policeman questioned us? They (police) only chased the SCs off. Can't they (police) chase our van or us? Can't they book us under the SC/ST (PA) Act? We have also made video recording of the whole procession. Let them book us under this Act at least by using these videotapes. They will not do that" (p.201-202).

The above narration of a common man belonging to *Maravar* caste and of others vividly portray the reality that majority of the police dealing with PCR/POA Act cases often do not respond positively to the SCs seeking justice under the special laws and do not give due importance to their grievances. This also portrays the biased mindset of majority of the caste Hindus against the SCs in Tamil Nadu.

This necessitates a specialised approach by committed and specially trained police force to curb effectively such inhuman behaviours and practices (abusing the SCs in the name of their castes and practising untouchability) prevailing among the non-SCs particularly in rural areas. Professional intervention is sought also to help, if not the entire non-SC/ST communities practising untouchability and committing atrocities against the SCs/STs, at least those police officials dealing with the PCR/POA Act cases at various levels are to rise above caste prejudice and to do justice to their profession. Only then, they, as custodians of laws, will be able to win the confidence of people in general and of the SCs and STs in particular.

(3) Factors Responsible for Acquittal

Effective implementation of the PCR and POA Acts has not been possible due to number of factors, resulting in acquittal of most of the cases registered under these laws. The attempt here is to bring to focus such factors under four broad categories: (a) gaps in the prosecution processes, i.e., from the stage of filing the FIR to the final pronouncement of judgement, (b) structural limitations leading to functional failures of the concerned police officials, (c) the inability of the police and (d) Judiciary dealing with untouchability and atrocity cases to function purely as professionals, transcending their primordial (caste and communal) loyalties and sentiments, and (e) the victims' inability to pursue their cases till their logical ends. A detailed discussion based on the views of different respondents has been attempted here for arriving at logical conclusions.

(a) Gaps or Failure in the Prosecution Processes

The effectiveness of any law depends on its implementation. It depends on the will of the implementing authority. It depends on how strict, meticulous and careful the concerned officials are in following the due procedure. In a situation where the accused is more powerful, every failure on the part of the prosecution and other officers in following the due and relevant procedure, becomes an opportunity for him to escape punishment due under the special laws. In most cases of untouchability or atrocity, the accused happen to be the powerful ones. Many a time, the accused happens to be those whom the victim depends on for his/her livelihood and physical protection. In such a state, obviously, the victim can not dare going against his own master. If he has to achieve justice, it then depends entirely on the sincerity of the police and other officials concerned in implementing the laws effectively. It also depends on the confidence that the police give to the victims to take up the case till its logical end. To examine how the police and other officials dealt with each of the chosen 15 acquitted cases and why they ended in acquittal, relevant portion of Chapter 4 may be looked into.

Table 6.2 gives the consolidated picture of the gaps and failures in the prosecution processes, which resulted in the acquittal of the chosen cases. The lack of will on the part of the law enforcing authority, particularly the police, is evident from the way in which the police responded to the victims. As listed in the table, even for serious violent crimes such as "rape with murder" and "murder" (Case No. 1, 2 and 3), the police refused to take proper and timely action. Every time the victims had to resort to public protest to make them take appropriate action. In case of Case No. 1 and 3, the police demanded money to pursue the case, and victims had no option but to yield to their demands. In all these cases, the witnesses were either bribed by the accused or threatened with dire consequences, but the police did not ensure them due protection. As a result, the witnesses could not give evidence in the Court of law, and hence the acquittal of these cases. The case No. 4 is a case of illegal occupation of Dalit land by the Muslim accused. The victim could not take control of his legitimate land despite having two judgements in his favour. It was reported that the police were bribed not to help the victims to reclaim his land. Instead, the police filed a counter case against the victims who sought their formal help to implement the Court's decision and get his due land back. The police played a vital role in getting the case acquitted by not sending the required document to the Court in time, as it happened in Case Nos. 6, 13 and 14. Cases get acquitted also due to delay on the part of the police in registration of cases without valid reasons, as was the case with Case Nos. 7, 8, 9, 13 and 14. It is most revealing that the accused of case No. 9 himself said that he could influence the Magistrate through money power and political connections to give judgement in his favour. The victim also confirmed the same.

Another way in which the prosecution fails is the manner in which the police tutor the witness and prepare him to depose the case effectively. For instance, in Case No. 8, the police tutored the witnesses in such way that their own statement, which was as per the suggestion and advice of the police, went against their interest, and subsequently the case got acquitted. Not only the police can change the fate the case by making certain changes

Table 6.2

Factors Responsible for Acquittal in PCR/POA Act Cases

Sl. No	*Nature of Offence*	*Acquittal Factors*
1	Rape with murder (1991)	(1) The police refused to register the case; (2) They filed case only after victims', NGOs' protest; (3) Accused was arrested only after being caught by victims; (4) Witnesses faced threat to life and fear of being chased away from village. (5) The police threatened and demanded money from victims.
2	Rape with murder (1996)	(1) The police registered the case only after victims & NGOs' public protest; (2) Main witnesses were bribed and threatened; (3) Witnesses did not come to the Court to give evidence.
3	Murder (1997)	(1) The accused accepted the offence in the police station; (2) Victim's brother & relatives were arrested & tortured for 11 days to be the guilty; (3) Witness could not depose the case properly due to threat to his and his family members' life; (4) The police had to be given money to pursue the case.
4.	Illegal occupation of land by Muslims (1999)	(1) Despite two favourable judgements the victim could not get his land; (2) When attempted again to get the land with the help of POA Act, the police filed counter case; Court verdicts not honoured by the police; and were bribed not to pursue the case.
5	Denial of access to common path (1998)	(1) Being poor could not pursue the case; (2) Accepted for a compromise as demanded by the accused
6	Denial of access to common path (1998)	The police did not send to the Court a few vital documents
7	Denial of due wage & discriminatory remarks (1992)	Judgement: (1) Delayed registration of case-due to the police; (2) The police gave no valid reason for the delay; (3) Witness being the caste person of accused, favoured the accused; (4) Benefit of doubt for the delay was given to the accused.
8	Stealing of SCs' fire-wood & attempt to assault with brooms (1991)	(1) Wrongly tutored by the police, the witness could not depose the case properly; (2) Delayed reporting caused doubt, benefit of doubt to accused

Contd...

Contd...

9	Denial of equal rights in religious festivals (1991)	(1) The police delayed the registration of case; no action against police; (2) Both victim and accused said that the latter could influence Magistrate through money power and political connections.
10	Physical assault and discriminatory remarks (1999)	(1) Error in FIR: wrong date of reporting; (2) the fact that the victim remained tied to the lamp post, and cow-dung mixture was poured on his head and tortured the whole night not recorded. (3) Money and muscle powers used; (4) Advocate of accused whom the victims too trusted got some documents signed by the complainants without letting them know what the documents meant for. (5) Though the policeman was witness to the incident, he did not stand as witness to the victims
11	Threat to life & discriminatory remarks for apprehending illegal fishing (1998)	Being poor and numerically a minority in village, accepted for compromise.
12	False allegation of attempting to assault a caste Hindu (1991)	Witness having accepted money from the accused and being the caste person of the accused turned hostile.
13	Discriminatory remarks (1991)	(1) Delayed reporting (because the dept. head did not take action against the accused in time); (2) The police did not produce the officer concerned in Court; (3) The police did not send relevant documents to the Court; (4) Witness was the neighbour and co-worker of the victims
14	Discrimination and harassment at work place (1999)	(1) Delay of 6 months in reporting; (2) Inspector and DYSP did not send vital documents to the Court; (3) Witness' statement was twisted by the typist of Court in favour of accused;
15	Attempt of murder and discriminatory remarks (1992)	(1) Victim himself said that he was not abused and there was no such incident at all; (2) Instead of probing the cause for his denial, the case was acquitted.

with regard to the nature of offences, date and time of incident, but the advocate of the accused can also influence the victims and get certain documents signed by them with or without their knowledge. This is what happened in the case of Case No. 10.

This is an act of clear violation of Section (2) (ii) of the POA Act. Though the police, when he had come to the rescue of the victim, witnessed the incident in which the victim remained tied to the lamp post, and cow-dung mixture had been poured on his head and tortured the whole night, he neither recorded these details in the FIR nor came forward to be the witness for the victims. The police's failure to produce the witnesses in Court of law on the specified date was also the factor responsible for the acquittal of cases. Case No. 13 is an ideal example in this regard. Despite the fact that the police have to play a vital role in ensuring justice to the Dalit victims by earnestly and effectively implementing these two special laws, they themselves have been found guilty of violating some of the provisions of the POA Act. More alarming is the fact that in the very Court itself, and that too in the presence of Magistrate, the witness's statement was twisted by the typist while typing out the statement to suit the interest of the accused. And it was with the help of such a twisted statement, the Case No. 14 was defeated. For more details regarding each case, refer to Chapter 4.

(b) Structural Limitations

The term "structure" here refers to the administrative structure of the office of the PCR/HR/SJ in charge of implementing and monitoring the PCR and POA Acts at the State, district and local levels. For a successful implementation of any law or a programme, there should be a well-defined administrative structure from top to local levels with exclusive powers and clear line of authority. For the purpose of implementation and monitoring of the two special laws in Tamil Nadu, there is a State level office at Chennai. This State level office is headed by the Additional Director General of Police (ADGP) and Inspector General of Police (IGP). Functioning under the supervision of these officers there are three Supervisory Squads, each headed by a Deputy Superintendent of Police (DYSP) with headquarters at Chennai, Trichy and Madurai respectively. And for covering all the 34 police districts of the State, there are 34 Mobile Squads each headed by an Inspector and also 34 Statistical Units each consisting of a Sub-Inspector and a Statistical Inspector (see Chapter 3).

Ironically, this structure has neither the police personnel in required numbers to reach out to the SCs and STs who are subjected to discriminations, harassment and atrocities, nor the scope and powers sufficient enough to enforce upon the local police officials (law and order) to reach out to such victims and to implement the PCR and POA Acts effectively. Yet, the ADGP and the IGP (PCR/Social Justice) with the support of their Supervisory Squads and Mobile Squads have been entrusted with the task of ensuring the safety and security of the SCs and STs. To this effect, every now and then, appropriate instructions and guidelines are issued to the SPs and Collectors at the district level whose primary concern is "law and order". Moreover, the ADGP and the IGP (PCR) function under the control of the Director General of Police (DGP) who is the head of the State police force and whose primary concern in the State is also "law and order". The DGP's direct involvement in the implementation of these two special laws is therefore bound to be limited. The concern for and commitment towards earnest implementation of the two special laws of other police officials who are under the direct control of the DGP, and whose primary concern is "law and order', is therefore likely to be limited. In such a structural arrangement, the implementation of the two special laws and the issues arising therein are bound to receive a half-hearted treatment at all levels, particularly when the implementation of these laws depends ultimately on the local level "law-and-order" police on whom the PCR Police officers have very limited (sometime no) administrative control.

Another anomaly arising out of the structural limitations of the PCR office is that when it comes to the investigation of PCR cases, no police officer below the rank of an Inspector is permitted to do that, but in the case of POA Act cases investigation is to be carried out by officers not below the rank of a DYSP. This difference of power vested in these two different investigating officers limits the scope and power of the officer who is the head of PCR office at the district level, and who is also in charge of implementation and monitoring of PCR and POA Acts. It is so because the officer is just a Police Inspector. For instance, the Police Inspector (PCR) can not put pressure beyond a point either on the Police Inspector (law and order) investigating PCR cases because the latter is on an equal rank, or on the DYSP investigating POA Act cases because the latter (DYSP) is above his level. More importantly, neither of these police officers are under the direct control PCR/HR/SJ police officials. As stated before, the DYSP is under the control of the concerned district level SP (law and order) and not under the control of IGP or ADGP (PCR/SJ).

In such a difference of power relations between the PCR police officers and the law and order police officers, where the latter enjoy more power and have direct control over the local police, who often end up investigating most of the PCR and POA Act cases (owing mainly to their physical proximity to the place of incident of atrocity), the role of the office of PCR or the Inspector (PCR) in the effective implementation of PCR and POA Acts at the district level becomes very limited. Often it is limited only to registering cases and maintaining records of cases reported and cases disposed.

The half-hearted treatment given to PCR office in general and the PCR cases in particular is reflected also by the fact that in most districts the office of PCR unit did not even have a proper office. For instance in Ramanathapuram district, at the time of this study, the PCR Unit office had been functioning from a vehicle shed, despite being located next to the office of the SP in the district town. Another observation to be recalled is that whenever vehicle was needed in the office of the district Mobile Squad (PCR) to reach out to the spot of atrocity, it was not available, though the sixth annual report on the POA Act claims that each Mobile Squad in Tamil Nadu has been provided with a jeep and a driver (Government of India, 1999:46). Perhaps this is one of the reasons why the Dalit victims and the NGOs which took up their cause maintained that the police in the Ramanathapuram district PCR office asked for money whenever the victims wanted the police's presence at the place of incident of atrocity. They said that the PCR police asked money from the victims under the pretext that it was needed either for filling petrol into their vehicle or for hiring a vehicle to reach the place of incident (p.184-185). In this regard what the IGP (PCR) had said may be worth noting:

"Vehicle cannot be provided immediately, because it is under the control of the SP (man-power). Presently, vehicles, their maintenance and man-power are under the control of the SP. I am not controlling them though I get the pay and allowance, and I get funds from the Government" (p.139-140).

The IGP's helplessness in enforcing the PCR and POA Acts with the help of local police who are under the control of the district level SP (law and order) is evident also from his another statement:

"the IGP can not control even the Sub-Inspector of a local police station, because they are posted by the SP and the SP is posted by the DIG. For the DYSPs and SPs (law and order), the DIG is everything" (p.142).

Another limitation with the present structure of the PCR office is, as argued, that the law and order police officers are unable to give due importance to the PCR/POA Act cases as they have too little time at their disposal for this purpose. They often seem to be preoccupied with resolving law and order problems. According to the IGP (PCR):

"Implementation of the PCR and POA Acts should not be left to the law and order police who are already burdened with general cases" (p.142). "Since the Sub-Divisional Officer (DYSP) has many other responsibilities and work, he cannot give due importance to the PCR cases. The SP finds it difficult to spare even five minutes in a month for the PCR cases. As a result, he is unable to review the cases in depth and unable to finalise any proceedings. But we are not like that. We, our officers, now review each and every case in depth. But my DGP thinks that I (IGP) cannot do that work. But I can" (p.140).

To overcome this limitation, the IGP suggested that all such cases should be investigated only by a specialised agency namely the office of the IGP (PCR/SJ).

The then IGP (PCR), Maharashtra Mr. T.K. Chaudhary also expressed similar concern. He said, "The PCR branch itself should investigate PCR cases as they are not involved in resolving law and order problems". He further said, "The Chief

Minister of Maharashtra is keen to have a separate investigation agency to investigate earnestly all PCR and POA Act cases". For this, he suggested strengthening of the PCR branches by appointing DYSP above the Inspector as the head of each PCR unit in the district (p.150).

The point to be noted here is that such a suggestion for strengthening the existing administrative structure has come from the State, which already has a relatively stronger administrative structure for the PCR office. The PCR office in the State of Maharashtra has an IGP (PCR) at the top, and an SP and others to assist him, supported by four regional level PCR offices each headed by an SP. Under each region, there are two to three PCR divisions, each consisting of 3 to 4 districts and headed by a DYSP. There is a PCR unit in every district, headed by an Inspector. The former IGP (PCR), Maharashtra went a step further in stating that the IGP (PCR) should report directly to the Home Department of the State instead of the State's DGP, and the confidential report of the IGP (PCR) be written by the State Home Department rather than by the DGP.

He also suggested that issues related to human rights violation should also be brought under the purview of the PCR office. But in the case of Tamil Nadu, the administrative structure of the PCR office is not only slightly different but also lacking in both powers and personnel required.

The major difference in the two structures is that in the case of Maharashtra the head for each of the four regional level offices is the SP, whereas in the case of Tamil Nadu it is the DYSP who functions as the head in each of its Supervisory Squads at regional levels. Another major difference is that in the case of Maharashtra the head of divisional level PCR office is DYSP, but in the case of Tamil Nadu there is no such structure. This may be one of the valid reasons for the gradual decline in the number of atrocities on the SCs in the case of Maharashtra, particularly from 1995 onwards, and the same not being the case in Tamil Nadu (see Table 2.3).

Whatever be the kind of instructions the IGP or ADGP (PCR) gives to the law and order district level police officials – be it the Sub-Divisional Officer or the SP or DYSP or the local police – it does not seem to be well-received and responded. Unless such instructions come directly from their superior police officers, who write their confidential reports and decide on their promotion, the local and higher-level police officers would not attach due importance to them. So, to ensure greater accountability on the part of the police officers (law and order) investigating PCR/POA Act cases, the merit and promotion of these officers may be subject to the consent of the PCR police officials who are higher in ranks/positions. This may not be possible given the present structure.

Suggestions

1. It is, therefore, suggested that the PCR office in Tamil Nadu be strengthened particularly at the regional level by appointing an SP above the existing position of DYSP in all the three Supervisory Squads, and by creating Divisional level PCR offices below the level of Supervisory Squads, each covering 2 to 3 districts with DYSP as the head in each of these.
2. The suggestion that the IGP (PCR) may report directly to the Home Department rather than to the DGP, his confidential report be written by the Home Department rather than by the DGP, and that he may also be allowed to function with more exclusive powers can not be ignored, especially in view of the fact that the DGPs of the States have often been confronted with an increasing number of law and order problems and that there were also a few instances where the DGPs did not let the IGP (PCR) to investigate the PCR/POA Act cases earnestly as happened with the then IGP (PCR), Maharashtra.
3. It is further suggested that an effective administrative mechanism should be evolved at the Central government level, so that, every DGP of the State is not only reminded that his concern for maintaining law and order in the State can not be at the cost of the lives, properties and dignity of the SCs and STs living over there, but also made more accountable to the Home Ministry or to the Ministry of Social Justice and Empowerment or to the National Commission for the SCs and STs or to a Committee consisting of members from these three or from other such

bodies of the Government for his/her (DGP) failures in protecting the interests of the SCs and STs.

Experiences of the Special Public Prosecutor

In the entire process of taking every case to its logical end, the Special Public Prosecutor (SPP), who is specially appointed to prosecute all those accused under these special laws, plays a very crucial role and therefore his experiences assume vital importance here. Not so surprisingly, compared to the victims, the experience of SPP is no better. He also seemed to have experienced a left-handed treatment. While sharing his experiences, the SPP said:

> "I am the SPP for 7 districts of (south) Tamil Nadu to deal with cases registered under the PCR/POA Act. But I don't have an office, and don't even have a clerk to assist me. I have not received my fee or remuneration in the last one and a half years of my appointment as SPP here. I sent bills, but never got paid. The response often given by the Government is "lack of funds". Without getting paid, I find it difficult even to maintain myself" (p.168).

The SPP, who is the vital and only support for the victims seeking justice under the special laws, seems to enjoy no importance in the justice process. Regarding the SPP's role, the then IGP (PCR), Maharashtra said that the role of SPP in deposing a case is very limited (p.157).

The lack of importance given to the SPP (as evident from his statements) and the IGP (PCR) indicates in a way the lack of importance given to the PCR/POA Act cases themselves. The Government should therefore seriously look into the grievances of SPPs and resolve them at the earliest. The Government also should make the police realise the importance of the role of SPP in deposing every PCR/POA Act cases earnestly through periodical meetings with and issuing instructions to the concerned police officials.

(c) Caste Prejudice in Police

Though no police personnel is recruited exclusively for monitoring and implementation of these special laws, and those involved in it are very much part of the general police force, but specially deputed for the purpose, our attempt here is to arrive at first a theoretical understanding on whether or not the police dealing with the PCR/POA Act cases lack professional commitment, and if so, why? Answer to this vital question could be found from the views expressed by the victims of caste atrocities. The victims' or the respondents' answer to this question is "yes". It is "yes" because the POA Act is so comprehensive and powerful enough to punish not only those committing atrocities on the SCs and STs and those party to it, but also those police officers failing to perform their lawful duty. There is hardly any scope for any case registered under the POA Act ending in acquittal unless the concerned police lack professional approach and fail or refuse to perform their earnest lawful duty. Moreover, the law has provisions to have an independent administrative structure for its monitoring and implementation and a Special Court for the speedy trial of all PCR/POA Act cases. Yet, why should there be a high rate of acquittal in such cases? What is that that derives the police away from their professional commitment, especially when they deal with cases registered under the PCR and POA Acts?

The answer is "caste". In India it is rare to find an individual particularly among the Hindus, who is free from caste prejudices. In Indian society caste plays a dominant role in every thing. India is caste and caste is India (Weber, 1958:3). Most Indians and most decisions are therefore bound to be under the influence of caste in one form or the other. The police alone cannot be an exception to it, though they are supposed to be so. After all, the police are not aliens to the society. The police for the society are very much from the society and very much by the society. Therefore, in their efforts to eliminate or control elements that are inimical to egalitarian social values or to uphold the agreed upon constitutional conducts particularly those that are meant to protecting the basic human rights and values of people in general and of the SCs and STs in particular, the police are bound to be influenced by their own affinity towards their castes and communities.

Though the police is committed to their profession and therefore supposed to adhere to the ethics of impartiality and to take all decisions only as per the given laws, they find it difficult to do so. Often their primordial loyalties and sentiments come in the way of objective decision making processes. Most of the decisions they take as police officers in-charge of implementing the PCR/POA Act are invariably bound to reflect the interests of their own caste and community members. Not only most of the police in general and those in-charge of the implementing the PCR/POA Act in particular belong to caste Hindus but the potential offenders to be booked under these Special laws also belong to the to the same castes.

The influence of caste in the core personality of every non-SC/ST police officers cannot be undermined. From the stage of infancy till they assume the position of policemen, they are groomed not according to the code of conducts that the police have to follow, but according to the values, norms, and ethics which are mostly rooted in the institution of caste which is in-egalitarian and inimical to healthy social relationships. Caste conducts obviously go in contravention to those egalitarian ideals enshrined in the Indian Constitution and reflected in the sprit of special laws such as the PCR and POA Acts.

The police – whose personality is primarily rooted in such in-egalitarian social values which have been successful so far only in dividing people as lower castes and upper castes – are suddenly expected to adopt egalitarian principles not only for their office dealings but also in their day to day social life as role models. Accordingly, they are also expected to change their personality from the day they become police or the moment they get into their police uniform. This is nothing but expecting a born deaf to become a master over night in singing songs with *sruthi* (scale/pitch) and to dance with the *tal* (rhythm). This is a rare possibility. *The kind of orientations and training the police undergo are not enough even to break the tip of the Himalayan problem of caste prejudice.* This may be possible if the policeman concerned is from a family, which discourages caste system and its 'code of conduct'. This is possible in two situations: (a) when the members of the family themselves are affected by the caste system like the Dalits, and (b) when they have been groomed in egalitarian values and principles and therefore there is no place in their personality for any birth-ascribed social status (caste), though they may be from upper castes. While for the former category, the entire Dalit caste groups can be the examples, for the latter, the examples are very few, and bound to be very few, since there would be hardly persons born in an upper caste but not considering themselves as upper caste and also discouraging the caste system that has given them high social honour as upper caste.

Taking into consideration the vigour with which caste system operates and influences decisions of individuals and professionals including the police, one may conclude that it would not be easier for the police in general and the dominant caste police in particular, to function purely as professionals without giving any room to their caste sentiments. This theoretical understanding may now be verified with the help of views expressed by the victims and other respondents of this study. To begin with, the views of victims on the police's caste prejudice against the SCs may be looked into.

Victims' Views on Police's Caste Prejudice

As concluded in chapter four the victims' experiences with the PCR police had been neither cordial nor encouraging. It was often deceiving and disheartening. The observations made by the victims and their witnesses, as seen in Chapter 3, indicate that the police had often gone out of their way doing things against their professional ethics and commitment and resorted to unlawful means to help the accused. Though it is not necessary to reproduce all such observations here, highlighting one such observation may serve the purpose. One of the victims (case No. 2) said:

> ".....if the accused gives little more money, the police file case against the victims themselves. In this way we (the victims) get beating not only from the caste Hindus, but also from the police" (p. 69).

The above observation clearly reflects the police's covert support to the accused on the one hand and their prejudice and enmity against the SCs on the other. For more specific details regarding the kind of observations the victim had made regarding police's caste prejudice, Chapter 3 may be referred to.

Views of PCR Police

To understand police's prejudice against the SCs in general and the victims in particular, the views of the PCR police may be recalled (Chapter 5). The following are some of the responses of the police, which are directly related to present discussion. Though the IGP (PCR), Tamil Nadu, the then IGP (PCR), Maharashtra and the DYSP, Ramanathapuram, Tamil Nadu stated that the police were for the interest of everyone and they would not be partial towards or biased against any caste and were committed to the strict implementation of the PCR and POA Acts, the DYSP, Ramanathapuram, when probed further, said:

> "If we go strictly by this Act, it will only aggravate the situation and will result in more and more problems..... If we implement this law strictly as we do in the case of other laws, there will only be conflicts and problems in the society. We can not solve such problems by strictly implementing these laws"(p.162).

The IGP (PCR), Tamil Nadu, when requested to comment on the above statement of the DYSP, said:

> "That DYSP's views may be his personal views. He did not take into consideration what is widely practised. He might have been from other communities (non-SCs). If the DYSP is not a SC person, it is likely that he does not understand the SCs' problems, and that is why he said so regarding the POA Act"(p.141).

Views of NGOs

About the functioning of PCR police one of the representatives of an NGO observed:

> "Their (police's) aim is always to brush aside the case. They are not for punishing the accused....Even when we manage to register the case under the POA Act, the police close the case when they frame charge-sheet. In this way, those (police) officers responsible for implementing this Act are not doing their duty earnestly" (p.186). "The police is responsible for most of the cases ending in acquittal. Even

> now, many police stations do not register cases under the POA Act deliberately. The entire case is in the hands of police. If they want, they can punish the accused" (p. 191).

Similarly, another NGO representative said:

> Most of the Backward Caste police, in general support their fellow caste accused in various ways. The police and the accused caste Hindus work in league with the support of ruling caste and political leaders denying justice to the SC victims (p.187).

Views of the Accused

The police's caste prejudice can be verified also from the points of views of the accused. One of the accused, Sakti (case No.10) said:

> "They (SCs) cannot do any thing, because we, the caste Hindus, are together. We resolve our problems with the help of police. It is all money; everything is money. We have so much money, because we are together. They have no money. ... What case that we have not seen? The policemen are with us, and so we have no problem" (p.104).
>
> Another accused, Ganapathi (case No. 9) said:
>
> "... if we give money the police will talk in our favour" (p. 100).

The police's inability to transcend their caste prejudice and function as professionals is reflected also in the way a local police Inspector at Parthibanur police station treated one of the Research Assistants (RA) of the present study who approached him for some information as directed by the Statistical Inspector, PCR Unit, Ramanathapuram. When the RA made a request for the data regarding a case under study, the Inspector concerned humiliated him by directly enquiring about his caste background and proudly proclaiming his superior caste *(Thevar/Maravar)* background, and by questioning him as to what calibre he had to be associated with such a study (p.174).

Another source of understanding the police's caste prejudice against the SCs and favouritism towards the caste Hindus is evident from the bold declarations made by one of the caste Hindu common men interviewed for this study. In the course of discussion, the common man Mr. Periyasamy Thevar, a caste Hindu, said to one of the RAs of this study as under:

> "These SC/ST Acts (PCR and POA Acts) can not be useful even to pluck 'our hair'. It may be a big thing for them (SCs/STS). They can give petition in the police stations saying that they have been abused as Pallan, Parayan and *Chalakiliyan*. They can give in writing. That is all. Indeed, we are happy that the fact that we abused them is being recorded. Which SI has arrested us so far? For this, there is DSP also (abuses here)" (p.201).

> "The SP himself stands for our protection when we go in vans and lorries in large numbers to Posumpon to celebrate the birth anniversary of our leader (Mr. Mutthuramalingam). What could the police pluck from us? They just talk big of the SC/ST Act. No Act can pluck anything from us" (p. 199)

> "Let me now abuse the SCs. We abuse them using loud speakers when we go on a procession every year for the *Pasumpon Muthuramalinga Thevar Guru Pusai.* Be it the IG or DIG – all stands for our security. Let me see whether these sons of a bastard can come and arrest us. Has the government not heard that we abuse the SCs? Has the SP not heard of it or have all those police standing in line not heard of it? Have the reserve police not heard of it? They bring 2000 to 4000 police. Last time, Kalaignar (the then Chief Minister of Tamil Nadu) sent police even in the airplane for our security. We went all the way abusing them (SCs). We stopped at every village and abused the SCs over there using our loud speakers. We challenged them saying *You bastard Pallans (SCs).* Which police questioned us? They (Police) only chased them (SCs) off. Can they chase us or our van? Can't they book us under the SC/ST Act? We have also made video recording of the whole procession. Let them book us under this Act at least by using these video taps. They will not do that" (p.201-202).

The caste Hindu common man further said to the RA:

> "If our people come to know that you are a SC person, your pant and shirt will be removed; they will beat you, abuse

> you saying, *yannada Pallapayale, yennanda Parapayale, yennada chakkiliya pundamayane.* What can you do?"
>
> "What case? Let them (SCs) give the case to the police. We will give Rs. 500/- to the police and the case will be withdrawn. After all, that SI has to work there. Why then we have our own MLAs? Why we have our MPs? What for our police officers there"? (p.200).
>
> "We indulge in murder. We indulge in rape and lute, and do any thing we like. Can the police question us? If they can, we will uproot our *Thevar varkam* (caste) itself" (p.202)

The confidence with which the common man made the above statements reflects clearly the police's open support to the caste Hindus and their prejudice against the SCs. It also indicates the caste Hindu's utter disrespect to those policemen trying to protect the interests of the SCs.

In another incident, when an NGO representative Mr. Sundarajan, Periyavallikulam village, (president of *Arundhadiyar* (SCs) Association), was asked by the police as to how he would like to resolve the problem that had been brought to the police, the former requested the police to proceed as per the law. In response, the accused said at the police station itself: "In our village, we have already taken a decision. You tell all your caste fellows" (p.192). To this open threat to the head of an NGO by the accused, the police did nothing. This in turn caused immense fear in the minds of the victims, and therefore none came forward to be the witness for this case. Though this was the case in which the police himself had gone to the spot and rescued the victim who had been tied along with the street lamp-post and beaten, the police, instead of being supportive to the victims, filed a counter case against the victims and forced covertly to settle the case out of Court (p.192). Such incidents, which were very common in southern districts of Tamil Nadu, speak volumes about the police's prejudice against the SCs.

(d) Caste Prejudice in Special Courts/Judiciary

The judiciary is ought to be beyond caste, religion, creed and, gender-based prejudices. But the decease of caste prejudice does not seem to have spared it. Like the PCR police, who, despite being appointed as professionals to protect the interest of the Dalits, did and could not refrain from caste prejudice, some of the Magistrates of the Special/ Designated Courts pronouncing judgements on the PCR and POA Act cases also seem to be prejudiced against the Dalits. Some of the observations of the respondents of this study are evidences to such conclusions.

Views of the Accused

The prevalence of caste prejudices against the SCs within the Court of law has been verified with the experiences of no less than an accused himself. One of the accused persons Ganapathi (Case No. 9) said:

> "...We have closed the case with the help of the Magistrate". "The accused escaped punishment successfully by bribing the advocates and others in the Court" (p. 100).

NGO's Views

About the Magistrates' roles in judging the validity of each case tried in the Special Courts, the State Secretary of *Thiyagi Imanuvel Peravai,* Paramakudi town, Ramanathapuram district, Mr. Shanmugavel said:

> "Most of the judges in courts belong to the dominant castes. The advocates and judges themselves approach the accused and suggest what the latter should do. In Madurai Special Court, ...there seems to be an internal understanding ....to close down all cases registered under the POA Act without taking due action (proper judgement). Looking at the kind of judgements delivered with regard the cases filed under the PCR and POA Acts, I have come to this conclusion" (p. 178).

In another interview, an advocate who tried to help a victim by taking up his POA Act case (Crime No. 72/99) said:

> "If we look into the Court side, atrocities against the Dalits are more severe than in the police stations. I know, we should not comment on the judgement of the Magistrate. But how many witness does he want to prove or disprove a

particular case – one or two or five? It is obvious that the victim would not say anything against his own interest and would obviously say what was reported in the FIR. The first witness, i.e., the police, for the case under reference, also gave evidence as per the FIR. The witness who came with the victim also deposed the facts correctly. How many more witness do we need to prove the case? Yet the case was acquitted" (p.170).

But what is more alarming in the above case was what happened inside the Court during and after the trial of the case. The advocate further said:

"When the witness made his oral statement before the Magistrate in the Court of law, his statement was typed out differently twisting the case in favour of the accused. When the witness wanted to know what was being typed out as his statement, the Magistrate himself asked the witness as to who instigated him to counter-check his statement. This incident reflects that such practice of twisting the witnesses' statements and typing it in a manner that would help the accused might have been in practice for a long time. This also reflects the Magistrate's concern for the accused; he is supposed to be impartial and be concerned that the victims get justice" (p.170-171).

Victim's Views

While narrating his experience in seeking justice through Court of law, one of the victims (Case No. 4) said:

"When we go to Court for justice, it favours the accused and thereby uphold the unjust practices as if it were meant for unjust practices. In this scenario, it is doubtful that we will get justice through the POA Act. If this has been the experience of a person like me who is educated to some extent, what would be the fate of common village men who are illiterate and ignorant" (p.85).

The advocate referred earlier said:

Court is meant for *Dharma* and justice, and the Judge is for ensuring these ideals. If the Judge himself favours overtly

> the accused, how can we say that the Court is for justice and how can the POA Act be implemented effectively? Such attitude of Judges of Special Courts results in acquittals of most of the POA cases, and this in turn gives an impression to the public that the SC and ST people unnecessarily file cases under the PCR and POA Act. But in reality, this is not true. Why should we then file cases under these laws and what is the use of these laws? At least in some cases the Court should convict the accused, and let the people see the offenders undergoing punishment behind the bars. If the Court cannot do this what is the use of it and why should Courts be there at all? (p.171)

From the above observations and discussion, it may be concluded that even the judiciary (Special Courts) does not seem to be free from caste prejudice against the SCs, particularly in southern Tamil Nadu, though the manifestations of such prejudices was more subtle and covert and the magnitude of it was lesser compared to those found in the police and other departments. Therefore the argument that both the police and the judiciary dealing with PCR/POA Act cases are not free from caste prejudice, and such prejudice has been responsible for number of PCR/POA Act cases ending in acquittal can not be overlooked. In all, such prejudices reflect that there is an absolute breach of trust on the part of the custodians of laws viz., the police and the judiciary dealing with PCR/POA Act cases. It should therefore be tackled at the structural level within the two systems.

Suggestions

In view of the above observations, it is suggested that unless the SCs/STs have their own people in the police department, and the judiciary dealing with the PCR/POA Act cases, their grievances would not get due attention, and justice would ever remain a distant dream for them. The IGP (PCR), Tamil Nadu therefore suggested 50 per cent reservation for SCs/STs in all such departments. If implemented, this suggestion will no doubt ensure justice to the victims of untouchability and caste-based atrocities and discriminations.

Justification for Such Reservation

When women as a category like the SCs and STs do not trust men as custodians of women's rights and privileges, and therefore, prefer women in large numbers in all statutory bodies deciding on their affairs, why not the same logic or rationale be applied in the case of the SCs and STs. For instance, the National Commission for Women (NCW), which came into operation formally from January 31, 1992 to protect and promote the interests of women as a whole, has been successful in appointing women in all key positions that is directly concerned with the women's safety, security and dignity, development and empowerment. During 1996-97, out of the 8 members of the NCW, which include one position of chairperson, two member secretaries and the rest all members, as many as 7, were women. There was only one male member.

In the same way, it would be difficult for the SCs and STs, to trust the non-SC and ST 'custodians of law' especially in view of their bitter experiences with these as protector of their rights and dignity. And therefore, the need for the SCs and STs representing their cause in all major decision-making bodies including the National Commission for the SCS and STs is more than obvious. If not to the extent of 80 to 90 per cent as followed in the case of NCW, the SCs and STs should represent at least to the extent of 70 to 80 per cent in all major decision making bodies including the National Commission for the SCs and STs which are meant for ensuring the safety and security of these communities. As stated before, the SCs/STs should represent their cause both in PCR police stations and PCR Special Courts.

- For tackling caste prejudice among the PCR police, at least 50 per cent of police personnel positions in each PCR police station may be reserved for the SCs and STs, as suggested by the IGP (PCR).
- For tackling caste prejudice in the judiciary and ensuring free and fair trial of at least all criminal cases registered under the POA Act, a two member bench – in which one member should be either SC or ST, preferably a SC/ST woman particularly when it is a case of rape or rape with murder – may be introduced.

(e) The Victims' Inability to Pursue their Cases

The victims' inability to pursue their cases till their logical end has been yet another major factor responsible for the high rate of acquittal in the cases registered under the PCR and POA Acts. Though there can be number of factors or reasons for high acquittal rate, all these are the result of their state of "powerlessness".

The SCs in general and the victims of caste system living in remote villages, in particular, suffer mainly from cumulative deprivation of power and social status. Being mostly landless or marginal farmers and depend often on the caste Hindus to eke out their basic livelihood, they lack economic power. Being mostly illiterate and ignorant, they lack the power of knowledge – the knowledge so essential to effectively use the given protective measures to protect their interests. Groomed as lower caste and as untouchables, they are deprived of self-esteem, self-confidence, self-respect and dignity, which are essential for their personality development. Scattered as they are in villages into few families, they lack numerical strength, which is necessary not only for self-defense but also for political power. In short, they suffer from total powerlessness. Though their conviction to fight against oppression and exploitation is largely determined by their level of consciousness (Oommen, 1990), their consciousness is determined largely by their power and status. Since they suffer from cumulative deprivation of power and status, joint or collective action against caste oppression and exploitation still remains unachievable particularly in rural areas.

The above conclusion is very much valid in the case of almost all cases studied here and also in the opinion of every respondent interviewed. While narrating the experiences in seeking justice under the POA Act for a case of "rape with murder", one of the witnesses (case No.2) said:

> "Since there seems none to support us, we are forced to give up the case. We have to live with all these things since we are small in number in our village and therefore cannot oppose the caste Hindus overtly" (p.69).

Moreover, the magnitude of economic deprivation is so high among the SCs in general and the victims of caste atrocities in southern Tamil Nadu in particular that even for meagre and momentary monetary gains, the SC victims give up their struggle for justice.

In this regard, an NGO representative said:

> "The SCs' economic backwardness drives them go against their own interests. Meenakshipuram case (Case No.1: case of rape with murder) failed because of internal fight among those who took up the case with regard to sharing of the amount given as compensation as per the provisions of the POA Act". Accepting bribe from the accused, one of the witnesses turned hostile and gave evidence in favour of the accused (p.190).

However, it may be noted that such cases were few in numbers. One of the witnesses of case No. 2 said:

> "After the Panchavarnam's incident (the incident of rape with murder), we are harassed by these Naidus (the caste Hindus/accused) in many ways. We cannot do our agricultural work after 4 in the evening. They threaten us. When our girls stand alone anywhere, they abuse them with all possible filthy words. They destroy our crops. They let their cattle scot-free in our farms and damage all our crops. When we try to chase these cattles away, we, particularly our women and daughters, are abused. If we raise voice against such acts, they threaten us with dire consequences. They say, "we would cut you into pieces and nobody could stop us. What can you do to us with your law?" All these experiences make us question ourselves as to why at all we stay in this village, and why not move into other places" (p.70).

The witness further said:

> "They (the accused) are not at all afraid of the POA Act, since they are getting lots of money from abroad. They also have lots of lands and pump-sets for irrigation purposes. They settle all such (POA Act) cases by bribing the officials concerned" (p.68-69).

He also said:

> "We cannot live in this place if we do not have this law. There is no other support for us to live here except this law.

> This law has to be implemented vigorously. Only then, we, the oppressed people, can live here. The law is a must" (p.69).

One of the NGO representatives maintained:

> "The basic problem faced by the Dalits is their economic dependence on the caste Hindus (CHs). Once they are made economically independent, the CHs will also come to know, over a period of time, the worth of the Dalits. If the Dalits think of their self-respect and dignity at this stage (and fight against the CHs), their family will suffer. But there is no escape. The benefits of all the efforts of government are in fact eaten away by the middlemen. If the Dalits get these economic benefits and become economically independent, the scope for atrocities on Dalit will be very much limited" (p.194).

Summary

The above analysis, which is based on the qualitative data obtained from Dalit victims, the accused, the police involved in the implementation of the PCR and POA Acts, NGOs, and common men on issues such as the context in which the SC victims sought justice under the two special laws, the victims' experiences with the police in the process of seeking justice, the various factors that lead to the acquittal of their cases, and suggestions for effective implementation of the two laws, has enabled the researcher to arrive at the following conclusions. It may be noted here that a detailed list of findings emerged in Chapters 4 and 5 have already been presented as summary at the concluding part of the respective chapters. The following are the findings that emerged out of a comparative analysis of views of the victims, witnesses, and the accused on the one hand and of the police, Special Public Prosecutor, NGOs, common men and others on the other as are presented in Chapters 4 and 5 respectively.

Context

With regard to the context in which the SC victims sought protection or justice under the PCR and POA Acts, the following conclusions may be worth noting.

1. In general, the SCs, given their socio-economic backwardness and vulnerable living condition, seldom dared going to the police seeking justice under the special laws.
2. The SC victims sought police intervention only when the gravity of the losses they suffered was high, and when there was hardly any support from any source to cope with their crisis situation. This is evident from the fact that most of the acquitted cases studied here were of such nature.
3. Most of the victims had bitter experiences of struggling on their own, without any support from any source, through the tiresome investigation and trial process only to get defeated finally in the Court of law.
4. On the whole, the experiences of the victims and others associated in the process of seeking justice through the special laws vividly indicates the fact that mere presence of such laws does not mean they would come to the rescue of the victims or the victims could easily make use of them. The police, as custodians of laws and protectors of the rights of the SCs and STs, have a major role in making these laws accessible to them.

The Police's Attitude Towards Victims

5. According to the experiences of most of the victims, their witnesses and NGOs associated with them, the responses of the police towards them, whenever they tried seeking justice under the two special laws, had neither been cordial nor encouraging. Their responses had often been unlawful and undesirable.
6. In view of the fact that both the victims, their fellow caste people and associates, and the accused and their fellow caste Hindus had expressed a very low opinion about the police in charge of implementing the two special laws in general and about those local police whom the victims approached for any immediate help in particular, the honesty and credibility of such police officials come under doubt and disbelief.
7. According to the opinion of most of the respondents, the police in general supported the accused (non-SCs/STs) in

very many ways as most of them too belonged to the non-SCs/STs. The various ways in which the police were of help to the accused included one or more of the following:

- The police either delayed or did not register the case at all.
- They often tried to find out some loop-hole in the petitions and converted every serious case to be registered under the POA Act into an ordinary case by applying inappropriate sections, and thereby protected the accused from severe punishment due under the POA Act.
- Though it was the duty of police, as per the POA Act, to provide necessary protection and ensure their presence before the Court of law as witnesses, they often refrained from doing so under some pretext or the other.
- The police took money from the victims to pursue their cases, and also from the accused to acquit the case or to settle it outside the Court.

8. Therefore, it is felt necessary that the police should first demonstrate their professional honesty through earnest implementation of these laws, transcend their primordial affinity to and loyalty towards their own caste groups.

Factors Responsible for Acquittal

9. The existing administrative structure for the effective implementation of the special laws in Tamil Nadu neither has police officials in required numbers to reach out to the needy SCs and STs living in villages and remote corners, nor the scope and powers sufficient to enforce upon the police officials at the district and local levels to implement the special laws earnestly and effectively. The implementation of these laws has been receiving half-hearted treatment since it depends ultimately on the local police whose primary concern is "law and order" and who are controlled by the SP (law and order), and not by the SP or IGP (PCR).
10. From the experiences shared by the various respondents, it is concluded that it had not been easier even for the police to

be free from caste prejudice and to act strictly as per the rules as professionals.

11. The caste Hindu accused feel that the SC victims can do nothing to them despite registering cases against them, under the POA Act, since they enjoy the support of the police. They can bribe the police to work in their favour.
12. Though the IGP (PCR), Tamil Nadu, the DYSP, Ramanathapuram, Tamil Nadu and the then IGP (PCR) Maharashtra stated that the police were for everyone and would never be partial to any caste, it was revealed from some of the observations made by the IGP (PCR) and the DYSP, Ramanathapuram that the caste Hindu police officers harboured from caste prejudice against the SCs and were thus reluctant to implement the PCR and POA Acts earnestly.
13. The fact that one of the Research Assistants of this study himself was discriminated and humiliated overtly within the police station by none other than the police Inspector, just because he belonged to the Scheduled Caste, reflects clearly the police's caste prejudice against the SCs.
14. The fact that one of the common men representing the views of accused said that the caste Hindus enjoyed the support of police officers, MLAs and MPs belonging to their own castes and therefore they could not be punished under the POA Act cases filed against them. It was due to such support, they could continue treating the SCs as their slaves and could also indulge in committing murder, rape and loot. They could prevent the police taking action against them under the POA Act by bribing and also by way of threatening them occasionally, if need be.
15. In view of the fact that majority of those in the police force in general and those concerned with the implementation of the PCR and POA Act cases in Tamil Nadu in particular belonged to the non-SC/ST communities (mostly backward caste Hindus), the fact that the police, under some pretext or the other, had often failed to be of support to the victims in punishing the accused in the Court of law, and the fact that there had been instances in which the police had gone out of their ways helping the accused escape due punishment, it may be concluded that there is immense amount of caste

prejudice against the SCs among the police in general and those directly dealing with the PCR and POA Act cases in particular. It may also be concluded that such prejudice has been one of major factors responsible for many PCR and POA Act cases ending in acquittal.

16. The analysis has also revealed that even the judiciary is not free from caste prejudice against the SCs in southern Tamil Nadu, and such prejudice had been an important factor responsible for the high rate of acquittal in the PCR/POA Act cases.
17. Victims' inability to pursue their cases has been yet another important factor responsible for the high rate of acquittal in PCR/POA Act cases. In all, the victims' state of powerlessness is seen to be the most important factor making them incapable of pursuing their cases to logical ends.
18. The basic problem faced by the Dalits/SCs in general and the SC victims in particular is their economic dependence on the caste Hindus who often commit atrocities on the SCs. The magnitude of economic deprivation is so deep among them that even for meagre and momentary monetary and material gains they give up their struggle for justice. The analysis reveal that they sometimes said and did things that lead to acquittal of their cases. Thus, there is a need for support in meeting their basic needs on a permanent basis.

Unless such needs are met on a priority basis, whatever, legal measures that we come out with will not be of much use to ensure the safety and security of this scattered, oppressed and pilloried caste groups.

7

Conclusion

Major Findings and Recommendations

In the previous chapters the focus was on the first five objectives of this study. It may be recalled that the main findings emerged in Chapters 4, 5 and 6 have been highlighted at the end of respective chapters under the sub-title "Summary". The purpose of present chapter is to consolidate few major findings that have emerged in the previous chapters of this study and also to make a few recommendations based on the experiences and suggestions of the various stakeholders of the PCR and POA Acts as shared in Chapters 4 and 5. It is hoped that these recommendations would help implement the two special laws effectively. The present chapter brings to light only those major findings for which recommendations have also been made. The following are the major findings and recommendations:

1. The PCR Office throughout Tamil Nadu may be strengthened in such a way that all the PCR and POA Act cases are investigated, charge-sheeted and prosecuted exclusively by its own police personnel, instead of depending on the local police. It should function similar to the way in which the CID (civil supplies) functions both at the Sate and local levels. It should be strengthened

particularly at the regional level by appointing an SP above the existing position of DYSP in all the three Supervisory Squads, and by creating Divisional level PCR offices below the level of Supervisory Squads, each covering 2 to 3 districts with DYSP as its head.

2. The ADGP/IGP (PCR) may report directly to the Home Department rather than to the DGP of the State, and accordingly his confidential report be written by the Home Department rather than by the DGP. This would ensure greater freedom for the ADGP/IGP (PCR) to do justice to the responsibilities assigned to him. To some extent, this would also help the DGP to devote maximum time for resolving the "law and order" problems in the State. The DGP, instead of directly getting involved on issues pertaining to PCR/POA Act cases, may extend necessary support to the ADGP/IGP (PCR) to ensure the safety and security of the SCs and STs in the State.
3. An effective administrative mechanism be evolved at the Central Government level, so as to consistently facilitate and remind, every DGP of the State that his/her concern for maintaining law and order in the State can not be at the cost of the lives, properties and dignity of the SCs and STs living over there, and to make them accountable either to the Home Ministry or to the Ministry of Social Justice and Empowerment or to the National Commission for the SCs and STs, or to a new Committee constituting members from these three or other such bodies of the Government so as to protect the interests of the SCs and STs.
4. Presently, the concerned SP of the district does the streamlining of investigation process of the PCR/POA Act cases registered in the district. In view of the enormous amount of other cases that the SP at the district level needs to look into, the above responsibility may be left exclusively to the office of the ADGP/IGP (PCR).
5. District level PCR police stations may be adequately equipped with necessary infrastructure facilities such as proper office, vehicles and other necessary facilities exclusively under its control.

6. The Scheduled Caste people should refrain from performing defiling, unpaid or underpaid occupations such as sweeping, scavenging, disposing of dead cattle etc. They should be accommodated in more dignified employment. The Government should actively take up such initiatives. In the longer run, this would help prevent the SCs becoming the victims of caste discrimination and untouchability.
7. Most of the SCs were unaware of the POA Act, and most of those who were aware of it were unaware of the manner in which this could be used to ensure justice to the victim of caste atrocities and discriminations. It is therefore recommended that the PCR office may undertake special programmes at various levels making people aware of the PCR and POA Acts, the sprit behind these laws and their usefulness to protect the SCs and STs. The police departments may carry out such responsibilities in collaboration with the academic/research institutions, and civil society organisations/NGOs.
8. The police personnels in general seem unaware of the various provisions, particularly of the POA Act. The police may therefore be properly trained and guided to use these laws effectively and to ensure justice to the victims.
9. In view of the fact that the victim in most cases could not get the TA and DA as per the provisions of the POA Act, and they had also been subjected to harassment of running from police station to Collector's office and to the Special Court, it is recommended that the due TA/DA be given to the victims and their witness in the Court itself.
10. The Special Public Prosecutor should be given the due recognition by meeting at least his/her basic requirements such as proper office, clerical assistance and the due remuneration, so that he/she is able to perform the due task effectively.

All the above recommendations shall be of definite help in implementing the Acts effectively. However, the following six recommendations shall be of much value for the purpose of bringing down the acquittal rate in the PCR and POA Act cases and to protect the SCs from all forms of exploitations on a permanent basis.

11. In view of the fact that most of the police officials dealing with the PCR and POA Act cases belong to the upper castes and they have not been able to win the confidence of the SCs/STs, particularly of those in rural areas, it is recommended that out of the total number of police officials directly dealing with the PCR/POA Act cases, at least 50 per cent of them may be from the SC/ST communities. More importantly, as suggested by the ADGP (PCR) and most others, of the two top PCR police officials, ADGP and IGP, who presently manage the PCR/HR/SJ Office of the State, one should always be represented by either a Scheduled Caste or Scheduled Tribe officer to ensure just and fair treatment to the cases processed.
12. The police may be sensitised and the SCs may be made aware of Section 12 of the PCR Act and Section 8 of the POA Act which make the accused responsible for proving his/her innocence.
13. Treating the close relatives and friends of the victim as "interested witness" has been one of the reasons for many cases ending in acquittal, as it had happened in more than one case of those examined in this study. Given the economic power and political and bureaucratic connections of the upper caste Hindus (potential accused), it is obvious that none other than the close relatives and friends of the victims would dare antagonizing the accused caste Hindus/non-SCs and coming forward to be the witness for the victims. It is therefore recommended that the Honourable Court may recognize the close relatives and friends of the victims as their "eligible witnesses".
14. There were instances in which the provisions of the POA Act were violated within the Court by the Court staff themselves. It is therefore recommended that at least all the criminal offences reported under the POA Act be tried in front of a qualified and committed two member Bench, in which one member should be from either Scheduled Caste or Scheduled Tribe, preferably a Scheduled Caste woman.

15. Despite the fact that the police had been found guilty of not producing the required witness in the Court by none other than the Magistrate, and due to which many cases end in acquittal, there has hardly been any judgment punishing such police officials. Therefore it is hoped that the judiciary plays a proactive role pronouncing punishment against such police officials as per Section 4 of the POA Act.
16. As long as the SCs live in villages in small numbers, they will not be able to protect themselves from the atrocities and exploitations by the caste Hindus, who are not only large in number and politically well connected but also enjoy the support of fellow caste policemen who are in majority in the police force. It is therefore recommended that all the Scheduled Caste families living in those villages predominantly inhabited by the dominant caste Hindus may be shifted to other villages where their fellow caste members are in large numbers and where there is no or very limited scope for the caste Hindus to discriminate and exploit them. The Government may help such families by buying whatever quantum of land they own and providing the same, if not more and better, quality of land, at the newly settled place. Such an arrangement would permanently put an end to this otherwise perennial problem.

The proposed suggestion for separate settlement for the Dalits/SCs is not something new.

Dr. B.R. Ambedkar made such a suggestion and also demanded the same through his Scheduled Caste Federation in a resolution dated September 23, 1944. The conclusions of the present volume merely reiterates the relevance of Ambedkar's demand.

Annexures

ANNEXURE 1

Protective Legislations Passed During 1943 – 1950

1. The Bihar Harijan (Removal of Civil Disabilities) Act, 1949 (Bihar Act XIX of 1949).
2. The Bombay Harijan (Removal of Social Disabilities) Act, 1946 (Bombay Act X of 1974).
3. The Bombay Harijan Temple Entry Act, 1947 (Bombay Act XXXV of 1974).
4. The Central Provinces and Berar Scheduled Castes (Removal of Civil Disabilities) Act, 1947 (Central Provinces and Berar Act XXIV of 1947).
5. The Central Provinces and Berar Temple Entry Authorisation Act, 1947 (Central Provinces and Berar Act XIII of 1947).
6. The East Punjab (Removal of Religious and Social Disabilities) Act, 1948 (East Punjab Act XVI of 1948).
7. The Madras Removal of Civil Disabilities Act, 1938 (Madras Act XXI of 1938).
8. The Orissa Removal of Civil Disabilities Act, 1946 (Orissa Act XI of 1946).
9. The Orissa Temple Entry Authorisation Act, 1948 (Orissa Act XI of 1948).

10. The United Provinces Removal of Social Disabilities Act, 1947 (U.P. Act XIV of 1947).
11. The West Bengal Hindu Social Disabilities Removal Act, 1948 (West Bengal Act XXXVII of 1948).
12. The Hyderabad Harijan Temple Entry Regulation, 1358F (No. LV of 1358F Fasli).
13. The Hyderabad Harijan (Removal of Social Disabilities) Regulation, 1358F (No. LVI of 1358F Fasli).
14. The Madhya Bharat Harijan Ayogta Nivaran Vidhan, Samvat 2005 (Madhya Bharat Act No. 15 of 1949).
15. The Removal of Civil Disabilities Act, 1943 (Mysore Act XLII of 1943).
16. The Mysore Temple Entry Authorisation Act, 1948 (Mysore Act XIV of 1948).
17. The Saurashtra Harijan (Removal of Social Disabilities) Ordinance (No. XL of 1948).
18. The Travancore – Cochin Removal of Social Disabilities Act, 1125 (Travancore-Cochin Act VIII of 1125).
19. The Travancore-Cochin Temple Entry (Removal of Disabilities) Act, 1950 (Travancore-Cochin Act XXVII of 1950).
20. The Coorg Scheduled Castes (Removal of Civil and Social Disabilities) Act, 1949 (Coorg Act I of 1940).
21. The Coorg Temple Entry Authorisation Act, 1949 (Coorg Act II of 1949).

ANNEXURE 2*

The Scheduled Castes and Scheduled Tribes (Prevention of Atrocities) Act, 1989

No. 33 of 1989

(11th September 1989).

An Act to prevent the commission of offences of atrocities against the members of the Scheduled Castes and the Scheduled Tribes, to provide rehabilitation of the victims of such offences and for matters connected therewith or incidental thereto.

Be it enacted by Parliament in Fortieth year of the Republic of India, as follows:

CHAPTER I: PRELIMINARY

1. (1) This Act may be called the Scheduled Castes and the Scheduled Tribes (Prevention of Atrocities) Act, 1989.
   (2) It extends to the whole of India except the State of Jammu and Kashmir.
   (3) It shall come into force on such date as the Central Government may, by notification in the Official Gazette, appoint.
2. (1) In this Act, unless the context otherwise requires-
   (a) "Atrocity" means an offence punishable under section 3;
   (b) "Code" means the Code of Criminal Procedure, 1973;
   (c) "Scheduled Castes and Scheduled Tribes" shall have the meanings assigned to them respectively under clause (24) and clause (25) of article 366 of the Constitution;
   (d) "Special Court" means a Court of Session specified as a Special Court in section 14;
   (e) "Special Public Prosecutor" means a Public Prosecutor specified as a Special Public Prosecutor or an advocate referred to in section 15;
   (f) words and expressions used but not defined in this Act and defined in the Code or the Indian Penal Code shall have the meanings assigned to them respectively in the Code, or as the case may be, in the Indian Penal Code.

---

* As noted on page No. 3 of Chapter 1

(2) Any reference in this Act to any enactment or any provision thereof shall, in relation to an area in which such enactment or such provision is not in force, be construed as a reference to the corresponding law, if any, in force in that area.

CHAPTER II: OFFENCES OF ATROCITIES

3. (1) Whoever, not being a member of a Scheduled Caste or a Scheduled Tribe:
   - (i) forces a member of a Scheduled Caste or a Scheduled Tribe to drink or eat any inedible or obnoxious substance;
   - (ii) acts with intent to cause injury, insult or annoyance to any member of a Scheduled Caste or a Scheduled Tribe by dumping excreta, waste matter, carcasses or any other obnoxious substance in his premises or neighbourhood;
   - (iii) forcibly removes clothes from the person of a member or a Scheduled Caste or a Scheduled Tribe or parades him naked or with painted face or body or commits any similar act which is derogatory to human dignity;
   - (iv) wrongfully occupies or cultivates any land owned by, or allotted to, or notified by any competent authority to be allotted to, a member of a Scheduled Caste or a Scheduled Tribe or gets the land allotted to him transferred;
   - (v) wrongfully dispossesses a member of a Scheduled Caste or a Scheduled Tribe from his land or premises or interferes with the enjoyment of his rights over any land, premises or water;
   - (vi) compels or entices a member of a Scheduled Castes or a Scheduled Tribes to do 'begar' or other similar forms of forced or bonded labour other than any compulsory service for public purposes imposed by Government;
   - (vii) forces or intimidates a member of a Scheduled Caste or a scheduled Tribe not to vote or to vote to a particular candidate or to vote in a manner other than that provided by law;
   - (viii) institutes false, malicious or vexatious suit or criminal or other legal proceedings against a member of a Scheduled Caste or a Scheduled Tribe;
   - (ix) gives any false or frivolous information to any public servant and thereby causes such public servant to use his lawful power to the injury or annoyance of a member of a Scheduled Caste or a Scheduled Tribe;

5. Whoever, having already been convicted of an offence under this Chapter is convicted for the second offence or any offence subsequent to the second offence, shall be punishable with imprisonment for a term which shall not be less than one year but which may extend to the punishment provided for that offence.
6. Subject to the other provisions of this Act, the provisions of section 34, Chapter III, Chapter IV, Chapter V, Chapter VA, section 149 and Chapter XXIII of the Indian Penal Code, shall, so far as may be, apply for the purposes of this Act as they apply for the purposes of the Indian Penal Code.
7. (1) Where a person has been convicted of any offence punishable under this Chapter, the Special Court may, in addition to awarding any punishment, by order in writing, declare that any property, movable or immovable or both, belonging to the person, which has been used for the commission of that offence, shall stand forfeited to Government.
   (2) Where any person is accused of any offence under this Chapter, it shall be open to the Special Court trying him to pass an order that all or any of the properties movable or immovable or both, belonging to him, shall, during the period of such trial, be attached, and where such trial ends in conviction, the property so attached shall be liable to forfeiture to the extend it is required for the purpose of realisation of any fine imposed under this Chapter.
8. In a prosecution for an offence under this Chapter, if it is proved that:
   (a) the accused rendered any financial assistance to a person accused of, or reasonably suspected of committing, an offence under this Chapter, the Special Court shall presume, unless the contrary is proved, that such person had abetted the offence;
   (b) a group of persons committed an offence under this Chapter and if it is proved that the offence committed was sequel to any existing dispute regarding land or any other matter, it shall be presumed that offence was committed in furtherance of the common intention or in prosecution of the common object.
9. (1) Notwithstanding anything contained in the Code or in any other provision of this Act, the State Government may, if it considers it necessary or expedient so to do:
      (a) for the prevention of and for coping with any offence under this Act, or
      (b) for any case or class or group of cases under this Act, in any district or part thereof, confer, by notification in the

Official Gazette, on any officer of the State Government, the powers exercisable by a police officer under the Code in such district or part thereof or, as the case may be, for such case or class or group of cases, and in particular, the powers of arrest, investigation and prosecution of persons before any Special Court.

(2) All officers of police and all other officers of Government shall assist the officer referred to in sub-section (1) in the execution of the provisions of this Act or any rule, scheme or order made thereunder.

(3) The provisions of the Code shall, so far as may be, apply to the exercise of the powers by an officer under sub-section (1).

CHAPTER III: EXTERNMENT

10. (1) Where the Special Court is satisfied upon a complaint or a police report that a person is likely to commit an offence under Chapter II of this Act in any area included in 'Scheduled Areas' or 'tribal areas', it can direct the person to move out beyond the limit of that area for a period not exceeding two years.

(2) The Special Court is to communicate to that person stating the grounds on which he has been asked to move out.

(3) The Special Court may revoke or modify the order made under sub-section (1), for the reasons to be recorded in writing, on the representation made by the accused or by some one on his behalf.

11. The Special Court may cause him to be arrested and removed from that area under police custody,

(1) (a) if that person fails to remove himself from that area as directed; or

(b) if he enters that prohibited area within the specified period,

(2) The Special Court may, by order, permit him to return to the area and subject to such conditions as specified in such order and may require him to execute a bond with or without surety for the due observation of the conditions imposed.

(3) The Special Court may at any time revoke any such permission.

(4) The person with the permission to return to his area for a temporary period, shall observe the conditions imposed and return back to the specified area and shall not return to his place within the remaining period without a fresh permission.

(5) The Special Court may cause him arrested, and sent to the specified place under police custody as prescribed by the Special Court, if he fails to observe any of the conditions imposed.

12. (1) Every person against whom an order has been made under section 10 shall, if so required by the Special Court, allow his measurements and photograph to be taken by police officer.

(2) If he resists or refuses, it shall be lawful to use all necessary means to secure his measurements and photographs.

(3) Such refusal or resistance under sub-section (2) shall be an offence under section 186 of the IPC.

(4) When an order under section 10 is revoked, all photographs (including negatives) taken under sub-section (2) shall be destroyed or handed over to the person against whom such order is made.

13. Any person contravening an order of the Special Court made under section 10 shall be punishable with imprisonment for a term not exceeding one year with fine.

CHAPTER IV: SPECIAL COURTS

14. For the purpose of speedy trial, the State Government shall, with the concurrence of the Chief Justice of the High Court, by notification in the official Gazette, specify for each district a Court of session to be a Special Court to try offences under this Act.

15. For every Special Court, the State Government shall, by notification in the Official Gazette, specify a Public Prosecutor or appoint an advocate who has been in practice as an advocate for not less than seven years, as a Special Public Prosecutor for the purpose of conducting cases in the Court.

CHAPTER V: MISCELLANEOUS

16. The provisions of section 10A of the PCR Act, 1955 shall, so far as may be, apply for the purposes of imposition and realisation of collective fine and for all other matters connected therewith under this Act.

17. (1) A District magistrate or a Sub-divisional Magistrate or any other Executive Magistrate or any police officer not below the rank of a Deputy Superintendent of Police may, after having valid reasons, declare an area to be an area prone to atrocities, and take necessary preventive actions to maintain peace, good behaviour, public order and tranquillity.

(2) The provisions of Chapters VIII, IX and XI of the Code shall, so far as may be, apply for the sub-section (1).

(3) The State Government may, by notification in the Official Gazette, make one or more schemes specifying the manner in which the officers referred to in sub-section (1) shall take appropriate action specified in such scheme or schemes to prevent atrocities and to restore the feeling of security amongst the members of the Scheduled Castes and Scheduled Tribes.

18. Nothing in section 438 of the code shall apply in relation to any case involving the arrest of any person on an accusation of having committed an offence under this Act.

19. The provisions of section 360 of the Code and the provisions of the probation of offenders Act, 1958 shall not apply to any person above the age of eighteen years who is found guilty of having committed an offence under this Act.

20. Save as otherwise provided in this Act, the provisions of this Act shall have effect notwithstanding anything inconsistent therewith contained in any other law for the time being in force or any custom or usage or any instrument having effect by virtue of any such law.

21. (1) Subject to such rules as the Central Government may make in this behalf, the State Government shall take such measures as may be necessary for the effective implementation of this Act.

(2) In particular, and without prejudice to the generality of the foregoing provisions, such measures may include

(i) the provision for adequate facilities, including legal aid, to the persons subjected to atrocities to enable them to avail themselves of justice;

(ii) the provision for travelling and maintenance expenses to witnesses including the victims of atrocities, during investigation and trial of offences under this Act;

(iii) the provision for the economic and social rehabilitation of the victims of atrocities;

(iv) the appointment of officers for initiating or exercising supervision over prosecutions for the contravention of the provisions of this Act.

(v) the setting up of committees at such appropriate levels as the State Government may think fit to assist that Government in formulation or implementation of such measures.

(vi) provisions for a periodic survey of the working of the provisions of this Act with a view to suggesting measures for the better implementation of the provisions of this Act;

(vii) identification of areas where the members of the SCs and the STs are likely to be subjected to atrocities and adoption of such measures so as to ensure safety for such members.

(3) The Central Government shall take steps as may be necessary to coordinate the measures taken by the State Governments under sub-section (1)

(4) The Central Government shall, every year, place on the table of each House of Parliament a report on the measures taken by itself and by the State governments in pursuance of the provisions of this section.

22. No suit, prosecution or other legal proceedings shall lie against the Central Government or State Government or any other officer or authority of Government or any other person for anything which is in good faith done or intended to be done under this Act.

23. (1) The Central Government may, by notification in the official Gazette, make rules for carrying out the purposes of this Act.

(2) Every rule made under this Act shall be laid, as soon as, may be after it is made, before each House of Parliament, while it is in session for a total period of thirty days which may be comprised in one session or in two or more successive sessions, and if, before the expiry of the session 7 immediately following the session or successive sessions, aforesaid, both Houses agree in making any modification in the rule or both Houses agree that the rule should not be made, the rule shall thereafter have effect only in such modified form or be of no effect, as the case may be; show however, that, any such modifications annulment shall be without prejudice to the validity of any thing previously done under that rule.

ANNEXURE 2A*

The Scheduled Castes and the Scheduled Tribes (Prevention of Atrocities) Rules, 1995

NOTIFICATION

G.S.R. 316 (E) – In exercise of the powers conferred by sub-section (1) of Section 23 of the Scheduled Castes and the Scheduled Tribes (Prevention of Atrocities) Act, 1989 (33 of 1989), the Central Government hereby makes the following rules, namely:

1. *Short Title and Commencement*:
   (1) These rules may be called the Scheduled Castes and the Scheduled Tribes (Prevention of Atrocities) Rules, 1995.
   (2) They shall come into force on the date of their publication in the Official Gazette.
2. *Definitions*: In these rules, unless the context otherwise requires:
   (a) "Act" means the Scheduled Castes and the Scheduled Tribes (Prevention of Atrocities) Act, 1989 (33 of 1989);
   (b) "dependent", with its grammatical variations and cognate expression, includes wife, children, whether married or unmarried, dependent parents, widowed sister, widow and children of pre-deceased son of a victims of atrocity;
   (c) "identified area" means such area where State Government has reason to believe that atrocity may take place or there is an apprehension of reoccurrence of an offence under the Act or an area prone to victim of atrocity;
   (d) "Non Government Organization" means a voluntary organization engaged in the welfare activities relating to the Scheduled Castes and the Scheduled Tribes and registered under the Societies Registration Act, 1866 (21 of 1866) or under any law for the registration of documents or such organization for the time being in force;
   (e) "Schedule" means the Schedule annexed to these rules;
   (f) "Section" means section of the Act;
   (g) "State Government", in relation to a Union Territory, means the Administrator of that Union Territory appointed by the President under Article 239 of the Constitution;

---

* As noted on page No. 3 of Chapter 1.

(h) Words and expressions used herein and not defined but defined in the Act shall have the meanings respectively assigned to them in the Act.

3. *Precautionary and Preventive Measures*: 1. With a view to prevent atrocities on the Scheduled Castes and the Scheduled Tribes, the State Government shall:

(i) identify the area where it has reason to believe that atrocity may take place or there is an apprehension of re-occurrence of an offence under the Act;

(ii) order the District Magistrate and Superintendent of Police or any other officer to visit the identified area and review the law and order situation;

(iii) if deem necessary, in the identified area cancel the arms licenses of the persons, not being member of the Scheduled Castes or the Scheduled Tribes, their near relations, servants or employees and family friend and get such arms deposited in the government Armoury;

(iv) seize all illegal fire arms and prohibit any illegal manufacture of fire arms;

(v) with a view to ensure the safety of person and property, if deem necessary, provide arms licenses to the members of the Scheduled Castes and the Scheduled Tribes;

(vi) constitute a high power State-level committee, district and divisional level committees or such number of other committees as deem proper and necessary for assisting the Government in implementation of the provisions of the Act;

(vii) set-up a vigilance and monitoring committee to suggest effective measures to implement the provisions of the Act;

(viii) set-up Awareness Centres and organize Workshops in the identified area or at some other place to educate the persons belonging to the Scheduled Castes and the Scheduled Tribes about their rights and the protection available to them under the provisions of various Central and State enactments or rules, regulations and schemes framed thereunder;

(ix) encourage Non-Government Organizations for establishing and maintaining Awareness Centres and organizing Workshops and provide them necessary financial and other sort of assistance;

(x) deploy special police force in the identified area;

(xi) by the end of every quarter, review the law and order situation, functioning of different committees, performance of Special Public Prosecutors, Investigating Officers and other Officers responsible for implementing the provisions of the Act and the cases registered under the Act.

4. *Supervision of Prosecution and Submission of Report:*

(1) The State Government on the recommendation of the District Magistrate shall prepare for each District panel of such number of eminent senior advocates who has been in practice for not less than seven years, as it may deem necessary for conducting cases in the Special Courts. Similarly, in consultation with the Director Prosecution incharge of the prosecution, a panel of such number of Public Prosecutors as it may deem necessary for conducting cases in the Special Courts, shall also be specified. Both these panels shall be notified in the Official Gazette of the State and shall remain in force for a period of three years.

(2) The District Magistrate and the Director of prosecution/in-charge of the prosecution shall review at least twice in a calendar year, in the month of January and July, the performance of Special Public Prosecutors so specified or appointed and submit a report to the State Government.

(3) If the State Government is satisfied or has reason to believe that a Special Public Prosecutor so appointed or specified has not conducted the case to the best of the ability and with due care and caution, his name may be, for reasons to be recorded in writing, denotified.

(4) The District Magistrate and the officer-in-charge of the prosecution at the District level, shall review the position of cases registered under the Act and submit a monthly report on or before 20th day of each subsequent month to the Director of Prosecution and the State Government. This report shall specify the action taken/proposed to be taken in respect of investigation and prosecution of each case.

(5) Notwithstanding anything contained in sub-rule (1) the District Magistrate or the Sub-Divisional Magistrate may, if deem necessary, or if so desired by the victims of atrocity engage an eminent Senior Advocate for conducting cases in the Special Courts on such payment of fee as he may consider appropriate.

(6) Payment of fee to the Special Public Prosecutor shall be fixed by the State Government on a scale higher than the other panel advocates in the State.

5. *Information to Police Officer-in-Charge of a Police Station:*

(1) Every information relating to the commission of an offence under the Act, if given orally to an officer-in-charge of a police station shall be reduced to writing by him or under his direction, and be read to the informant, and every such information, whether given in writing or reduced to writing as aforesaid, shall be signed by the persons giving it, and the substance thereof shall be entered in a book to be maintained by that police station.

(2) A copy of the information as so recorded under sub-rule (1) above shall be given forthwith, free of cost, to the informant.

(3) Any person aggrieved by a refusal on the part of an officer-in-charge of a police station to record the information referred to in sub-rule (1) may send the substance of such information, in writing and by post, to the Superintendent of Police concerned who after investigation either by himself or by a police officer not below the rank of Deputy Superintendent of Police, shall make an order in writing to the officer-in-charge of the concerned police station to enter the substance of that information to be entered in the book to be maintained by that the police station.

6. *Spot Inspection by Officers*:

(1) Whenever the District Magistrate or the sub-Divisional Magistrate or any other Executive Magistrate or any police officer not below the rank of Deputy Superintendent of Police receives an information from any person or upon his own knowledge that an atrocity has been committed on the members of the Scheduled Castes or the Scheduled Tribes within his jurisdiction, he shall immediately himself visit the place of occurrence to assess the extent of atrocity, loss of life, loss and damage to the property and submit a report forthwith to the State Government.

(2) The District Magistrate or the sub-Divisional Magistrate or any other executive Magistrate and the Superintendent of Police, Deputy Superintendent of Police after inspecting the place or area shall on the spot:-

(i) draw a list of victims, their family members and dependents entitled for relief;

(ii) prepare a detailed report of the extent of atrocity, loss and damage to the property of the victims;

(iii) order for intensive police patrolling in the area;

(iv) take effective and necessary steps to provide protection to the witnesses and other sympathisers of the victims;

(v) provide immediate relief to the victims;

7. *Investigating Officer*:

(1) An offence committed under the Act shall be investigated by a police officer not below the rank of a Deputy Superintendent of Police. The investigating officer shall be appointed by the State Government/Director General of Police/Superintendent of Police after taking into account his past experience, sense of ability and justice to perceive the implication of the case and investigate it along with right lines within the shortest possible time.

(2) The investigating officer so appointed under sub-rule (1) shall complete the investigation on top priority within thirty days and submit the report to the Superintendent of Police who in turn will immediately forward the report to the Director General of Police of the State Government.

(3) The Home Secretary and the Social Welfare Secretary to the State Government, Director of Prosecution, the officer-in-charge of Prosecution and the Director General of Police shall review by the end of every quarter the position of all investigations done by the investigating officer.

8. *Setting Up of the Scheduled Castes and the Scheduled Tribes Protection Cell*

(1) The State Government shall set up Scheduled Castes and the Scheduled Tribes Protection Cell at the State head quarter under the charge of Director of Police/ Inspector General of police. This Cell shall be responsible for:

(i) conducting survey of the identified area;

(ii) maintaining public order and tranquillity in the identified area;

(iii) recommending to the State Government for deployment of special police force or establishment of special police post in the identified area;

(iv) making investigations about the probable causes leading to an offence under the Act;

(v) restoring the feeling of security amongst the members of the Scheduled Castes and the Scheduled Tribes;

(vi) informing the nodal officer and special officer about the law and order situation in the identified area;

(vii) making enquiries about the investigation and spot inspections conducted by various officers;

(viii) making enquiries about the action taken by the Superintendent of Police in the cases where an officer in charge of the police station has refused to enter and information in a book to be maintained by that police station under sub-rule (3) of rule 5;

(ix) making enquiries about the willful negligence by a public servant;

(x) reviewing the position of cases registered under the Act; and

(xi) submitting a monthly on or before 20th day of each subsequent month to the State Government nodal officer about the action taken/proposed to be taken in respect of the above.

9. *Nomination of Nodal Officer*: The State Government shall nominate a nodal officer of the level of a Secretary to the State Government preferably belonging to the Scheduled Castes or the Scheduled Tribes, for co-ordinating the functioning of the District Magistrates and Superintendent of Police or the offices authorised by them investigating officers and other officers responsible for implementing the provisions of the Act. By the end of the every quarter, the nodal officer shall review:

(i) the reports received by the State Government under sub-rule (2) and (4) of rule 4, rule 6, clause (xi) of rule 8.

(ii) the position of cases registered under the Act;

(iii) law and order situation in the identified area;

(iv) various kinds of measures adopted for providing immediate relief in cash or kind or both to the victims of atrocity or his or her dependent;

(v) adequacy of immediate facilities like rationing, clothing, shelter, legal aid, travelling allowance, daily allowance, and transport facilities provided to the victims of atrocity or his/her dependants;

(vi) performance of non-governmental organisations, the Scheduled Castes and the Scheduled Tribes Protection Cell, various committees and the public servants responsible for implementing the provisions of the Act.

10. *Appointment of a Special Officer*: In the identified area a Special Officer not below the rank of a Additional District Magistrate, Superintendent of Police or other officers responsible for implementing the provisions of the Act, various committees and the Scheduled Castes and the Scheduled Tribes Protection Cell. The Special Officer shall be responsible for:

    (i) providing immediate relief and other facilities to the victims of atrocity and initiate necessary measures to prevent or avoid re-occurrence of atrocity;

    (ii) setting up an awareness centre and organising workshop in the identified area or at the district head quarters to educate the persons belonging to the Scheduled Castes and Scheduled Tribes about their rights and the protection available to them under the provisions of various Central and State enactments or rules and schemes etc. framed therein;

    (iii) co-ordinating with the non-Governmental organisations and providing necessary facilities and financial and other type of assistance to non-governmental Organization for maintaining centres or organising workshops.

11. *Travelling Allowance, Daily Allowance, Maintenance Expenses and Transport Facilities to the Victim of Atrocity, His or Her Dependent and Witnesses*:

    (1) Every victim of atrocity or his/her dependent and witnesses shall be paid to and fro rail fare by second class in express/mail/passenger train or actual bus or taxi fare from his/her place of residence or actual bus or taxi fare from his/her place of residence or place of stay to the place of investigation or hearing of trial of an offence under the Act.

    (2) The District Magistrate or the sub-divisional Magistrate or any other Executive Magistrate shall make necessary arrangements for providing transport facilities or reimbursement of full payment thereof to the victims of atrocity and witnesses for visiting the investigating officer, Superintendent of Police, Deputy Superintendent of Police, District Magistrate or any other Executive Magistrate.

(3) Every women witness, the victim of atrocity or her dependent being a woman or a minor, a person more than sixty years of age and a person having 40 per cent of more disability shall be entitled to be accompanied by an attendant of her/his choice . The attendant shall also be paid travelling and maintenance expenses as applicable to the witness or the victim of atrocity when called upon during hearing, investigation and trial of an offence under the Act.

(4) The witness, the victims of atrocity or his/her dependent and the attendant shall be paid daily maintenance expenses, for the days he/she is away from the place of his/her residence or stay during investigation, hearing and trial of an offence, of such rates but not less than the minimum wages, as may be fixed by the State Government for the agricultural labourers.

(5) In addition to daily maintenance expenses the witness, the victim of atrocity (or his/her dependant) and the attendant shall also be paid diet expenses at such rates as may be fixed by the State Government from time to time.

(6) The payment of travelling allowances, daily allowance, maintenance expenses and reimbursement of transport facilities shall be made immediately or not later than three days by the District Magistrate or the Sub-divisional Magistrate or any other Executive Magistrate to the victims that dependants attendant and witnesses for the days they visit the investigating officer or in-charge police station or hospital authorities or Superintendent of Police/ Deputy Superintendent of Police or District Magistrate or any other officer concerned or the Special Court.

(7) When an offence has been committed under Section 3 of the Act, the District Magistrate or the Sub-Divisional Magistrate or any other Executive Magistrate shall reimburse the payment of medicines, special medical consultation, blood transfusion, replacement of essential clothing, meals and fruits provided to the victim(s) of atrocity.

12. *Measures to be Taken by the District Administration*:

(1) The District Magistrate and the Superintendent of Police shall visit the place or area where the atrocity has been committed to assess the loss of life and damage to the property and draw a list of victim their family members and dependents entitled for relief.

(2) Superintendent of Police shall ensure that the First information Report is registered in the book of the concerned police station and effective measures for apprehending the accused are taken.

(3) The Superintendent of Police, after spot inspection, shall immediately appoint an investigation officer and deploy such police force in the area and take such other preventive measures as he may deem proper and necessary.

(4) The District Magistrate or the Sub Divisional Magistrate or any other Executive Magistrate shall make arrangements for providing immediate relief in cash or in kind or both to the victims of atrocity, their family members and dependents according to the scale as in the schedule annexed to these Rules (Annexure – I). Such immediate relief shall also include food, water, clothing, shelter, medical aid, transport facilities and other essential items necessary for human beings.

(5) The relief provided to the victim of the atrocity or his/her dependent under sub-rule (4) in respect of death, or injury or damage to property shall be in addition to any other right to claim compensation in respect there of under any other law for the time being in force.

(6) The relief and rehabilitation facilities mentioned in sub-rule (4) above shall be provided by the District Magistrate or the Sub-Divisional Magistrate or any other Executive Magistrate in accordance with the scales provided in the Scheduled annexed to these rules.

(7) A report of the relief and rehabilitation facilities provided to the victims shall also be forwarded to the Special Court by the district Magistrate or the Sub-Divisional Magistrate or the Executive Magistrate or Superintendent of Police. In case the Special Court is satisfied that the payment of relief was not make to the victim or his/her dependent in time or the amount of relief or compensation was not sufficient or only a part of payment of relief or compensation was made, it may order for making in full or part the payment of relief or any other kind of assistance.

13 *Selection of Officers and Other Staff Members or Completing the Work Relating to Atrocity:*

(1) The State Government shall ensure that the administrative officers and other staff members to be appointed in an area

prone to atrocity shall have the right aptitude and understanding of the problems of the Scheduled Castes and the Scheduled Tribes.

(2) It shall also be ensured by the State Government that person from the Scheduled Castes and the Scheduled Tribes are adequately represented in the administration and in the police force at all levels, particularly at the level of police posts and police station.

14. *Specific Responsibility of the State Government*: The State Government shall make necessary provisions in its annual budget for providing relief and rehabilitation facilities to the victims of atrocity. It shall review at least twice in a calendar year, in the month of January and July the performance of the Special Public Prosecutor specific or appointed under Section 15 of the Act, various reports received, investigation made and preventing steps taken by the District magistrate, Sub-Divisional Magistrate and Superintendent of Police, relief and rehabilitation facilities provided to the victims and the reports in respect of lapses on behalf of the concerned officers.

15. *Contingency Plan by the State Government*:

(1) The State Government shall prepare a model contingency plan for implementing the provisions of the Act and notify the same in the Official Gazette of the State Government. It should specify the role and responsibility of various departments and their officers a different levels, the role and responsibility of various departments and their officers at different levels, the role and responsibility of Rural/Urban, Local Bodies and Non-Government Organisations. Inter alia this plan shall contain a package or relief measures including the following:

(a) scheme to provide immediate relief in cash or in kind or both ;

(b) allotment of agricultural land house sites ;

(c) the rehabilitation packages;

(d) scheme for employment in Government or Government undertaking to the dependant or one of the family member of the victim;

(e) pension scheme for widows, dependant children of the deceased, handicapped or old age victims of atrocity;

(f) mandatory compensation for the victims ;

(g) scheme for strengthening the socio-economic condition of the victim;

(h) provisions for providing brick/stone masonry house to the victims;

(i) such other elements as health care, supply of essential commodities, electrification, adequate drinking water facility burial/cremation ground and link roads to the Scheduled Castes and the Scheduled Tribes habitats.

(2) The State Government shall forward a copy of the contingency plan or a summary thereof and a copy of the scheme, as soon as may be, to the Central Government in the Ministry of Welfare and to all the district Magistrates, Sub-Divisional Magistrates, Inspectors General of Police and Superintendent of Police.

16. *Constitution of State-Level Vigilance and Monitoring Committee*:

(1) The State Government shall constitute a high power vigilance and monitoring committee of not more than 25 members consisting of the following:

(i) Chief Minister/Administrator-Chairman (in case of a State under President's Rule, Governor- Chairman).

(ii) Home Minister, Finance Minister and Welfare Minister-Members (in case of a State under the President's Rule Advisors-Members).

(iii) all elected Members of Parliament and State Legislative Assembly and Legislative Council from the State belonging to the Scheduled Castes and the Scheduled Tribes-Members.

(iv) Chief Secretary, the Home Secretary, the Director General of Police, Director/Deputy Director National Commission for Scheduled Castes and the Scheduled Tribes-Members.

(v) The Secretary in-charge of the Welfare and Development of the Scheduled Castes and the Scheduled Tribes – Convenor.

(2) The high power vigilance and monitoring committee shall meet at least twice in a calendar year, in the month of January and July to review the implementation of the provisions of the Act, relief and rehabilitation facilities provided to the

victims and other matters connected therewith, prosecution of cases under the Act, role of different officers/agencies responsible for implementing the provisions of the Act and various reports received by the State Government.

17. *Constitution of District Level Vigilance and Monitoring Committee*:

(1) In each district within the State, the District Magistrate shall set up a vigilance and monitoring committee in his district to review the implementation of the provisions of the Act, relief and rehabilitation facilities provided to the victims and other matters connected therewith, prosecution of cases under the Act, role of different officers/agencies responsible for implementing the provisions of the Act and various reports received by the District Administration.

(2) The district level vigilance and monitoring committee shall consist of the elected Members of the Parliament and State Legislative Assembly and Legislative Assembly and Legislative Council, Superintendent of Police, three group 'A' officers/Gazetted officers of the State Government belonging to the Scheduled Castes and the Scheduled Tribes, not more than 5 non-official Members belonging to the Scheduled Castes and the Scheduled Tribes and not more than 3 members from the categories other than the Scheduled Castes and the Scheduled Tribes having association with Non-government Organisations. The District Magistrate and District Social Welfare Officer shall be Chairman and Member Secretary respectively.

(3) The district level committee shall meet at least once in three months.

18. *Material for Annual Report*: The State Government shall, every year before the 31st March, forward the report to the Central Government about the measures taken for implementing provisions of the Act and various schemes/plans framed by it during the previous calendar year.

Norms for Relief Amount
(As per Rule 12 (4) of PA Rules, 1995)**

Sr. No.	*Nature of Offence*	*Sections*	*Minimum Eligible Relief Amount*
1.	Forcing a person to drink or eat inedible or obnoxious substances	3(I) (I)	Rs. 25,000/- or more to each victim depending on the gravity of the offence. Payment as follows: • 25% when the charge sheet is sent to the Court • 75% when accused are convicted by the lower Court
2.	Causing injury, insult or annoyance	3(1) (ii)	Rs. 25,000/- or more to each victim depending on the gravity of the offence. Payment as follows: • 25% when the charge sheet is sent to the Court • 75% when accused are convicted by the lower Court
3.	Derogatory Act	3(1) (iii)	Rs. 25,000/- or more depending on the gravity of the offence. Payment to be made as follows: • 25% when the charge sheet is sent to the Court • 75% when accused are convicted by lower Court
4.	Wrongful occupation or cultivation of land etc	3(1) (iv)	Atleast Rs. 25,000/- or more to each victim. • The land/premises/water supply to be restored where necessary at government cost. • Full payment when charge sheet is sent to the Court.
5.	Relating to land, premises and water	3(1) (v)	Atleast Rs. 25,000/- or more to each victim • 25% payment at FIR stage • 75% on conviction in the lower Court.
6.	Begar or forced or bonded labour	3(1) (vi)	At least Rs. 25,000/- to each victim • 25% at FIR stage • 75% on conviction in the lower Court

Contd...

Contd...

7.	Relating to right to franchise (vote)	3(1) (vii)	Upto Rs. 20,000/- to each victim depending upon the nature and gravity of the offence.
8.	False, malicious or vexations legal proceedings	3(1) (viii)	Rs. 25,000/- or reimbursement of actual legal expenses and damages or whichever is less after conclusion of the trial of the accused.
9.	False and frivolous information	3(1) (ix)	Rs. 25,000/- or reimbursement of actual legal expenses and damages or whichever is less after conclusion of the trial of the accused.
10.	Insult, intimidation and humiliation	3(1) (x)	Upto Rs. 25,000/- to each victim. • 25% after charge sheet. • The rest on conviction.
11.	Outraging the modesty of woman	3(1) (xi)	Rs. 50,000/- to each victim. • 50% amount to be paid after medical examination. • Remaining at the conclusion of the trial
12.	Sexual exploitation of a woman	3(1) (xii)	Rs. 50,000/- to each victim. • 50% amount to be paid after medical examination. • Remaining at the conclusion of the trial
13.	Fouling of water	3(1) (xiii)	Upto Rs. 1,00,000/- or full cost of restoration of normal facility. • Payment to be made at the stage as deemed fit by district Administration.
14.	Denial of customary rights of passage	3(1)(xiv)	Upto Rs. 1,00,000/- or full cost of restoration of right of passage and full compensation of the loss suffered, if any. • Payment of 50% after charge sheet • Payment of rest 50% on conviction in the lower Court.
15.	Making one desert place of residence	3(1) (xv)	• Restoration of site/right to stay • Rs. 25,000/- compensation to each victim, and • Reconstruction of the house at government cost, if destroyed • Compensation to be paid in full when charge sheet is sent to the lower Court.

Contd...

Contd...

16.	Giving false evidence	3(2) (I) and (ii)	Atleast Rs. 1,00,000/- or full compensation of the loss or harm sustained. • 50% to be paid after charge sheet • 50% on conviction.
17.	Committing offences under the IPC punishable with imprisonment for 10 or more years	3(2) (V)	Atleast Rs. 50,000/- to each victim and or his dependents. • The amount would vary if especially otherwise provided in the schedule.
18.	Victimization at the hands of a public servant	3(2)(vii)	Full compensation on account of damages or loss or harm sustained. • 50% to be paid after charge-sheet sent to the Court. • The rest on conviction by lower Court.
19.	Disability: (Refer notification No.4-2/83-HW III dated 6.8.1988 of Ministry of Welfare, GOI as amended from time to time). Compensation for the disability caused: (a) 100% incapacitation (i) Non earning member of a family (ii) Earning member of a family (b) Where incapacitation is less than 100%		At least Rs. 1,00,000/- to each victim. • 50% on FIR • 25% at chargesheet • 25% on conviction by the lower Court. At least Rs. 2,00,000/- to each victim of offence. • 50% to be paid on FIR/medical examination stage • 25% after charge sheet • 25% at conviction in lower Court. The rates as laid down in (a) (i) and (ii) above shall be reduced in the same proportion, the stages of payments also being the same.
20	(a) Murder/Death of non-earning member of a family (b) Murder/death of an earning member of a family		At least Rs. 1,00,000/- to each case. • Payment of 75% after postmortem • 25% on conviction by the lower Court At least Rs. 2,00,000/- to each case. • Payment of 75% after post mortem • 25% on conviction by the lower Court

Contd...

Contd...

21	Victim of murder, death, massacre, rape, mass rape, and gang rape, permanent incapacitation and dacoity	• In addition to relief amounts paid under above items, relief may be arranged within three months of date of atrocity as follows: (i) Pension to each widow and/or other dependents of deceased SC and ST @ Rs. 1000/- per month, or • Employment to one member of the family of the deceased, or • Provision of agricultural land and house, if necessary by outright purchase (ii) (Full cost of the education and Maintenance of the children of the Victims. • Children may be admitted to Ashram Schools/residential schools. Provision of utensils, rice, wheat, pulses, etc. for a period of three months.
22	Complete destruction/burnt houses	• Brick/stone masonry house to be constructed or provided at government cost where it has been burnt or destroyed.

Source: Government of India (2000), National Commission for Scheduled Castes and Scheduled Tribes: Hand Book, New Delhi, pp. 64(I) – (v).

ANNEXURE 3

Recommendations of National Commission for SCs STs

The National commission for SCs and STs, has made 12 major observations and recommendations for effective implementation of the two special laws. On the basis of general analysis of macro level data pertaining to atrocities on SCs/STs and the various issues dealt within the Commission (See Government of India, April 25, 1998: 245-46). However, some of the specific observations and recommendations proposed by the conference of Home Secretaries, and Director Generals, Inspector General of Police of State/UTs on the subject of crime and atrocities on SC/ST held on 16.12.96 at Vigyan Bhawan, New Delhi are more specific and comprehensive and thus worth reproducing here (ibid, 233-34). Of all, the conference emphasised the following three points:

- The Conference emphasised the point that the preventive measures mentioned in the Act should be enforced to create an environment in which the SCs and STs live with dignity and feel secure.
- Strict vigilance and prompt action was also emphasised.
- It was stressed that the police personnel and all the officers concerned with the implementation of the SCs and STs (Prevention of Atrocities) Rules, 1955 should be properly trained. They came out with the following specific recommendations:
  The specific recommendations include the following:

1. Since the number of officers at DYSP level are not adequate for investigating into all the cases resulting in delays, Rule 7 of the SC and ST (POA) Rules, 1995 should be amended to make investigations possible by officers lower in rank than DYSP to facilitate proper investigation. It was recommended to amend the Rule to enable the State Governments to have the power to designate the officers who will conduct the investigation.
2. It was agreed that Section 4 of the SC & ST (POA) Act, 1989 should be amended to include all the officers including SC/ST for neglecting their duties. As such the words 'but not being the member of SC/ST' in line 2 of the Section should be deleted.
3. In order to ensure speedy trial and disposal of the case in the courts it was necessary to make prosecution accountable to Police, especially at the district level.
4. Presently the offences have been listed in Section 3(1) & 3(2) of the SC &ST (POA) Act, 1989. It was suggested by a number of officers that the punishment for all the offences under Section 3(1) is the

same though the nature of these offences varies from minor to severe. As such total revision of the offences is required and some offences can then be deleted.

5. The proper enforcement of the Act requires the support of other agencies and can't be done by the police machinery alone. Awareness needs to be created through involvement of NGOs and Panchayats.

6. The judgment of full Bench, M.P. High Court in Anand Swaroop Tiwari Vs. Ram Ratan Jatav and two others (decided on 23.8.95) may be referred here for the procedure for trial. In this judgment the Court has held that the Special Court has the status & level of Court of Session, but is not a Session Court. It is not bound by the provision of Section 193 Cr.P.C. and can take cognizance in circumstances referred to in Section 190 of Cr.P.C. The judgment of Madhya Pradesh High Court regarding the powers of Special Courts to take cognizance of the cases directly was circulated to all the officers for action accordingly.

7. Where the number of registration of cases is high and the pendancy is substantial, the state Governments should take immediate steps to set up exclusive Special Courts and seek financial assistance from the Ministry of Welfare.

   The Commission has recommended these amendments to the Ministry of Welfare so that necessary changes be made in the Acts and appropriate instructions issued to the concerned authorities.

   Commission had also conducted State level review meetings in a number of States/UTs. The observations made in these meetings have been reproduced here (see Ibid.:236).

1. Only a few States such as M.P., Rajasthan, Andhra Pradesh had set up exclusive Special Courts. The infrastructure of the Court was also inadequate to cope up with the high number of cases.

2. As per some judicial observations by Allahabad High Court many of the designated Special Courts are not taking cognizance of the offences directly under SC & ST (POA) Act 1989 because of Sections 190 & 193 of Cr.P.C. There is a need to clarify this issue following the observations of the M.P. High Court and amend rules etc., if necessary.

3. A large number of cases are ending in acquittal because witnesses are not turning up and prosecution is not effective. It is the responsibility of the prosecution officers and the police to ensure that witnesses are present in the Courts. Further, Courts are sometimes treating SC/ST witnesses as interested witnesses. This view needs to be revised.

4. The SC & ST (POA) Act, 1989 provides for setting up of monitoring, vigilance and implementation committees at various levels. These committees have not been set up in all the States and

where set up, they are not meeting or monitoring cases as regularly as they should.

5. The Orientation of police personnel and their proper training also needs to be improved. It has also been observed that many police stations don't have the translated copies of the Act. As a result the police officers are not able to use proper sections.

- It was also stressed that awareness should be created amongst people about the provisions of these Acts and the police authorities should also take quick action. Such a situation only would ultimately help in the prevention of crimes.
- Commission has observed that the designated Special Courts are not in position to do justice with these cases of atrocities against Scheduled Castes and Scheduled Tribes because of prolonged proceedings, lack of interest by witnesses and their preoccupation with other Sessions Cases. The Commission is of the opinion that there should be exclusive Special Courts, not just designated courts, for speedy trial of the atrocity cases (Ibid.,239).

Sensitisation of Police Personnel

The Commission held a workshop with U.P. Police at Ghaziabad on sensitisation of police personnel to Civil Rights of Scheduled Castes and Scheduled Tribes which was organised by the District Police Ghaziabad on 31.8.1996. The recommendations of the workshop are as follow (Ibid, 239-40):

1. The objective of the PCR Act 1955 and the SC & ST (POA) Act 1989 is primarily to take preventive steps and also to change the attitude of the people towards the downtrodden Scheduled Castes and Scheduled Tribes.
2. Immediately on receipt of a complaint or a report in the police station the designated police officer should rush to the scene of incident for investigation of the case, so that the correct and first hand information is collected. This will also boost the morale of the SC/ST victims on the one hand and put psychological pressure on the accused and other people of the area.
3. Police should register the FIR in the cases covered under SC/ST (POA) Act and PCR Act promptly. These cases may not be closed by the police during investigation. This violates the provisions and the spirit of these two Acts. These cases must be sent for trial in the Court.
4. The number of cases of atrocities on SC/ST pending for disposal before the courts is very large, while intake of cases is also increasing every year. This problem can be resolved by setting up Exclusive Special Courts in required number in each district.

5. It was observed that speedy trial of cases under SC/ST (POA) Act is hampered by treating SC/ST witnesses as interested witness. Further, general category people are reluctant to come forward to give evidence. Sometimes, the prosecution is unable to get evidence for fear amongst witnesses that they may be punished for fabricated evidence. Prosecution should take all possible steps to give confidence and security to the witnesses. Such an approach combined with exclusive Special Courts taking direct cognizance of case will facilitate speedy trial as envisaged in the Act.

- In view of the increasing number of atrocities on the SCs and STs despite stringent penal provisions and special laws, the Commission has laid emphasis over and again on the need to step up preventive action as provided in the POA Act and Rules (Ibid.241).
- The Commission has also expressed overtly its dissatisfaction over the fact that the police who are supposed to be the protectors of the SCs/STs have themselves indulged in inhuman crimes against the SCs and STs. And it has appealed to the State to initiate strict measures against such police officers. But till April 1998 only the State of Rajasthan and Orissa have sent information regarding involvement of police officials in crime and atrocities against the SCs and STs (Ibid, 243).

References

Action Aid (2002), *People's Report on the Status of Untouchability in Rural Maharashtra,* (Executive Summary), Mumbai.

Ambedkar, B.R. (1979), 'Status and Minorities', in *Dr. Babasaheb Ambedkar: Writings and Speeches,* Vol.5. Government of Maharashtra, Bombay.

— (1987), 'Philosophy of Hinduism', in *Dr. Babasaheb Ambedkar: Writings and Speeches,* Government of Maharashtra, Bombay. Vol. 3: 28-41.

— (1989), 'Their Wishes are Laws Unto Us' *In Dr. Babasaheb Ambedkar: Writings and Speeches,* Vol.5. Government of Maharashtra, Bombay.

Cotterrel, R. (1984), *The Sociology of Law,* Department of Social Welfare.

Dalit Human Rights Watch, (2001), *Dalit Human Rights Monitor – 2000: Andhra Pradesh, Sakshi,* A.P.

Das, Bagwan (1995), 'Socio-economic Problems of Dalits' in Bagwan Das and James Massey (eds.), *Dalit Solidarity,* ISPCK, Delhi.

Galanter, Marc (1972), 'The Abolition of Disabilities: Untouchability and the Law', In J. Michael Mahar (Ed.), *The Untouchables of Contemporary India,* The University of Arizona Press, Tucson.

Ghosh, S.K. (1980), *Protection of Minorities and Scheduled Castes,* Ashish Publishing House, New Delhi.

Ghurye, G.S. (1969), *Caste and Race in India,* Popular Prakashan, Bombay.

Government of India (1984), *Sixth Report, April 1983 – March 1984,* Report of Commission for Scheduled Castes and Scheduled Tribes, New Delhi.

– (1990), *Atrocities on Scheduled Castes and Tribes: Causes and Remedies,* Report of the National Commission for the Scheduled Castes and Scheduled Tribes, New Delhi.

– (1998a), *Third Report: 1994-95 & 1995–96, (Vol.I),* National Commission for Scheduled Castes and Scheduled Tribes, New Delhi.

– (1998b), *Fourth Report: 1996-97 & 1997–98, (Vol.I),* National Commission for Scheduled Castes and Scheduled Tribes, New Delhi.

– (2001), *Annual Report on The Scheduled Castes and Scheduled Tribes (Prevention of Atrocities) Act, 1989 (Sixth Report, 1999),* Ministry of Social Justice and Empowerment, New Delhi.

– (2004), *Report on Prevention of Atrocities against Scheduled Castes,* National Human Rights Commission, New Delhi.

Government of Madhya Pradesh (2002), *The Bhopal Conference: Charting a New Course for Dalits for the 21st Century,* Conference held during 12-13 January 2002, Bhopal.

Iyer, Krishna (1989), *Social Democracy and Dalit Egalite,* University of Madras, Madras.

Jayaram, N. (1986), Can Law Save Scheduled Castes?, *Mainstream,* (May 17), New Delhi.

– (1981), Fresh Look at Harijan Question, *Mainstream,* (May 23), New Delhi.

Jayshree, P. M., et al. (2000), Dalit Human Rights Violations: Atrocities against Dalits in India, Volume 1 – Case Papers: Summary & Jury's Intrim Observations and recommendations, National Campaign on Dalit Human Rights.

Mendelsohn, O. and Vicziany, M. (2000), *The Untouchables: Subordination, Poverty and the State in Modern India,* Cambridge University Press, New Delhi.

Nandu Ram (1986), 'Law and the Atrocities on the Weaker Section in India' in R.G. Singh (ed.), *The Depressed Classes of India: Problems and Perspectives,* B.R. Publishing Corporation, New Delhi pp.111-12.

— (1995), *Beyond Ambedkar: Essays on Dalits in India,* Har-Anand Publications, New Delhi.

Naval, T.R. (2001), *Law of Prevention of Atrocities on the Scheduled Castes and the Scheduled Tribes,* Concept, New Delhi.

Oommen, T.K. (1985), *From Mobilization to Institutionalization,* Popular Prakashan, Bombay.

— (1990), *Protest and Change: Studies in Social Movements,* Sage, New Delhi.

Pandit, Vivek (1995), *A Handbook on Prevention of Atrocities (Scheduled Castes and Scheduled Tribes),* A Vidhayak Sansad Publication, Mumbai.

Ramaiah, A. (1992), Identifying Other Backward Classes, *Economic and Political Weekly,* Vol. XXVII, No.23, June 6.

— (1998), *Protest Movements and Scheduled Caste Identity: The Impact of Constitutional Provisions on Scheduled Caste in Selected Villages of Tamil Nadu,* Ph.D. Thesis submitted to JNU, New Delhi.

— (1998a), 'The Plight of Dalits: A Challenge to Social Work Profession' in Murli Desai, Anjali Monteiro and Lata Narayan, *Towards People-Centred Development* – Part 1 (eds.), TISS, Mumbai.

— (2002), *Factors Responsible for High Rate of Acquittal in Cases Registered under the PCR Act 1955 and the SCs and STs (Prevention of Atrocities) Act 1989: The Case of Southern Tamil Nadu,* Tata Institute of Social Sciences, Mumbai.

Sharma, M. (2004), *Unquiet Worlds: Dalit Voices and Visions,* Heinrich Boll Foundation, New Delhi.

Srinivas, M.N. (1987), *The Dominant Castes and Other Essays,* Oxford University Press, New Delhi

Strauss, A.L. (1997), *Grounded Theory in Practice,* Sage, London.

Weber, M. (1958), *The Religion of India: The Sociology of Hinduism and Buddhism,* Glencoe, Illinois.

Index